Macintosh 3D Handbook

Macintosh 3D Handbook

CRAIG LYN

CHARLES RIVER MEDIA, INC.
Rockland, Massachusetts

Publisher: David F. Pallai
Interior Design/Comp.: Reuben Kantor
Cover Design: Gary Ragaglia
Printer: InterCity Press, Rockland, MA.

CHARLES RIVER MEDIA, INC.
P.O. Box 417
403 VFW Drive
Rockland, Massachusetts 02370
617-871-4184
617-871-4376 (FAX)
chrivmedia@aol.com

This book is printed on acid-free paper.

Macintosh 3D Handbook
By Craig Lyn
ISBN 1-886801-17-7
Printed in the United States of America

96 97 98 99 00 7 6 5 4 3 2

CHARLES RIVER MEDIA titles are available for site license or bulk purchase by
institutions, user groups, corporations, etc. For additional information, please contact the Special Sales Department at 617-871-4184.

DEDICATION

To Thalia and Michael Lyn, for everything...

Contents

ABOUT THE AUTHOR xxi

ACKNOWLEDGEMENTS xxiii

FOREWORD xxv

1 Welcome 1

SECTION ONE: HOW TO GET THE MOST FROM THIS BOOK 2
What Is This Book About? 2
What Do I Have to Know? 3
What Software and Hardware Do I Need? 3
    SOFTWARE 3
    HARDWARE 3
What Do I Have to Know About 3D? 4
How Should I Use This Book? 4
    BEGINNERS 4
    INTERMEDIATE TO ADVANCED 5

SECTION TWO: OVERVIEW OF THE MACINTOSH 3D PROFESSIONAL 5
Part 1: Chapters 1–4 5
Part 2: Chapters 5–11 5
Part 3: Chapters 12–16 6
The Chapters, Tutorials, and Animations 6

SECTION THREE: ABOUT THE CD-ROMS 6
Formats 7
    MODELS 7
    TEXTURE MAPS 7
    ANIMATIONS 7
The CD-ROM 8

2 What Is 3D? 11

SECTION ONE: PERSISTENCE OF VISION 13

SECTION TWO: THE STAGES OF CREATING AN ANIMATION 13
Storyboarding 14
Modeling 14
Texture Mapping 15
Lighting or Scene Building 15
Animation 16
Rendering 16
Postproduction 16

SECTION THREE: USES FOR 3D 17
Multimedia 17
Product Design 18
Broadcast and Film 19

3 Choosing the Right Hardware and Software 21

SECTION ONE: HARDWARE HARDSHIPS 22
The Savvy Shopper 23
The CPU 24
PowerPC Versus 68K 24
  NUBUS VERSUS PCI 25
  CLOCK ACCELERATORS 26
  APPLE VERSUS THE CLONES 26
RAM 27
Monitors 28
  COLOR DEPTH 29
QuickDraw 3D Accelerator Cards 29
Multiple Processor Cards 30
Flatbed Scanner 30
3D Digitizers 31
Storage 31
  WORKING STORAGE 31
    Hard Drives 32
    Medium-Capacity Removable Storage 32
  OLDER REMOVABLE STORAGE FORMATS 34
  OPTICAL MASS STORAGE SOLUTIONS 34
  ARCHIVAL STORAGE 35

CD-R 36
DAT 36

SECTION TWO: SOFTWARE RECOMMENDATIONS 37
All-Inclusive Packages 38
Modeling Software 38
POLYGONAL BASED MODELERS 39
SPLINE-BASED MODELERS 40
Modeling Tools 42
TOOL SETS 42
Primitives 42
Lathe 44
Extrude 47
Sweep or Extrude on Path 48
Twist and Taper 51
Mirror 52
Bevel 52
Loft and Skin 53
Boolean Functions 54
Rendering and Animation Software 56
RENDERING 57
LIGHTING 57
TEXTURE MAPPING 58
ANIMATION TOOLS 58
QuickDraw 3D 59

4   Storyboarding 61

SECTION ONE: THE SCRIPT 63

SECTION TWO: CREATING THE STORYBOARD 64
The Nontraditional Storyboard 69
Casting Call 70

5   The Modeling Process 71

SECTION ONE: CONFIGURING YOUR COMPUTER 73
Freeing RAM 73
Monitor Depth 76
Screen Savers and Automatic Programs 77

SECTION TWO: HELPFUL MODELING TIPS 77
Perspective 78

Layers 78
Views 79
Names 80
Model Resolution 80
Overmodeling 81

SECTION THREE: THE MODELING PROCESS 82
Creating a Model 82
   ▪ *TOY SOLDIER TUTORIAL* 84
Layers 89

SECTION FOUR: MODELING A ROUGH DRAFT OF A 3D SCENE 90
Composition 93
   CENTER OF INTEREST 93
   BALANCE 94

SECTION FIVE: EXPORTING YOUR MODEL 94
DXF 95
   N x M MESH 95
   3D FACE 95
   POLYLINE 95
RIB 96
Apple's 3D MetaFormat 96

6   Advanced Modeling 97

SECTION ONE: EPS TEMPLATES 99
Using EPS Templates 100
   BOOLEAN FUNCTIONS 100
   ▪ *SIMPLE BOOLEAN TUTORIAL* 100
   ▪ *MODELING COMPLEX 2D SHAPES TUTORIAL* 102
   ▪ *GEARS TUTORIAL* 104
   ▪ *CREATING 3D TEXT FROM 2D SHAPES TUTORIAL* 105
   ▪ *BOOLEANS AND TEXT TUTORIAL* 109
   CREATING RIBS WITH EPS TEMPLATES 111

SECTION TWO: TERRAIN MODELING 112
   DEDICATED TERRAIN MODELERS 112
   GRAYSCALE BITMAP TERRAIN 114
   ▪ *CREATING A TERRAIN TUTORIAL* 114
   ▪ *CANYON TUTORIAL* 118
   ▪ *CAVE TUTORIAL* 120

OTHER USES FOR TERRAIN MODELING 124
CYBERMESH 126

SECTION THREE: 3D DIGITIZERS 127
Mechanical Arm Digitizers 127
Ultrasonic Digitizers 128
Magnetic Digitizers 129
Laser Digitizers 129

SECTION FOUR: DEDICATED HUMAN BODY AND TREE MODELERS 130
Fractal Design's Poser 130
CONTORTIONISTS FOR HIRE 130
Onyx's Tree Professional 132
Tree Tricks 134
▪ *METHOD ONE* 134
▪ *METHOD TWO* 136

7   Materials and Texture Mapping 139

SECTION ONE: MATERIALS — THE VIRTUAL ALCHEMIST 141
Material Color Theory 142
DIFFUSE COLOR 142
SPECULAR COLOR 143
AMBIENT COLOR 144
Physical Properties 144
AMBIENT VALUE 145
DIFFUSE VALUE 145
SPECULAR VALUE 146
REFLECTIVITY 147
TRANSPARENCY 149
INDEX OF REFRACTION 149
GLOW 150
Putting It All Together 151
▪ *SPACESHIP TUTORIAL* 152

SECTION TWO: MAPPING BASICS 155
How It Works 156
Types of Mapping 156
PLANAR MAPPING 157
CUBIC MAPPING 158
CYLINDRICAL MAPPING 158

SPHERICAL MAPPING 159
Tiling Maps 160
TEXTURE CREATION APPLICATIONS 161
WHEN AND WHEN NOT TO USE SEAMLESS MAPS 161

SECTION THREE: CREATING CUSTOM MAPS 162
Size 162
Bit Depth 163
Proportions of Maps 164
CYLINDRICAL MAPPING 164
CUBIC MAPPING 165
SPHERICAL MAPPING 165
PLANAR MAPPING 166

SECTION FOUR: CREATING AND ALIGNING A BITMAP 166
■ *SPACESHIP COLOR MAPPING TUTORIAL* 167

8 Advanced Texture Mapping 175
A Mapping Background 178

SECTION ONE: SPECULAR MAPS 180
■ *SPECULAR WINDOW TUTORIAL* 181
■ *SPECULAR SPACESHIP TUTORIAL* 182

SECTION TWO: TRANSPARENCY MAPS 185
■ *TRANSPARENCY TUTORIAL* 186
■ *BOTTLE LABEL TUTORIAL* 189

SECTION THREE: DIFFUSE MAPS 193
■ *DIFFUSE SPACESHIP TUTORIAL* 193

SECTION FOUR: BUMP MAPS 194
How Bump Maps Work 194
Using a Bump Map 196
■ *BRICK WALL TUTORIAL* 197
■ *TILES TUTORIAL* 200
■ *TEXT-SHAPED BUMP MAP TUTORIAL* 202
MORE BUMP MAP EXAMPLES 204

SECTION FIVE: GLOW MAPS 206
■ *GLOWING SIGN TUTORIAL* 206
■ *SPACE STATION TUTORIAL* 209

SECTION SIX: REFLECTIVITY MAPS 213
   ▪ *FLASH OF LIGHT TUTORIAL* 214
   ▪ *RIPPLING REFLECTION TUTORIAL* 217

SECTION SEVEN: ANIMATED MAPS 218
Video Sources 219
Software Sources 220
Animated Color Maps 220
Animated Reflectivity Maps 222
   ▪ *ANIMATED FLASH OF LIGHT TUTORIAL* 222
Animated Bump Maps 225
   ▪ *ANIMATED BUMP TEXT TUTORIAL* 226
Animated Transparency Maps 228
   ▪ *FADING CUBE TUTORIAL* 228

9 Lighting 233

SECTION ONE: BASIC LIGHTING AND COLOR THEORY 235
Red, Yellow, Blue Color Model 235
RGB, CMYK, and HSL Color Models 235
   RGB COLOR MODEL 235
   HSL COLOR MODEL 237
      Hue 237
      Saturation 237
      Luminance 238
      Complimentary Colors 238
   COLOR AND MOOD 239
   COLOR TEMPERATURE 239
   DISTANCE AND COLOR 240

SECTION TWO: TYPES OF LIGHT SOURCES 240
   PARALLEL LIGHTS 241
   SPOTLIGHTS 243
   POINT OR RADIAL LIGHTS 244
   AMBIENT LIGHT 245
   TUBE LIGHTS 246
   BLACK LIGHTS 247

SECTION THREE: ANGLE OF INCIDENCE, LIGHT ATTENUATION,
      AND SHADOWS 248
Angle of Incidence 248
   ▪ *ANGLE OF INCIDENCE TUTORIAL* 248

Light Attenuation 250
  ATTENUATION OF POINT LIGHTS 251
  ATTENUATION OF SPOTLIGHTS 252
Shadows 253

SECTION FOUR: LIGHTING A SCENE 256
Three-Light Studio Setup 257
  KEY LIGHT 258
  FILL LIGHT 258
  BACK LIGHT 258
Four-Light Studio Setup 260
  GRAZED LIGHT 260
  ACCENT LIGHT 260
Basic Lighting Considerations 262

10 Simulating Environments with Lighting 265
Lighting a Real-World Environment 266
  ATMOSPHERE 266
  LIGHT COLOR, INTENSITY, AND ANGLE 266

SECTION ONE: SUNLIGHT 268
CAD Lighting 268
Quick and Easy Sunlight 268
  TIME OF DAY 269
    Setting the Solar Angle 269
    Setting the Intensity of the Light 270
    Setting the Color of the Light 271
    Seasons 272
    Global Location 273
  ▪ CHAIRS TUTORIAL 273

SECTION TWO: MOONLIGHT 274

SECTION THREE: FOG AND ATMOSPHERIC CONDITIONS 274
Fog . . . .
 275
  HOW FOG WORKS 276
  USING FOG 278
  DEPTH OF FIELD WITH FOG 280
Atmospheric Conditions 280
  POLLUTION 280
  RAIN AND SNOW 281
  SPECIAL LIGHTING CONSIDERATIONS 281

SECTION FOUR: OUTER SPACE 281
Vacuum 282
Ambient Light 282

SECTION FIVE: UNDERWATER 283
Depth 283
Fog . . . .
. . . . 284
Background 284
Lighting 284

SECTION SIX: ARTIFICIAL LIGHTING 285
Types of Artificial Lighting 286
   HALOGEN 286
   LIGHTBULBS 286
   FLUORESCENT 286
   SODIUM VAPOR 287
   NEON 287

11   Lighting Special Effects 289
The Lighting Toolbox 290

SECTION ONE: GELS, PROJECTORS, AND GOBOS 291
Simple Gels 291
   ▪ *SIMPLE GEL TUTORIAL* 291
   ANOTHER SIMPLE GEL 294
   ▪ *CREATING CUSTOM GELS TUTORIAL* 295
Complex Colored Gels 298
   ▪ *STAINED GLASS TUTORIAL* 298
Projectors 301
   ▪ *PROJECTOR BOX TUTORIAL* 302
   ▪ *SUBMARINE TUTORIAL* 304
Gobos 306
   ▪ *GOBO OF STARS TUTORIAL* 307

SECTION TWO: VISIBLE LIGHT SOURCES 308
Creating Visible Lights 308
Glowing Radial and Spotlights 309
   MAKING YOUR OWN VISIBLE LIGHT SOURCES 312
   ▪ *DESK LAMP TUTORIAL* 312
      Edge Density 314

SECTION THREE: LENS FLARES 319
Types of Lens Flares 320
Uses for Lens Flares 323
    LENS FLARES AND LIGHT SOURCES 323
    LENS FLARES AND EXPLOSIONS 324
    LENS FLARES AS STARS 324

12 Perspective and the Virtual Camera 327

  SECTION ONE: PERSPECTIVE 328
  Orthographic vs. Perspective Views 329

  SECTION TWO: THE VIRTUAL CAMERA 332
  All About Cameras 332
    FIELD OF VIEW 333
    THE VIRTUAL CAMERA 335

  SECTION THREE: DEPTH OF FIELD 338
    ▪ *DEPTH OF FIELD TUTORIAL* 339
  Layering for Depth of Field 342
    MOTION BLUR 342

13 Animation: The Magic of Movement 343

  SECTION ONE: A BRIEF HISTORY OF ANIMATION 344
  Cel-Based Animation 346
  Computer-Based Animation 346

  SECTION TWO: SCRIPTING YOUR ANIMATION 346
  Coordinate Systems 348
    WORLD COORDINATES 348
    OBJECT COORDINATES 348
  The Keyframe 349
    ▪ *KEYFRAME TUTORIAL I* 350
    ▪ *KEYFRAME TUTORIAL II* 352
  Model Hierarchy and Links 353
    HIERARCHY 354
    LINKS AND COORDINATE SYSTEMS 355
    ▪ *LINK AND COORDINATE SYSTEM TUTORIAL* 355
  Animation Sequencers 360

  SECTION THREE: MOTION THEORY 361
  Velocity 362
    VELOCITY CONTROLS 362

HOW FAST IS FAST? 363
    Scale 364
    Frame Rate 364
Human Motion or Character Animation 364
Motion Paths 366

SECTION FOUR: BASIC CINEMATOGRAPHY 367
Basic Camera Tips 367
Basic Camera Movements 368
   ZOOM IN 368
   MODEL FLY-BY 369
   CAMERA DOLLY 370

14   Animation Special Effects 373

   SECTION ONE: PYROTECHNICS 375
CD-ROMS 375
   EASY ALPHA CHANNELS 376
   INSERTING THE MAP INTO THE SCENE 377
Particle Groups 378
   3D PARTICLE GROUPS 378
      Northern Lights Productions 379
   2D PARTICLE GROUPS 381
      FinalEffects 382
Traditional Animation Methods 384
   LIGHTNING AND ELECTRICITY 384
   ■ *SMOKE AND FOG TUTORIAL* 385
   FIRE IN AFTER EFFECTS 388
   SHOCK WAVE TUTORIAL 390
Tying It All Together 393

   SECTION TWO: SPECIALIZED ANIMATION FEATURES 393
Align to Path 394
Velocity 396
Explode 396
Inverse Kinematics 398
Deformations 400
Morph 402
Metaballs 402

   SECTION THREE: BACKGROUNDS 402
Applying a Background in a Scene 403
Using Models as Backgrounds 403
   ■ *ENVIRONMENT SPHERES* 404

Environment Saucers 406
Infinite Planes 407
Environment Mapping 407
Perspective Matching 409
Modeling 409
The Photo Shoot 410
Matching the Perspective 411

15   Rendering 413

Section One: Rendering Algorithms 415
Surface Normals 415
Wireframe 416
Hidden Line 416
Flat Shading 417
Gouraud Shading 417
Phong Shading 419
Raytracing 420
Radiosity 421

Section Two: Configuring the Computer 421

Section Three: Special Rendering Considerations 422
Rendering Farms and Multiprocessors 422
SGI Rendering Engines 423
Hardware Acceleration 423

Section Four: Output Resolution 423
Multimedia 424
Television 425
Color 425
Interlacing 425
    Rendering for an Interlaced Monitor 427
Pixel Ratio 427
Film 427
Print 428

16   Postproduction 429

Section One: Postproduction Software 430
Editing Software 431

AFTER EFFECTS 3.0 431
PREMIERE 4.0 432
QuickTime and Codecs 432
   CODECS 432
      Cinepak 433
      Apple Video 433
      Animation 433
      JPEG 433
      MPEG 433
      Graphics 433
      None 433
Resolution 434
Hardware Editing Suites 434
   HARDWARE-BASED CODECS 435
   SCSI-1 VS. SCSI-2 435
   THE ARRAY 436

SECTION TWO: DIGITAL COMPOSITING 437
What Is the Alpha Channel? 437
   ▪ *ALPHA CHANNEL TUTORIAL* 438
   OTHER USES FOR THE ALPHA CHANNEL 441
Creating Your Own Alpha Channel 441
   ▪ *RENDERING AN ALPHA CHANNEL* 441
   SWITCHING CHANNELS 442
      Method One 442
      Method Two 442
   ▪ *ADDING AN ALPHA CHANNEL INTO A CLIP* 443
   ▪ *COMPOSITING WITH AN ALPHA CHANNEL* 445
Shadow Masks 448
   PLANNING 448
   MODELING 449
   LIGHTING AND RENDERING 450
   ▪ *COMPOSITING THE SHADOW MASK* 451
Chroma Keying 454
   LIGHTING CONSIDERATIONS 454
   PROCESSING THE FOOTAGE 455
Rotoscoping 455
   DEBABELIZER 455
   STRATA MEDIAPAINT AND FRACTAL DESIGN PAINTER 456
Adding Special Effects 456
   ▪ *LENS FLARES* 456
   PARTICLE GROUPS 459

SECTION THREE: PREPARING FOR OUTPUT 459
Multimedia 460
   CD-ROM 460
      Data Transfer Rate 461
      Optimizing Your QuickTime Movie 461
   KIOSKS 462
Television 462
   NTSC LEGAL COLORS 462
   INTERLACING 462
Film 463

SECTION FOUR: OUTPUT METHODS 464
Frame-Accurate Tape Decks 464
Digital Video Editing Suites 464

APPENDIX A: INDEX OF 3D COMPANIES 465

GLOSSARY 471

INDEX 479

About the Author

With roots in Canada, Jamaica, and Wisconsin, **Craig Lyn** is a recent transplant to the San Francisco Bay area. It was more by chance rather than by intention that Craig ended up in the computer graphics industry. Originally driven to the culinary profession by his love of food, a radical career switch to 3D computer graphics was made in 1993.

Since then Craig has been a freelance designer specializing in 3D modeling, texture mapping and animation for multimedia, broadcast television, and film. Also look for his regular articles in publications such as *MacWeek* and *Digital Video Magazine* on topics such multimedia production, non-linear editing, and 3D techniques.

He's currently working a CD-ROM title based on the clash of the famous ironclads the Monitor and the Merrimac. Also in the works is another book titled the *After Effects Handbook*.

Acknowledgements

This book is not the product of only one person, but of many. I would like to extend my warmest thanks and appreciation to the following people who have given me the support as well as expertise to write the *Macintosh 3D Handbook*. To Raymond Chang, who was the first one that helped me take the first steps towards my goals. Brian Clark and Victoria Anderson of Digital Video, it's good to know that both of you are only a phone call away.

I owe a debt of extreme gratitude to Ben Long and José Toledo. Ben is my toll free tech support hotline that can usually answer my most inane questions about anything dealing with computers or aboriginal music. Sean Wagstaff, whose book actually started it all and got me interested in 3D in the first place. Lucien Rhodes, who was there when I first started in this business and has offered me his invaluable advice and much needed encouragement all along the way. Wendy Bozigian of Electric Image, thank you for always looking out for the young aspiring talents in this industry.

Dave Pallai, my Publisher, for taking the chance on an untried author and for always telling me that I could do it. Reuben Kantor, for putting up with my foibles, absent-mindedness and missed deadlines. Scott Andreae, for just being Stock My Greatest Friend. John Skidgel, for your insight and advice on the later parts of this book. Ivan Rascanin, who's pride of my accomplishments rivals that of my father. And most importantly, to Katherine Torrence, who always believed in me and my crazy dreams. Thank you for your patience, understanding, and love.

I would also like to thank the following companies and their representatives for all that they have done for both this book as well as for my magazine articles: Patricia Payne and Kellie Bowman of Adobe, Alexandra Yessios of auto•des•sys, Scott Peterson of Byte by Byte, John Bass and Dale Wise of Fractal, Kristin Keyes and Craig Clevinger of MetaTools,

John Knoll of Knoll Software, Lynn Stadler of Macromedia, Pjer Zanchi of Onyx, Kathy Englar of RayDream, Dorothy Eckel and Chris Johnson of Specular, Josh Bevans of Strata, Roseanne Alspector of Valis, Ashley Sharp of Virtus, Nick Pavlovic of VIDI, Susie Woltjen of VRL, and Chiara Reeves of YARC.

To those that I've forgotten to mention and thank, I apologize. My addled brain is tired and will not forget in the future.

CRL
February 4, 1996

Foreword

When I first started in the field of computer graphics, in particular 3D design, there weren't that many sources from which I could learn. Yes there were many professional designers in the field, but they were about as accessible as the moon in the sky. What I wanted was a book from which I could learn all of the tips and tricks of the pros. But there weren't any available. My learning curve was unnecessarily long and difficult simply because there wasn't anyone out there that could teach me. I learned about 3D through trial and error, going to users groups meetings and just talking to professionals in the field. And that's why I wrote this book, to help you along the way so that maybe someday you can teach me a thing or two. Remember that knowledge is worthless unless it is shared. And I'm sure that you will find that just about anyone that you speak to in this field will be more than willing to lend a hand in either your endeavors or careers.

I want to wish you all the best of luck in your models, maps and animations. Please drop me an e-mail to let me know what you think of the book, and perhaps even show me what you've done.

Craig Lyn
craiglyn@aol.com

1
Welcome

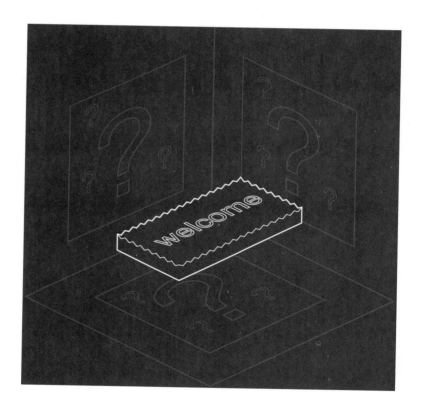

Welcome to the Macintosh 3D Handbook, your resource for 3D design on the Macintosh platform. This book is a comprehensive guide to software, hardware, modeling, animation, and lighting techniques. The Mac 3D Handbook also offers many hints and tips that can help you on your way to becoming a professional 3D designer.

SECTION ONE: HOW TO GET THE MOST FROM THIS BOOK

This section covers some of the more commonly asked questions about the book. The answers should give you an idea of what knowledge level you will need to get the most out of the book.

SECTION TWO: OVERVIEW OF THE MACINTOSH 3D HANDBOOK

The guide to the layout of the Mac 3D Handbook. This section describes the format of the book, how the chapters are broken down, and how the tutorials work.

SECTION THREE: ABOUT THE CD-ROMs

Section Three covers the content and organization of the CD ROM included with the book. Find out what is on the silver platter in this section. Everything from demo versions of 3D software to the most popular shareware titles are included.

SECTION ONE: HOW TO GET THE MOST FROM THIS BOOK

What Is This Book About?	This book is all about 3D. The Macintosh 3D Handbook illustrates the fundamentals of 3D, starting with building your first model. Several chapters discuss texture mapping and cover topics such as the different types of maps available and how to create your own custom maps.

After texture mapping, basic animation and lighting skills are discussed and finally we cover postproduction.

What Do I Have to Know?

This book is for the user that is already familiar with a Macintosh computer. You should have a good understanding of how your computer's operating system and hardware function. Do you know the difference between RAM and a hard drive? Can you create a folder on the Desktop? If you can't answer these questions then I would suggest learning a little bit more about your computer before starting this book. There are plenty of resources available to those who do not know that much about their computers. If you already consider yourself a Mac guru, you're in great shape for this book.

What Software and Hardware Do I Need?

SOFTWARE

The only piece of software you need is a 3D application. All of the models and texture maps used in each tutorial are included on the CD-ROM so you don't even have to worry about creating them yourself! The models are saved in a DXF.3DMF, and form•Z format, which just about every 3D application can import. The texture maps are saved as PICT files which is a standard file type for the Macintosh.

 Tip. You will benefit more from this book if you have a copy of Photoshop or Illustrator so you can create your own custom texture maps. There are save-disabled versions on the CD-ROM if you're interested in taking either application out for a test drive.

HARDWARE

You will need a computer of course, and I highly recommend using a PowerPC. 3D is perhaps the most processor-intensive application that you will ever use on your personal computer and a PowerPC is infinitely faster than a 68K machine.

In addition, your basic operating system should be System 7.5. If you're not running 7.5 consider upgrading. Your computer should have at least 8MB of RAM and be able to support at least 16-bit color on your monitor. See Chapter 3, Choosing the Right Hardware and Software, for a more comprehensive discussion on hardware and software recommendations.

What Do I Have to Know About 3D?

Contrary to popular opinion, 3D is not an arcane art or black magic to which only a select few are privy. You can do 3D just like the masters. All you need to have is a very basic understanding of a 3D package such as Strata StudioPro, Specular's Infini-D, or Macromedia Extreme 3D and the dedication and drive to learn something new.

OK, so now you're saying to yourself, what level of experience constitutes a *basic understanding* of a program? You should be familiar with the modeling tools at your disposal as well as how to use them. You also need to know how the texture mapping features specific to your application work, and how your animation sequencer functions. This book is not meant to replace your 3D application's instruction manual, but rather to supplement it.

In addition to knowing how to use your 3D application, it also helps to have a rudimentary understanding of a 2D graphics program such as Adobe's Photoshop or Fractal Design's Painter. And for the more advanced tutorials some knowledge of an illustration program such as Adobe's Illustrator or Macromedia's FreeHand will be beneficial but not absolutely necessary. Finally for postproduction work, familiarity with Adobe's Premiere or After Effects will also be beneficial. If you don't have a copy of any of these programs, don't worry, there are save-disabled versions included on the CD-ROM.

How Should I Use This Book?

BEGINNERS

There are two methods for using the Macintosh 3D Handbook. First of all you can read your 3D application's instruction manual cover to cover, do the included tutorials, and then once you feel more familiar with your program, pick up the Mac 3D Handbook. A better alternative is to use the Mac 3D Handbook as a supplement to your manual. Start by reading your instruction manual, and as you learn about each features that your application offers, refer to the Mac 3D Handbook on how to get the most out of that feature.

INTERMEDIATE TO ADVANCED

The Mac 3D Handbook can be used as a constant reference volume. You don't need to read this book from cover to cover or in any particular order. For those of you who have already gotten their feet wet and want to improve the quality of their renderings, there are hundreds of tips and techniques that you can easily pick up. Just flip to a section that interests you and then read what you need to know.

If you want to read the book cover to cover you will notice that the Mac 3D Handbook is designed to follow the typical creative process involved in producing an animation. If you come across material that seems familiar, then skip ahead to the next section. Even for the most seasoned veteran there is valuable information between the covers of this book. Use the Mac 3D Handbook if you're stumped on a project or if you're at a loss on how to create a certain special effect.

SECTION TWO: OVERVIEW OF THE MACINTOSH 3D HANDBOOK

The Mac 3D Handbook can be broken down into three distinct parts that correspond to the developmental process of an animation.

Part 1:
Chapters 1–4

The first part of the book offers a brief introduction to the technology and theory behind 3D. This section lays the groundwork for your entry into the world of 3D animation. All of your major concerns such as hardware and software recommendations, what 3D on the computer really is, as well as suggestions for formulating and organizing your ideas are discussed.

Part 2:
Chapters 5–11

The second part of the Mac 3D Handbook covers the nitty-gritty of 3D. This section is the heart and soul of the book. Topics such as modeling, texture mapping, and extensive discussions of lighting are covered in these chapters. Novices will find this part of the book extremely useful and should devote most of their attention here.

Part 3:
Chapters 12–16

Part 3 pulls everything together. You'll learn how to add movement to your ideas through animation. This section discusses how to use and place your camera and how to choose the right rendering algorithm. The book finishes up with the postproduction process and an index of software developers.

The Chapters,
Tutorials, and
Animations

Each chapter is broken down into separate sections. Each section usually consists of a brief discussion or explanation of some aspect of 3D as well as several tutorials. These tutorials are the key to improving your 3D skills. I'm a firm believer in learning by doing. The best way to learn and retain information is to do it yourself.

The tutorials, as well as the rest of the book, assume that you have a basic understanding of how your 3D application works. The tutorials cover the major features available in most 3D applications and offer several work-arounds for applications that don't support these features. All of the source files for each tutorial, such as models, textures, and even some animation samples, are included on the CD-ROM.

At the top of a chapter you might find the heading "Additional Chapter Requirements." This means that we might be straying away from our 3D application and using another program such as Photoshop or Premiere. Underneath this heading you'll see which additional programs we might be using, and the specific features of the program that you should know about. Don't worry because we won't usually do anything extremely complex, and if we do the tutorial will lead you through it step by step.

SECTION THREE: ABOUT THE CD-ROMs

Included with the Mac 3D Handbook is one CD-ROM, which includes the following:

- Color versions of all of the illustrations in the book
- All of the models and texture maps for every tutorial
- Sample animations
- An extensive collection of 3D software from the leading developers

The software libraries on the CD-ROM offer save-disabled and demo versions of some of the most popular 3D applications available today. Also included are a few limited feature versions of DeBabelizer as well as several powerful 3D shareware applications.

Formats

All of the information on the CD-ROM is configured for Macintosh computers so you will need a Mac to be able to read the files. Since each chapter usually has a series of tutorials assigned to it, there is the question of file formats and interprogram compatibility. Not everyone is using the same 3D application, but don't worry, all of that has already been taken care of.

MODELS

Each 3D model has been saved with two different types of common file formats: DXF and 3DMF. Your 3D application will probably be able to read either one or both of the files. In addition since most of the modeling was done in auto•des•sys' form•Z, that file format has also been included.

TEXTURE MAPS

All of the texture maps have been saved in a 24-bit PICT file format which is standard on the Mac. Any graphics program will be able to import and manipulate a PICT image. All of the Illustrator files have been saved as EPS documents to ensure complete interapplication compatibility.

ANIMATIONS

The animations included with the book are compressed in two formats: QuickTime and Electric Image Fastloader. The QuickTime animations use the Animation CoDec and are at 30 fps. They aren't really meant to be played off of the CD-ROM or with the Animation CoDec. Animations were compressed using this format to deliver the highest possible quality image. If you want to play back the animation, either recompress the movie with a faster CoDec or use the Fastloader version.

The Fastloader version of the animations are compressed using Electric Image animation format. The entire animation is loaded into

RAM to guarantee the fastest playback rate possible. What this means is that you will need a fair amount of RAM to play back these animations. That amount of RAM varies according to the size of the movie. Select the movie and then click **Get Info** in the **File** menu on the desktop. The RAM requirements to playback the animation are listed under **Memory Requirements** in the **Preferred Size** box.

FIGURE *The animations included on the*
1.1 *CD-ROM come in two formats. The Electric Image format is perhaps the best method for playback, but also requires the most RAM.*

The CD-ROM

All of the color images of the figures in the book as well as all of tutorials are in the folder named Tutorials and Color Images (see Figure 1.2). Within that folder are all of the source files needed to complete each tutorial.

Also on the CD-ROM are several animations saved in the Electric Image Fastloader format. These animations correspond to the various tutorials in the book. In the folder named Application Software (Figure 1.3) there are several great tryout versions of the most popular 3D applications around. There are also several fully functional shareware programs such as Terrainman which lets you create terrain from 2D grayscale images.

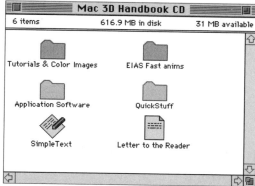

FIGURE 1.2 *The CD ROM included with the book has tutorials, color images, and several animation files.*

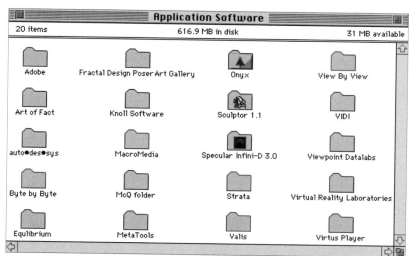

FIGURE 1.3 *The CD ROM also includes many save disable and shareware 3D applications.*

2

What Is 3D?

Just about everyone has seen those astounding special effects on television or have heard the media ramble on about computer-generated graphics, but the average person doesn't have the faintest idea of how this technology works. It's a popular misconception that the burden of the work done in 3D animation is handled by the computer. Unfortunately, this isn't the Holodeck from Star Trek where I can just talk to the computer and have it spit out a hologram. 3D design is a time-consuming, multidisciplinary field that has a learning curve that can scare off the most resolute.

3D design has been shrouded in mystery and cryptic symbolism for years by the high priests of the computer world. Computer jockeys are guilty of over-complicating the technology with useless jargon and technical mumbling such as *Boolean functions* and *inverse kinematics*. The techno-peasantry has been held in the dark, huddled around their flickering monitors, believing the unending rhetoric that the personal computer is not a viable 3D platform and that they'll never be able to create all of those flashy graphics that they see on television and in the movies. But that's why I'm here. Believe me, you can do more than just word processing and spreadsheets with your computer. But in order to be able to create a 3D animation, you have to first understand how animation and 3D works in the first place.

SECTION ONE: PERSISTENCE OF VISION

A brief introduction to the illusion of moving images and an explanation of how an animation appears to move.

SECTION TWO: THE STAGES OF CREATING AN ANIMATION

An introduction and general description of each phase of the animation process. Find out what rendering and postproduction really mean.

SECTION THREE: USES FOR 3D

3D can be used for more than just animation. Find out what other applications there are for 3D in the graphics industry.

Section One: Persistence of Vision

We're not some group of primitives living out in the depths of the Amazon, yet most people still think that the images on television or in the movies are actually moving. This isn't so far removed from thinking that there are little people walking around inside a magic box. Even though your cat might think that there are little animals or people in the television set, we know better.

What we actually see on a movie screen is a sequence of rapidly changing pictures being flashed before our eyes at a rate of 24 pictures or frames per second. Because of a wonderful phenomenon called *persistence of vision* an illusion occurs that the figures on the screen are moving. Our eyes recognize the trace images of the previous frame and with each sequential frame the image appears to move. It's like one of those old cardboard flip books that can be ruffled with your fingers to make the printed images appear to dance. On the other hand, your television set or computer monitor is not so far removed from the movie camera. A television or computer monitor uses an electron gun to rapidly flash an image on the view screen. A television updates this picture 29.97 times a second, while a computer can *refresh* this image at a much higher rate. Moving images on television, in the movies, or on a computer monitor all appear to move because of persistence of vision.

What does this have to do with 3D? At first glance, not much, but just consider it an introduction to what we're about to learn. We've gotten the idea of how images seem to move across the computer screen down pat. Now we need to try to understand how 3D computer graphics works and how it relates to persistence of vision.

Section Two: The Stages of Creating an Animation

No matter which way that you look at it, 3D is still only a two-dimensional image displayed on a flat screen. Whether you're looking at a computer monitor, television, or movie screen, the image is still flat. *So why do we call it 3D computer graphics?* The most simple answer to that question is because all of the images that are displayed are based on three-dimensional computer models.

You as the designer create the 3D models and then the computer takes a picture or *renders* each frame. Once all of the frames are rendered, each frame is then played back at the appropriate speed. And finally through persistence of vision, *voilà*, moving pictures or animation.

But what is the process behind creating an animation? It would be nice if I could just pick up my mouse and use it as a microphone to tell my computer what I wanted to see on the monitor. That unfortunately won't be happening anytime soon. The 3D design process can be long and sometimes very tedious. For example, for a shot that lasts only 10 seconds on the movie screen, a design company will often spend a couple of months creating the animation. This is how we do it — the process of creating an animation can be broken down into the following steps:

- Storyboarding
- Modeling
- Texture mapping
- Lighting or scene building
- Animation
- Rendering
- Postproduction

Storyboarding

Before the computer is even turned on, a company goes through the brainstorming process to plan the details of the animation. During the storyboarding process, a script is created and the details of the animation are sketched out in rough form. The storyboard itself serves as a guide in both the modeling and animation steps of production.

Modeling

This is the second stage in the production process. Once all of the plans and diagrams have been scratched out on cocktail napkins and yellow Post-It pads you can finally turn on your computer. The modeling step is where you start to build your 3D world.

During the modeling process, the designer creates shapes or *primitives* in three-dimensional space using a 3D modeling application. A primitive can be made up of anywhere from 20 to 200,000 points. Points are joined together to form lines, lines form polygons, and polygons finally form three-dimensional primitives such as cubes, spheres, cones, and so on. These primitives are then joined to other objects to form complete models. For example, if I wanted to build a 3D model of a snowman, I would use three spheres for the body, a cone for a nose, and two cylinders for a hat.

Texture Mapping

Once the model is built, the next step is to paint it. A designer doesn't use spray paint or a brush, but rather a material or texture map. 3D models are "painted" in much the same way as when you built small plastic models as a child or, in the case of my brother, still do. What he does with plastic and what the 3D designer does with a computer are not far removed.

After building and then priming a model, my brother paints the model with a coat of paint that resembles the real-world material that he's trying to mimic. For example, if he were building an airplane, the first coat of paint would be a shiny glossy aluminum. In the world of 3D, the designer would create an aluminum material in a 3D application and then apply it the model. For the next step, my brother would apply decals to the model for things such as the insignia and numbers. The 3D designer instead would use a 2D PICT in a program such as Photoshop and then apply it to the surface of the model as a color map. To make the model look a little worn and dirty, my older sibling would use a little sandpaper and then use an airbrush to muddy the paint job. The 3D designer would apply a bump map to the model and then apply a diffuse map.

Lighting or Scene Building

At this stage of the game the production team gets to switch jobs. They get to take off their construction hard hats, soak their paintbrushes, and finally take a seat in the director's chair. In the lighting or scene building stage, a cast of models is assembled. It is at this point that all of the models are placed on the stage, the scene composition is checked to see if it is balanced, and the scene is then lit. The entire lighting process is vitally important since this is generally what sets the mood for an animation.

In 3D the designer has a wide variety of lighting tools at his/her disposal. Spotlights, point lights, parallel lights, gels, masks, projectors, and gobos can all be used in 3D. Fortunately, a designer doesn't have to climb to the top of rickety scaffolding to mount lights. In 3D the designer can simply hang a light in 3D space and not even have to worry about where to plug it in or finding an extension cord.

Animation

Action! At this point in the process the models are made to move and dance in space. In the past, traditional cel-based animators relied on a staff of hundreds to finish a project. Now the task is up to the designers and their computers.

The majority of software available today relies on a linear keyframe timeline. Sounds tricky, but it really isn't. How does it work? In the most simple description the designer gets to play the key-person.

When Disney was first pioneering traditional cel-based animation, hundreds of people worked on a project but only a select few made the important artistic decisions. The select few were known as the key-men. The key-man would draw the frames at the important points in the action and then hordes of artists would fill in the sequences between the frames, a process now known as *tweening*. In 3D animation, the designer creates the keyframes and then the computer fills in action with everything from lighting intensity to camera movement being animated.

Rendering

At this point in the animation process, the computer truly takes over. Think of the rendering process as sending the film out to be developed. Now that all of the lighting, texture maps, and animation are completed, the computer takes a picture of every single frame in your animation. The rendering process can take anywhere from a couple hours to several days for an animation. In the past, Disney used scores of women to paint each cel individually; now we can let the good old PowerPC chip handle the mind-numbing details.

Postproduction

This process is kind of like the editing room. Clips of various types are joined to form a movie, special effects are composited over the action, or animation is overlaid on live-action footage. At this point in the process the animation is finally transferred to the delivery medium. The animation can be transferred to videotape, film, or converted into a QuickTime movie so everyone with a computer can play back the animation.

SECTION THREE: USES FOR 3D

Multimedia

In the past few years, more and more multimedia designers have been relying heavily on 3D to create games and presentations. On the most simple level, 3D is extremely useful in creating interfaces, buttons, or toggle switches.

FIGURE *This interface for a multimedia presentation was created entirely in*
2.1 *Strata StudioPro.*

On the game and entertainment side of multimedia applications, many of the larger studios are using 3D to create entire worlds. The advantage to using 3D is that once the model is built, all of the renderings of the different player perspectives are simply camera angles.

What makes 3D so versatile is the fact that since all of a model's geometry exists in 3D space, it can be rotated, moved, scaled, or viewed from every conceivable angle. Myst, Gadget, and the Journeyman Project are examples of multimedia games that were created with off-the-shelf 3D applications and multimedia authoring packages. It is entirely possible for a team as small as five dedicated professionals to create a best seller.

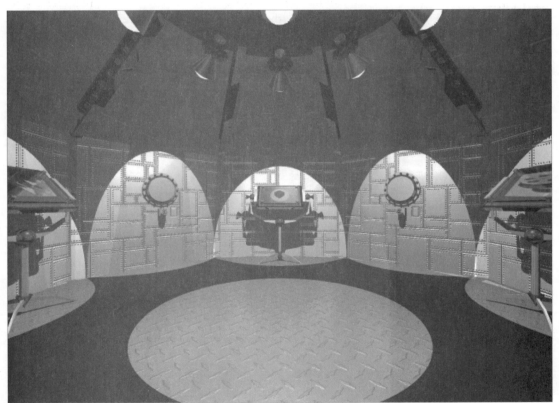

FIGURE *It's easy to build the interior of a room and then take multiple camera renderings for a game.*
2.2

Product Design   In the past, when an advertising or design agency needed to build a prototype for a product or try out different types of packaging design, they traditionally turned to expensive out-of-house fabricators. Now with 3D a competent designer can build the product in a 3D environment complete with all of the appropriate colors, materials and labels. If the client wants to move a knob or change the material, it's a simple enough task. Nowadays it is possible to see what a product will look like before it is ever built.

Broadcast and Film	The most obvious outlet for 3D animation is in the broadcast and film industries. Millions of dollars have been invested in high-end hardware and software to create the digital magic that we see on the silver screen. Don't despair if you feel that you don't have the budget to afford this high-priced technology. You'd be surprised to learn that many famous projects were produced on the lowly personal computer.

3

Choosing the Right Hardware and Software

There will come a time in your life when what you have just won't be enough, especially when it relates to both computer hardware and software. For me this feeling of malaise occurs just about every other day and I have to restrain myself from whipping out my credit card and dialing one of those catalog companies that can guarantee next day delivery.

This chapter is here to help you to comprehend the various aspects of computer hardware and 3D software, so you can make an informed decision when it comes to either purchasing a new system or simply upgrading your old one. This chapter also discusses the 3D software tools currently available and how they work and what you really need.

SECTION ONE: HARDWARE HARDSHIPS

Section One tells you all about your computer hardware. All of the new 3D specific peripherals such as multiple processors and 3D accelerator cards are discussed along with how to plan a system from the ground up and the basic hardware requirements of 3D design.

SECTION TWO: SOFTWARE RECOMMENDATIONS

Section Two describes the 3D software that you need to get started ranging from the right modeling application to the animation package. What modeling tools do you want and how do they work? What is QuickDraw 3D and how does it relate to you?

SECTION ONE: HARDWARE HARDSHIPS

Buying a computer is a lot like buying a car, and when you start to get into the rarefied atmosphere of the ultra fast and ultra new computers, the lines start to blur between the price of a new high-end Mac and a low-end automobile. For the new computer owner, perhaps the most unpleasant experience is to look at your nonfunctioning computer and think that for the same price you could be driving a shiny new convertible down to Tijuana for the weekend. But if you want to be able to produce high-end animation on schedule, you will need to forfeit your lusty wanton needs and concentrate on a solid computer platform.

So where do you start? This book assumes that you already have a computer in your life, but there will come a time when you will need to upgrade or buy another.

Tip. Before you think about selling your old computer, consider holding on to it for awhile. Why have more than one computer? When production time becomes tight, it helps to have one machine dedicated solely to rendering and another to model and script animations. Another reason to own several computers is so you can create a rendering farm that can break down a project into individual segments that each computer can work on separately.

The Savvy Shopper

Before you go off the deep end and start melting your credit card and getting your spouse in a huff, sit down and price out each piece of hardware carefully. Check the newspapers for sales or clearouts on old models. The best way to buy any new piece of hardware is through mail order.

Shop around the back of a reputable computer magazine. All of the numbers are toll free so you're calling on their dime anyway. It's easiest to get the best prices on a system this way. Don't be afraid to ask the salesperson to match a price that you were quoted from another company. Also, haggle over shipping costs; once you've been quoted a price that you are comfortable with, tell them you'll purchase the system right now if they'll cover the shipping. Another advantage of buying via mail order is that you avoid paying local sales tax.

Tip. Pay for everything with your credit card. There are disreputable dealers out there and the only way you have to protect yourself is by using the clout of your credit card company. It's far easier to contest a charge with a credit card company than to rush to place a stop payment on a personal, or even worse, a certified check. Don't send money orders, there is little to no chance of ever getting your money back!

When you buy hardware try to buy only what you need. Unfortunately when that purchasing frenzy sets in it's easy to go out shopping for an ink jet and end up buying a laser printer. But remember that it's often cheaper to buy all of the components at the same time rather than piecemeal. It's like having to install an air conditioning unit in your car after you've bought it. The dealership quotes you a ridiculously high price and you can only snarl in frustration. Buying a CD-ROM drive or extra RAM will give you that same level of anxiety. Try to get an entire package deal on a system. Also make sure that you have the salesperson send you an itemized list before you commit, just to make sure you are getting somewhat of a discount.

 Tip. One caveat of mail ordering anything is finding someone to service your hardware if something ever breaks, and believe me it will. But if you do purchase your CPU from Apple, for example, chances are there is a local service representative that can fix the problem.

The CPU

The central processing unit or CPU is the heart and soul of your entire system and will perhaps be the most expensive single item in your budget. Unlike a monitor or RAM, the CPU will probably need to be updated fairly regularly in order for it to stay competitive. It's a good idea to see if your computer manufacturer offers a good upgrade path.

The faster and more powerful your CPU, the faster your computer will render images and the easier it will be to work with complex files. Now that Apple has finally licensed out its previously proprietary operating system, many clone manufacturers are starting to release competitively priced systems. Since Apple is no longer the only fish in the pond, the problem is what brand and type of computer should you purchase. This is never an easy question, but if you're in the market for a new computer and you want to use it for 3D, you should seriously consider the following factors.

POWERPC VERSUS 68K

Comparing a PowerPC to a 68K machine is like comparing a Ferrari to a skateboard. The old CISC-based 68K chip set has definitely seen its day and in comparison to the PowerPC it just can't compete. That's not to say that any 68K-based machine is antiquated, but for sheer rendering speed the RISC-based PowerPC is infinitely faster. If you're buying a new computer, don't buy a used 68K machine unless you're getting an incredibly good deal. A new low-end PowerPC runs at twice if not three times the speed of the old top-of-the-line 68K machine. But if you are using one of the old machines, don't despair, they still can be useful for either modeling, setting up an animation or creating a texture map. The bottom line is that the PowerPC is a faster rendering computer.

Tip. Daystar Digital is producing multiple processor computers using the 604 PowerPC chip. These multiple processor wonders are supposed to be able to compete directly with dedicated graphics workstations. Once 3D software becomes optimized for multiple processor configurations, expect to see rendering times plummet.

When it comes to making a decision on how fast your processor should be, you should first consider your budget. Try to get the fastest computer that you can for your money, but do not spend your entire bankroll on the CPU. If you don't have enough RAM in your machine a fast processor is useless

Tip. There are several generations of PowerPC chips being released nowadays. The 604 has just replaced the first-generation 601 chip. Even though the megahertz or clock speed is the same on some 601s and 604s, a 604 is inherently faster when it is running software that is optimized for the CPU.

Important. Don't settle for anything less than a PowerPC machine if you can. The speed of a low-end PowerPC is up to two to three times as fast as the most powerful 68K machine.

NuBus Versus PCI

With the second generation of PowerPC Macintoshes, Apple released PCI-based machines to replace the older NuBus slot-type computer. Generally speaking, this doesn't mean much to the average 3D user unless they plan to use either a separate processing card such as the YARC Hydra or a QuickDraw 3D accelerator card. Only when you start getting into the high end of 3D should you be concerned about either of these options.

Tip. What is PCI? *Peripheral component interconnect* or the PCI format is a high-speed bus developed by Intel for their Pentium-based processors. Apple has recently adopted this standard. What this means for the Mac end user is that the new PCI bus is faster than the older NuBus and many PC card manufacturers might start releasing low-cost cards for the Mac.

CLOCK ACCELERATORS

Third-party manufacturers have begun offering clock accelerators for the PowerPC-based Macs. These little clip-on devices are attached to the processor on the mother board and increase the clock cycle of the CPU. Proponents of these devices claim that accelerators can give their machines a nice little boost, anywhere from 5% to 10%, which in the 3D world can mean shaving a couple of minutes off of a frame during rendering. On the other hand there are many who say that an accelerator can quickly burn out the processor on a machine and the performance advantage is not worth the initial price of the device.

I personally wouldn't risk strapping anything onto the processor of my machine, especially when Apple clearly states that the warranty on a computer is voided if you do something like that. If you do decide to get an accelerator, I would recommend buying one that has a cooling fan attached to it, or installing another fan in your machine just in case.

APPLE VERSUS THE CLONES

Once you've priced out your systems, it's time to make a decision. In most cases a computer is simply a computer, and after awhile they all perform at the same level. But it might be worthwhile spending the little bit extra to purchase an Apple computer. Apple does have the most experience as well as technical support and resources available to the consumer.

All of the other benefits aside the most important issue that you need to recognize is upgradability. Most of the newer computers have the processor located on a daughter card to the mother board. The primary advantage of this arrangement is that when it comes time to upgrade the computer, which in this industry occurs almost yearly, the processor can be simply swapped out with a minimum of fuss as well as cost. Also third-party manufacturers have planned to release their own low-cost speedy processor daughter cards sometime in the near future.

RAM

If I had to make a choice over buying a blisteringly fast CPU with a small amount of RAM, or purchasing a machine with a mid-speed processor with a lot of RAM, I would definitely go with the latter. After purchasing your CPU, RAM should be your next highest priority. 3D is perhaps one of the most RAM hungry applications you will ever encounter on your computer and the more RAM in your machine the better. Another consideration is that the RAM requirements of the Mac OS have been expanding with every passing generation. On an average, expect to see at least 6MB to 7MB allocated to the System Folder with System 7.5 and later.

Realistically speaking, the minimum amount of RAM that you should have in your computer is 16MB. You can get away with using far less, but rendering time will be extremely slow and you will have problems manipulating complex files. Some 3D applications might even flash an out-of-memory warning at you. Many professionals have upwards of 100MB worth of RAM in their computers, and for most users this might seem excessive. If you're interested in investing in more RAM I would recommend stocking your system with around 32MB. It's a good level to start at and it won't empty your wallet.

Why do you need so much RAM? First of all it speeds up rendering time by reducing the amount of time that the computer has to access the hard disk. With models and textures sometimes in the 10MB range its far faster to keep all of that information in RAM rather than on a hard disk. This stands true not only when it comes to rendering, but also when it comes to creating the models themselves. Having a large amount of RAM allocated to a modeling application will often reduce the amount of screen redraw or refresh rate after moving a model since the information does not need to be spooled to a hard drive. Another consideration is multitasking. It's a real time saver to have enough RAM to run several applications simultaneously. Being able to run Photoshop at the same time as your 3D application will make the texture mapping process a whole lot easier.

When it comes to buying RAM make sure you consider the following. The RAM should first of all be noncomposite. Also make sure that the RAM is new and not "refurbished." Try to get the fastest NS or nanosecond speed for your dollar, the lower the number the better. Also be sure to call around. The large mail order catalogs that are deforesting the world offer the worst prices. Try companies that specialize in

RAM; you can usually get the best deal and at the same time avoid paying sales tax.

Important. The minimum amount of RAM you should have in your computer if you're interested in 3D is 16MB. I would recommend at least 32MB for those more serious about their work.

Tip. With the PCI series of Macintoshes it's a good idea to buy sets of DIMMs (dual in-line memory modules) rather than one large DIMM. The computer can interleave several DIMMs, making access time faster. So instead of buying one 64MB DIMM, consider investing in two 32MB DIMMs. But remember that you only have a limited number of slots to place memory on the board.

Monitors

A good monitor is something that you will keep with you for the rest of your life. This is your window onto the world and it had best be good. In this case, the bigger it is the better. For the graphics professional I would suggest settling for nothing less than a 16- or 17-inch monitor. Anything smaller might lead to serious headaches or constant squinting.

One of the features that the Macintosh OS is famous for is supporting multiple monitors. Several monitors can be connected to the same computer to create a virtual desktop. This feature is extremely handy when it comes to 3D or Photoshop. When I work in my modeling program, I use three monitors, one 17-inch and two 14-inch displays. The advantage of this type of setup is that I can look at the same model from three different perspectives simultaneously. For applications such as Photoshop, I like to keep the image that I'm working on in the large screen, and all of my palettes and tools in the smaller ones. This technique also works well for scripting an animation or working in multimedia authoring applications.

If you're interested in getting a second monitor for your system, I would recommend going with a smaller 14-inch display rather than another large screen. This is of course if you already have a 17- or 21-inch monitor. Multiple monitors on your desktop can soon overcrowd a small workspace. Depending on the Macintosh model you have, you might have to buy an additional video card to support another monitor or there might be an additional monitor port on your computer.

COLOR DEPTH

As any graphics professional will tell you, if you want to do computer graphics your computer will have to support a bit depth of 24-bit. What is bit depth? Bit depth is the maximum number of colors that can be supported on screen at any given time. It works like this:

2-bit monitor depth = black and white
4-bit monitor depth = 16 colors
8-bit monitor depth = 256 colors
16-bit monitor depth = thousands of colors
24-bit monitor depth = 16.7 million colors

Why do you need to see all of those colors at any given time? If your computer does not support 24-bit color and you tried to look at a 24-bit image, the picture would look pixelated or blocky on the screen. This is most noticeable when you have subtle shading gradations such as on the surface of a sphere.

How do you increase the number of colors on screen? You can either buy a 24-bit video card or increase the amount of VRAM (video RAM) in your computer. Buying more VRAM depends on the size of your monitor. A larger monitor requires more VRAM to display a higher bit depth than does a smaller monitor. Also a 24-bit video card that can support 24-bit color on a 21-inch monitor is more expensive than a video card that can support 24-bit color for a 17-inch monitor.

Important. Do not settle for anything less than 24-bit color on your machine. 16 bit will do temporarily, but the difference between the two is astounding.

QuickDraw 3D Accelerator Cards

Many people, including several industry professionals, are confused over what QuickDraw 3D accelerator cards can do. 3D accelerator cards accelerate Apple's new QuickDraw3D API, which lets you view an animation or manipulate a model in real time using a cross between Gouraud and Phong shading. For example, when you're creating a model, and you want to see what it looks like with Gouraud or Phong shading, you usually click a button and the computer performs a quick rendering of the model. Since the Gouraud or Phong shading algorithm is fairly fast, the entire rendering process only takes a few seconds.

Now imagine being able to render the object using Gouraud or Phong shading in real time, which is what 3D accelerator cards do. This was previously possible only on high-end SGI graphics workstations that cost more than my car. But with the advent of the PowerPC chip, QuickDraw 3D, and PCI-based 3D accelerator cards, all of that has changed. Any PowerPC Mac can take advantage of QuickDraw3D without any hardware assistance, but an accelerator card will let you view a complex model faster and at a higher frame rate. For more on QuickDraw 3D be sure to read the section at the end of this chapter.

 Tip. A 3D accelerator card will only work on a PowerPC computer since Apple has no plans of porting QuickDraw 3D to the 68K Mac platform. Also for those using NuBus-based PowerPC systems, you probably won't see a 3D accelerator card for awhile, if at all. Development seems aimed at PCI-based PowerPC computers.

When it comes to purchasing a 3D accelerator card you should consider how many polygons per second it can display on the screen. The more polygons, at the greater bit depth, at the highest frame rate, at the larger screen size the better. Also, different 3D accelerator cards support different features such as reflectivity, texture mapping, and transparency all in real time.

Multiple Processor Cards

We've all heard the expression "Two heads are better than one." The same axiom can applied in the computer world. Apple Computer and Daystar Digital have designed a symmetrical multiprocessing system that allows for several CPUs to work on the same task at the same time. The bottom line is that for 3D users rendering time should be drastically reduced. The technology is still in its infancy, and will not be fully integrated into mainstream use until the advent of Copland, which is the next-generation operating system. Daystar has already proven that it is possible to swap out the daughter card on the 8500 and 9500 Macs and replace it with one of their multiprocessor cards. It remains to be seen if they will offer an upgrade path.

Flatbed Scanner

While not as essential as the other pieces of hardware, a flatbed scanner makes a good addition to your studio. A scanner can be used to create your own texture or color maps quite easily. For example, if you wanted a pebble finish, you could simply scan in a plastic bag full of pebbles. It's a lot cheaper than having to go out and buy a lot of CD-ROMs with texture maps on them.

3D Digitizers

3D digitizer hardware starts to head into the range of the high-end 3D user. These digitizers can be used to input real-world spatial coordinates to create a 3D model. For a more thorough description, refer to Chapter 6, Advanced Modeling.

Storage

I remember my first computer. It had 512K worth of RAM and I did everything from floppy disk including launching the computer. When I finally invested in a 20MB hard drive, I had thought that never in my wildest dreams would I ever fill it. Today my computer has more than 80MB worth of RAM and I measure storage in the gigabyte rather than in the megabyte range.

All too often I've been faced with the problem of putting all of the information that I have someplace safe. For the 3D designer, storage considerations have to be paramount. When your models alone start to creep up in the 8MB range, and a folder full of texture maps for one project starts peaking out at 20MB, you should be concerned. Also consider the fact that one frame in an animation can be upwards of 1MB, and one second for an NTSC animation consists of 30 frames, one minute of uncompressed computer animation can equal 1.8 gigabytes. Yes, you can compress these files but the time involved for compressing and decompressing will cut into your productivity level.

Your storage concerns can be broken down into two categories: working and archival storage. Working storage implies on-line, easy random access, with high data transfer rates. Archival storage on the other hand needs to be both high capacity and inexpensive.

WORKING STORAGE

The key to working storage is fast and easy access. You need to be able to store and access your files directly from the device with a minimum of fuss.

Hard Drives

There are several solutions for on-line working storage. The most accepted and frequently used is the tried and true magnetic hard drive. The prices of hard drives have fallen in the past few years and the quality of the drives has improved. When it comes to buying an additional hard drive you should consider the following:

- Try to get a high-speed AV drive. The prices are slightly higher, but the drives are of a better quality. The sustained data transfer rate is in the 3MB to 4MB range for most AV drives which is ideal for playing back animations, digitizing video, or even burning a CD-R.
- Think of buying an external rather than an internal drive. An external drive will run around $100 more but the advantages are obvious. The external drive has its own power supply and cooling fan, it is far more portable than an internal device, and it's easier to install.
- The price difference between a 1GB and 4GB hard drive is around $500. If a 1GB drive costs $1000 and a 4GB drive costs $1500, which is the better deal? It's often cheaper to go ahead and buy a large-capacity drive right off the bat rather than postpone the inevitable storage crunch.

 Important. The bottom line regardless of what you buy — whether it be a magnetic hard drive or removable media — is that you will need at least a 500MB internal hard drive. This drive should be used to store both your System Folder and applications. Consider investing in another 1GB drive for project files.

Medium-Capacity Removable Storage

The cost of removable storage is at an all time low and the capacity of these devices has increased. The advantage of removable media is that if a cartridge becomes full, all you need to do is go out and buy another. These removable media drives might be destined to replace the industry standards, which are the 5.25-inch SyQuest cartridge and Bernoulli drive. Iomega's Zip and Jaz, Sony's MD Data Drive, and SyQuest's EZ135 offer portable, low-cost, midlevel capacity solutions.

- *Iomega.* The Zip drive utilizes 3.5-inch magnetic-based media that can store up to100MB worth of data. The drive weighs in at less than a pound, so if a remote site does not have a drive, it's a simple matter to take yours with you. Perhaps the most appealing aspect of both the drive and the media is the cost. The average street price of the unit is around $200 dollars and the media when purchased in quantity is around $10 a cartridge.

  Iomega's next generation of drive is an ultra high-capacity, high-speed drive that might change the way people think about storage. The Jaz drive is a SCSI 2 compatible device with a data transfer rate in the 6.73MB/sec range with a storage capacity of approximately 1GB. The most appealing aspect of this device is the price. The 3.5-inch media is expected to debut at around $125 with the drive itself coming in at $600. For video professionals the Jaz drive might just replace your old high-speed array. Several devices can be daisy chained to produce a Jaz array with a 10MB/sec synchronous data transfer rate. Unfortunately, the Jaz is not backwardly compatible with the Zip drive so you might end up purchasing both units.

- *Sony.* On the other hand Sony's MD Data Drive enters the market at the high end with a street price of around $700. The optical-based media can store upwards of 140MB and costs approximately $30 a cartridge. The primary advantage of this unit is that it is truly portable since it can be run off batteries, which makes it a great companion for laptop computers. Also since the media is MO based, the integrity of the information is almost guaranteed.

- *SyQuest.* The EZ135 3.5-inch media has a data transfer rate of 2.4MB/sec and a storage capacity of 135MB. SyQuest has released the drive at around the same price range as the Zip drive, trying to woo the consumer with a low $240 price tag. The manufacturers suggested retail price of the media is in the $20 range, which makes it much more affordable than their previous 5.5-inch 44MB and 88MB cartridges. The drive is based on Winchester Disk drive technology of which SyQuest has years of experience.

All three drives offer the user that is strapped for additional storage room a low-cost alternative. The capacity as well as data transfer rate allow the user the option of storing and launching an application directly from the disk. Since the media is reusable, it might even become more cost effective than a CD-R. Also because of the high data transfer rate of the micro media, it is better suited than a CD-ROM for the playback of a multimedia presentation. Since all of the units are small enough to slip into a briefcase, they are ideal for offsite multimedia demonstrations run from a laptop computer.

All of the drives just listed have a capacity in the 100MB to 150MB range, which is ideal for storing the source files for an animation or even a short animation itself. When purchasing any of these devices be sure to consider the following:

- *Reliability.* Will my information be there when I go back and look for it? How long is the shelf life of the media.
- *Cost.* How much is the price of the individual cartridge? How does the price of the drive compare with its competitors?
- *Speed.* What's the data transfer rate of the device? Is it fast enough to play back an animation?

OLDER REMOVABLE STORAGE FORMATS

The older 5.25-inch 44MB and 88MB SyQuest formats should not be considered as a storage option for the first-time buyer. They are notoriously unreliable as well as expensive when compared to the other options available to the consumer. The Bernoulli as well as the venerable floppy disk should also be put out to pasture as well.

OPTICAL MASS STORAGE SOLUTIONS

For storage-hungry applications such as nonlinear editing, 3D animation, and multimedia authoring, high-capacity storage is absolutely necessary. The main advantage magnetic media has over optical-based solutions is the access time to information and fast data transfer rate. The future of optical media lies not in increasing the speed of the media, but rather in increasing capacity. The storage capacity of both magneto optical (MO) as well as CD-ROM-based media will be taking a quantum leap forward. For the consumer, that will mean less media will be necessary to store larger amounts of data. And since the majority of optical media is removable, the user — depending, of course, on budget — has an almost infinite amount of storage available.

Even though MO drives have been around for several years, they really haven't gained a very large following. The drawback to MO technology is that the cost per megabyte of the media as well as the initial hardware price were generally too high for most consumers. On the other hand, because of the nature of MO technology, the media stored on a cartridge is extremely secure for upwards of 30 years. Another benefit to MO technology is that the 5.25-inch format has a data transfer rate of approximately 2MB/sec, which puts it into the range of magnetic media. The goal of MO manufacturers now is to offer the consumer a more cost-effective solution in regards to MO technology.

A recently introduced, high-density constant angular velocity (CAV) MO format might be able to give optical-based media a foothold above the average magnetic drive. The data transfer rate of these units easily surpasses the speed of the average stock hard drive included with most package systems. It's entirely possible to use a MO drive in the same manner as you would a magnetic device. The CAV MO drive will be large and fast enough to support either the storage or launch of applications directly from the drive. A magnetic device such as an array or a high-end multimedia drive does have a much higher sustained data transfer rate, but optical devices do have the advantage of low-cost removable media.

 Tip. Pinnacle has recently released a new high-capacity 4.6GB MO drive that retails for around $1700. The Apex has a data transfer rate in the 5MB to 6MB range and the media runs at around $200.

ARCHIVAL STORAGE

While not as high a priority as working storage, archival storage is another consideration that needs to be faced by the 3D designer. You've finished the animation for the client, and he's ecstatic with the work. But now, you need to clear off your hard drive so you can start on the new project. The problem is, where do you put it all? You can't keep it on a relatively expensive Zip or MO cartridge, and the high cost for the real estate on a hard drive is out of the question. The amount of time that you spend both on the modeling and then on rendering is far too extensive to simply erase the files. You need something that is inexpensive with a high capacity and also fairly reliable.

CD-R

In the past only multimedia developers and users that required mass storage capabilities used CD burners or CD-Rs. The cost of both the hardware and the media were too high for the average consumer. But that's all changing. The present goal of the CD-R manufacturer is to make the CD-R as ubiquitous as the floppy disk. Major changes in both price as well as technology will make the CD-R appealing to even the most conservative consumer.

The primary drawback to CD-R technology is that it's a write once/read many media. But the CD-R manufacturer is trying to make the media so cost effective that the write-once factor will not play such an integral role in the decision making process. The street price of a CD-R blank is about $10, and industry analysts feel that soon it should be less than $5. Even though the media is write once, many drives support multisession capabilities. In other words, the user does not have to fill the entire CD-R in one session, and can go back at a later time to add more data. For the frugal at heart, think of it this way: you can have over 400 floppy disks for only $5, the shelf life is measured in decades rather than in years, and the only drawback is that you can only write to each "disk" once.

But there are a few additional caveats to the technology. First of all the writing process to the blank is still a slow procedure. There are several 4x and higher burners available but they do require a high-speed dedicated drive which will increase the initial cost of a unit. Also 650MB does not go as far as you would want nowadays. The data transfer rate from a CD-ROM is also phenomenally slow, especially when compared to a magnetic hard drive. A 4x speed CD-ROM has a data transfer rate of around 600K/sec as compared to 2MB/sec on an average magnetic drive. On the other hand, the benefits to CD-R are numerous. The large installed base of CD-ROM readers almost guarantees compatibility across a variety of both platforms or sites. Also once burned, expect your files to be safe for around 100 years, more time than we need to even worry about.

DAT

While it's the most cost-effective form of storage, DAT or the DD-2 format is the most inconvenient. The simplest way to describe how a DAT drive works is that a directory or catalog is made of the contents of your hard drive. That information is then written to the DAT drive.

The write and verify speed is extremely slow in comparison to a standard hard drive, and an entire backup session can last hours.

When the user needs to restore from a DAT they need to first refer to the directory, and then the DAT drive has to wind the tape to the specific point to read the information. This method is considered not to be random access but rather linear, which can be extremely time consuming. The average DAT drive can transfer information at around 25MB a minute. But backup time needs to be doubled because the transferred information has to be verified.

The main advantage that DAT has over the other archival storage alternatives is the cost per megabyte. When the average 120-meter tape costs $25 and the capacity is in the 3GB to 4GB range, it definitely can be considered to be the most inexpensive means for storage. The drawback, of course, is that the archiving process is slow and many professionals recommend copying your data from the DAT to a hard drive and then back to a DAT every six months to ensure the integrity of your information.

SECTION TWO: SOFTWARE RECOMMENDATIONS

It's ironic that one of the primary advantages of 3D software for the Mac is it's largest limitation. A wide variety of software applications are available for the 3D enthusiast, yet the drawback is the fact that no one program is entirely self sufficient or self sustaining for serious production work. The bottom line is that you're going to need more than one program to get the job done.

 Tip. Don't start a project without having the appropriate tools. You should not be desperation buying! You also will not have the time to learn an entirely new program during the production process — you should be doing that on your own time and not on the client's.

The key to purchasing 3D software is to start at the beginning of the production process and then move onward. First of all, consider what sort of modeling package you want, and then choose an animation and then finally a postproduction application.

Tip. If you're a student or instructor, many software companies offer substantial educational discounts. Take advantage of this fact since you could save anywhere from 50% to 70% off of the list price of the software.

All-Inclusive Packages

Many companies are releasing packages that can handle the entire modeling, rendering, and animation process. I wholeheartedly recommend these packages for the beginner. Buying an all-inclusive package can save you some money and the feature sets are usually pretty good. Packages such as those marketed by Specular, Strata, and Macromedia offer the novice a solid user-friendly environment to learn all about 3D. But for serious production work, I would recommend looking into programs dedicated solely to either modeling or animation. I'm not saying that the all-inclusive packages cannot handle high-level production work, rather that it will be easier to produce higher quality animation in far less time with dedicated applications. On the all-inclusive packages, there are work-arounds for just about every single problem, the drawback is the time and effort spent implementing them.

Modeling Software

There's going to be a time when you reach a certain point in the production process and no matter what, you just can't get that model right. A deadline's looming over your head and you're running out of time. You need a model of a cowboy hat and the only thing you have on screen is a cylinder. No matter how persuasive you think you are, you know your client isn't going to believe that this is the latest trend in Western wear. Your arsenal of tools has begun to fail you and there's nowhere else to turn. What do you do? Your first option is to give up entirely and consider taking up another profession such as television repair. But if you want to stick with it, there are a couple of alternatives.

Tip. Before you go out and buy more software, take the time to learn the basics on the one you have. The learning curve for 3D modeling is the steepest out of the entire animation process. And while the inexpensive and less sophisticated programs do offer less in terms of modeling tools, generally speaking they are easier to learn. Once you feel comfortable with what you have, then it might be a good idea to start looking for another program.

If you are having problems creating a 3D model, and you feel that you've exhausted all of the tools at your disposal, you might consider learning another 3D package. But before you start to become enticed by amazingly long checklists of features of an application, you should first consider what type of model you need to create. Is it organic or soft such as human figures or racing cars? Or will your models contain hard-edged shapes such as buildings or spaceships?

3D modeling applications can be broken down into two distinct types of categories: polygonal- or spline-based modelers. As the 3D market for the Mac has matured, more and more programs have been blending the two types of modeling geometry together. But unfortunately no one program has successfully integrated both types of geometry into the same package with any degree of success. It's for that reason that I recommend purchasing one package to create one type of model, and another package to create another.

POLYGONAL-BASED MODELERS

Polygonal-based modelers are best suited for creating hard or straight-edged models. Any shape or primitive that you create with a polygonal modeler will be composed of individual polygons. The surface of a sphere, for example, that is created in form•Z is composed of hundreds of individual polygons. Since a polygon itself is composed of at least three straight lines, a polygonal-based object when rendered might appear faceted when viewed at close range.

 Tip. If your object does appear faceted, try increasing the amount of geometry used to define the object. In the case of a sphere, increase the density or resolution of the object. For a lathed object, increase the number of steps used in the lathing process. Another alternative is to increase the breaking angle used to define the smoothing of an object.

The advantage of using a polygonal-based modeler over a spline-based one is that it is usually easier to create and manipulate straight-edged objects such as squares, rectangles and planes. Also Boolean functions, which are some of the more essential modeling tools, work almost exclusively on polygonal-shaped objects. For most modeling applications, a polygonal modeler will be able to handle just about any task.

The problem with a polygonal modeler arises when it has to deal with curved shapes. Since any curved or rounded shape has to be

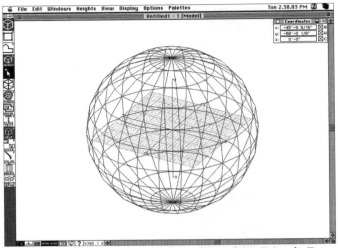

FIGURE *A sphere primitive from auto•des•sys form•Z RenderZone*
3.1 *2.7.5 is composed of several hundred polygons.*

constructed of straight lines, any object created will tend to look jagged or rough around the edges when viewed at close range. Since the only alternative is to increase the resolution or the amount of geometry of the model, performance is decreased. Polygonal-based models also tend to take up more storage space on your hard drive since they're usually composed of more information than a spline-based model.

SPLINE-BASED MODELERS

Spline-based modelers excel at handling rounded or curved shapes. Since the surface of an object is defined by a spline curve, which is in essence a mathematical formula, an object can be thought of as being resolution independent. When a spline-based object is viewed at close range, the object remains smooth edged. It is also considerably easier to create soft or organic shapes with a spline-based modeler since the majority of tools are designed specifically for this task.

Most spline-based modelers use the analogy of clay when describing the modeling process. Many of the 3D tools available in spline-based applications such as pinch, twist, and bend are directly derived from the physical process of molding clay. What makes spline-based modelers so powerful is the fact that the individual splines that define the

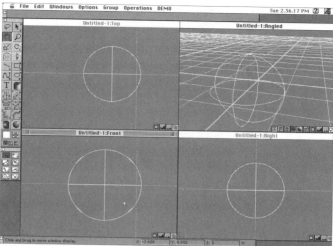

FIGURE **3.2** *This sphere, created in VIDI's ModelPro 3.0, is a spline-based object.*

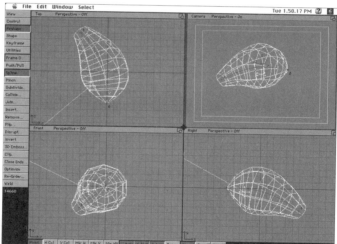

FIGURE **3.3** *Valis' Pixel Putty lets the user manipulate splines that run the length of an object. Also the surface of an object can be treated like modeling clay and molded into various shapes.*

surface of an object can be manipulated directly, which in turn affects the entire surface of the model.

The drawback is that most spline-based modelers do not handle straight-edged objects as well as polygonal-based modelers. If a spline modeler does have Boolean functions, for example, it must first convert the object into a polygonal shape before performing the function. But if you're interested in creating sweeping shapes or soft shaped models, a spline-based modeler will be the better choice.

Tip. For the novice 3D enthusiast I would recommend first learning a polygonal-based modeler, and then after becoming more experienced picking up a spline-based application. Generally speaking, the polygonal-based program will be more useful for most applications and will be easier to learn.

Modeling Tools

Many companies that produce 3D software pride themselves on their long checklists of features. The problem is deciding what you want, and what you will actually use on a day-to-day basis. For the lower level modeling tools such as lathe and extrude, most software packages offer virtually the same options. And when you're first starting out, these tools are going to be the ones that you use the most anyway. You won't miss the higher end features until you really start to become proficient in 3D. Unfortunately, it doesn't make sense to buy a program, spend the time learning it, and then realize that you have to upgrade to another package to get the additional features that you want.

Tip. Not all modeling programs are created equally. For example you might see two packages state that they both support Boolean functions, yet one will implement the feature better than the other. How would you know that without purchasing the program? Either phone the company for a demo version or download one from an on-line library. The CD-ROMs included with this book also have many try-out versions of the most popular 3D modeling software available.

TOOL SETS

The following is a description of some of the more essential tools that you should look for in your modeling package. These are the tools that you will get the most use out of on a day-to-day basis. The images are all from auto•des•sys form•Z RenderZone 2.7.5.

Primitives

Think of primitives as your building blocks in the 3D world, you'll be using these for just about any model that you create. There are two major types of primitives, 2D and 3D. Spheres, pyramids, cubes, cones, and cylinders all fall into the category of 3D primitives. Some of the higher level programs also support user-configurable polyhedron primitives.

2D primitives include squares, circles, ovals, and usually a line tool that can be used to create either coplanar 2D polygons or paths. On their own, the 2D primitives don't seem as useful as the 3D ones, yet in combination with the higher end functions of certain programs, 2D

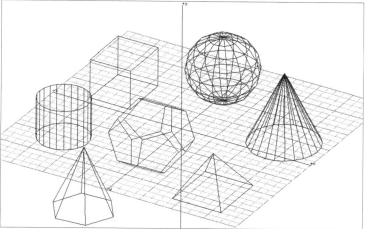

FIGURE *The shapes in this image are generally regarded as 3D primitives.*
3.4

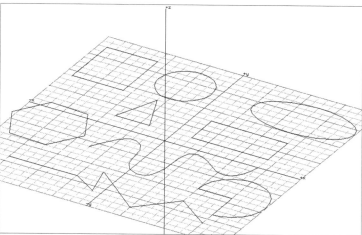

FIGURE *2D primitives when used in conjunction with the higher level*
3.5 *modeling tools can be used to create almost any shape imaginable.*

primitives become powerful modeling tools. Most 3D programs support the creation of 2D spline-based primitives.

Lathe

The lathe tool in a 3D program is much like a carpenter's lathe or a potter's wheel, but it's easier to use and requires much less skill to operate. The user starts with a 2D profile or shape and then chooses an axis (X, Y, Z) around which to rotate the object.

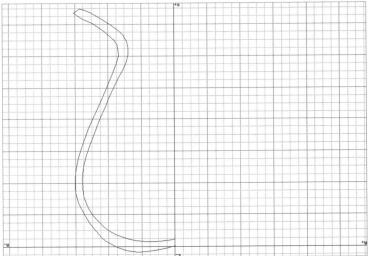

FIGURE   *This 2D shape or template can be revolved or lathed to produce*
3.6   *a 3D shape.*

Unlike a carpenter's lathe, the user can revolve a 2D template with varying degrees of rotation. For example you can create an object that has only been rotated 180° or 270°.

Don't limit yourself to thinking that the lathe tool should be used solely for creating wine glasses or vases. If your program for example does not have a cone-shaped primitives or toroid, you can create your own with the lathe tool.

By offsetting a 2D shape from the axis of rotation you can create shapes that would have been difficult to model. For example, by modeling the 2D cross section of a car tire rim, you can lathe the shape into a 3D object.

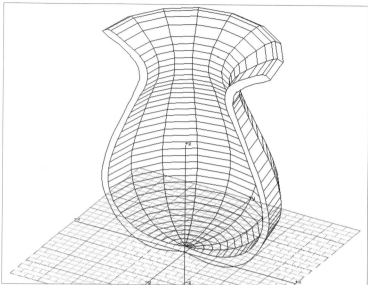

FIGURE *The 2D template has been lathed 180° to produce this 3D shape.*
3.7

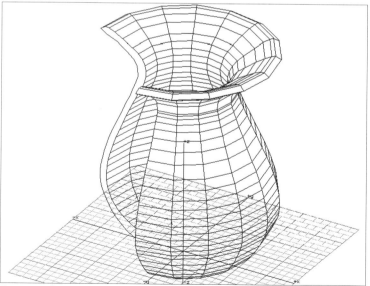

FIGURE *The 2D template has been lathed 270° to produce this 3D shape.*
3.8

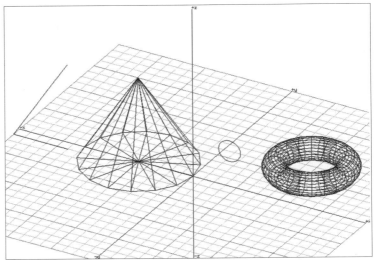

FIGURE   *Primitive shapes can be created easily with the lathe tool.*
3.9

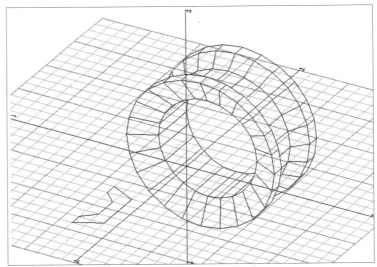

FIGURE   *A 2D shape can be offset from the axis of rotation to create a*
3.10   *hollow center.*

Tip. When creating an object that is hollow or one with a visible inside wall, remember to model both sides of the surface. For example, many beginners forget to model both the inside and outside surface of a wine bottle. If the bottle is opaque, then it really doesn't matter, but if the bottle is semitransparent, then the object will not look realistic when rendered.

Extrude

The extrude tool pushes a 2D profile or shape along the axis that is perpendicular to the surface of the shape. It's a lot like those pasta machines that you see on television. The user starts with a 2D shape and then pushes it out along a perpendicular axis. The extrude tool is particularly useful for creating shapes such as ribbed garbage cans or gears.

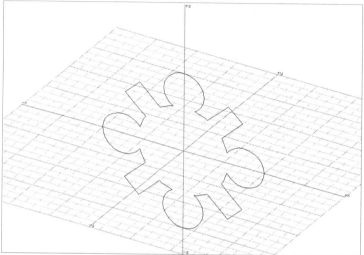

Figure *A 2D shape...*

3.11

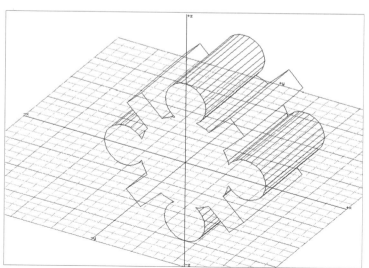

Figure *...can be extruded perpendicular to its surface.*

3.12

Sweep or Extrude on Path

The sweep tool is a derivative of the extrude tool. The major difference between extrude and sweep is that a 2D object can be extruded along 2D planar paths, 2D curved paths or nonplanar 3D paths.

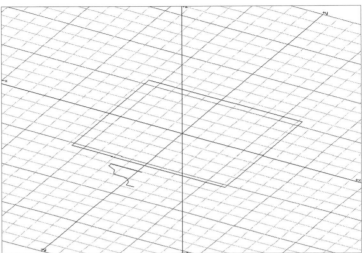

FIGURE **3.13**   *This 2D shape can be swept on the 2D planar path to produce...*

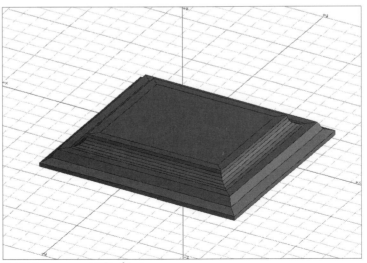

FIGURE **3.14**   *...a swept 3D object.*

Sweeping on a 2D planar path can be used to create objects such as picture frames, crown molding for a room, or bases for pedestals (Figures 3.13 and 3.14).

Sweeping a 2D shape along a planar curved path can be used for serpentine-like objects such as a winding fence or bendy bench (Figure. 3.15 and 3.16).

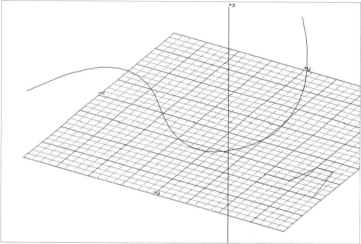

FIGURE *A 2D shape swept along a curved 2D path...*
3.15

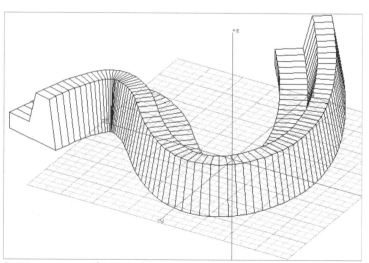

FIGURE *...can produce winding shapes such as this.*
3.16

Sweeping a 2D shape along a curved, 3D path can produce very complex shapes such as telephone cords or a banister for a spiral staircase (Figures 3.17 and 3.18).

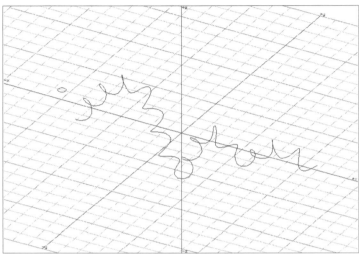

FIGURE *A 2D shape swept along a curved 3D path...*
3.17

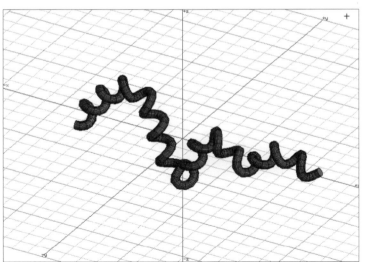

FIGURE *...produces very complex helical objects.*
3.18

Twist and Taper

The twist and taper tools go hand in hand with the sweep and extrude tools. A twisted shape is simply an extruded shape that has been rotated along the central axis of extrusion while a tapered shape can be scaled along the axis of extrusion.

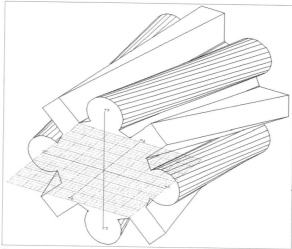

FIGURE **3.19** *A twisted shape is rotated along the axis of extrusion.*

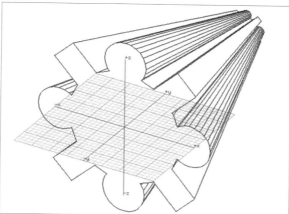

FIGURE **3.20** *A tapered shape is scaled along the axis of extrusion.*

Mirror

The mirror tool is one of the most overlooked tools in 3D yet one of the most essential. The mirror tool can be used to create a mirror reflection of an object.

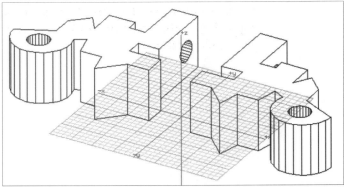

FIGURE *The mirror tool creates a mirror reflection of an object.*
3.21

Bevel

The bevel or rounding tool lets the user apply a beveled or softened edge to an object. This feature is particularly useful when applied to text-based objects. Beveling also works well on planar surfaces when you need to break up large even shapes.

Tip. Try to bevel the edges of all of your text when creating a flying logo. By beveling the text, you create more surfaces that catch reflected light.

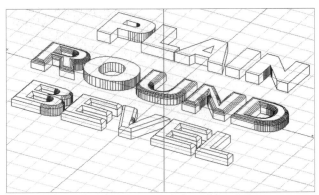

FIGURE *Examples of plain, rounded, and beveled text.*
3.22

Loft and Skin

One of the more complicated 3D tools available is the lofting or skinning tool. By using a series 2D shapes, which are often called *ribs*, the user can create a 3D lofted surface. The closest analogy to this process is building a boat hull. The boat builder starts by constructing a series of ribs to form the skeleton of the boat. A surface of planks is then applied over the skeleton to form the hull or shell. The process is almost identical in 3D.

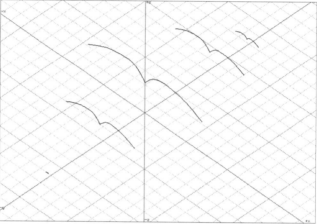

FIGURE 3.23   *Individual 2D shapes or ribs are drawn and aligned...*

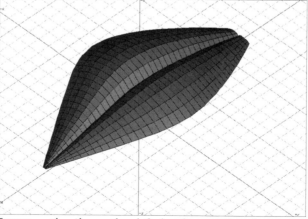

FIGURE 3.24   *...the ribs are then lofted to form a 3D surface...*

FIGURE   *...and then grouped to create a model of a flower.*
3.25

Boolean Functions

Boolean functions are perhaps the most important tool in the 3D modeling toolbox. Very few applications include Boolean functions, and even fewer still do them well. Booleans can be divided into two categories, 2D and 3D functions. Most programs claim to support 2D Boolean functions, which is fairly standard. The more important 3D functions can only be found in a few select applications.

Tip. If your program can import EPS files then you can have access to all of the 2D Boolean functions. Programs such as Adobe Illustrator and Macromedia FreeHand can add, subtract, and difference 2D shapes. It's a simple matter to then export the file as an EPS document and then import it into your 3D program as a 2D shape.

3D Boolean functions allow the user to either carve spaces out of 3D objects with other 3D objects, join several objects into one single volume, or split intersecting objects into individual volumes. Boolean functions enable you to create shapes that would have been impossible to make using more traditional modeling methods. Many programs offer work-arounds in order to substitute for Boolean functions but they are often time consuming and usually don't work.

3D Boolean functions can be divided into four different types: union, difference, split, and intersection. A Boolean union combines two objects into a single volume. A Boolean difference subtracts the intersecting area of one object from a second object. A Boolean split divides two intersecting objects into multiple volumes, with the surface of the intersecting volume defined by the surface of the two original objects. Finally, a Boolean intersection creates a single volume from the intersection of two objects.

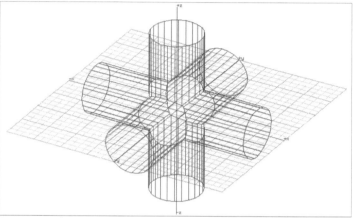

FIGURE **3.26** *Boolean union combines the intersecting area of two objects into a single volume.*

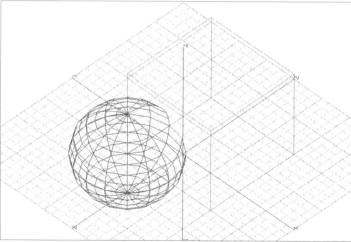

FIGURE **3.27** *Boolean difference subtracts the intersecting area of one object from a second object.*

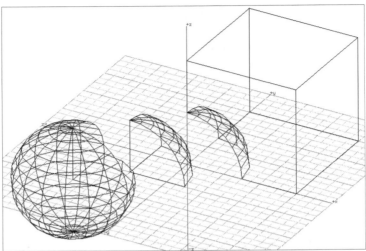

FIGURE **3.28** *Boolean split divides two intersecting objects into multiple volumes, with the surface of the intersecting volume defined by the two original objects.*

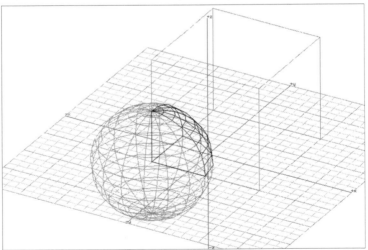

FIGURE **3.29** *Boolean intersection creates a single volume from the intersection of two objects.*

Rendering and Animation Software

Since the rendering and animation features of a package are so closely intertwined, it makes sense to consider them both when looking for a 3D program. This section covers the major features that are available in most packages, it is meant as a brief overview of the technology since most of the terms are covered in greater detail later in this book.

RENDERING

A program is only as good as its finished product. Perhaps one of the most influential factors is the rendering algorithm used to produce the image. The majority of programs offer the following rendering algorithms:

- Raytracing
- Phong
- Gouraud
- Flat shaded
- Hidden line
- Wireframe

Tip. For serious animation production work, most designers use the Phong rendering algorithm. For still work when only one frame is necessary, most designers can afford to use the slower, but more realistic, Raytracing method.

Try to find a program that offers all of the algorithms mentioned above. But don't limit yourself. Try not to exclude any package just because it is lacking one or two rendering engines. Remember that each rendering engine should be used for specific applications. Take a little time to think about what you want to use your 3D program for and then make a decision. For a more detailed description of each algorithm refer to Chapter 15, Rendering.

Tip. At the highest end of the algorithmic totem lies the fabled Radiosity. Radiosity, a derivative of the Raytracing algorithm, is perhaps one of the most resource demanding and time-consuming rendering engines available. On the other hand, it is perhaps the most realistic, mimicking the color bleed that occurs between closely placed objects of varying colors.

LIGHTING

Light sources add dimension and mood to your animations. It helps to have several different types at your disposal because chances are you will be using most of them at one point or another. Just about every program offers the following lighting options:

- Parallel or global
- Point
- Spot

For more specialized effects, you should look for the following types of lights:

- Ambient
- Tube
- Lens flares
- Projectors
- Gels
- Glowing lights

For a more detailed description of each type of lighting, refer to Chapter 9, Lighting, and Chapter 11, Lighting Special Effects.

TEXTURE MAPPING

When it comes to texture mapping, you will absolutely need the following types of maps in order to get the most out of 3D. At some point you will use each one of these types of maps in a project:

- Color
- Bump
- Reflection
- Environment
- Specular
- Ambient
- Diffuse

For the more adventurous at heart, animated texture mapping abilities are also a huge plus! Refer to Chapter 8, Advanced Texture Mapping, for more information on the various types of texture mapping.

Tip. One feature to definitely look for in a program is the ability to apply more than one map to an object at a time.

ANIMATION TOOLS

It's extremely difficult to codify any sort of standard to judge several animation packages since each one is so vastly different. The bottom line is that if you want to do any sort of serious animation, you need the following tools:

- Spline-based motion paths
- Point At and Align to Path functions
- Velocity controls
- Inverse kinematics for character animation

These are your basic animation tools. The rest is entirely up to you. Yes, it would be nice to have particle effects but you won't be using them everyday. You could give da Vinci and a chimpanzee the same pencil and piece of paper, but the result would be completely different. Don't get wrapped up in long lists of features and special effects, learn the basics first and then move on to an SGI.

QuickDraw 3D

QuickDraw 3D is the software that manages to blur the line between modeling, rendering, and animation. QuickDraw 3D or QD3D is a sophisticated 3D API (application programmers interface) that is integrated at the operating system level of your Mac.

QuickDraw 3D is specially designed software that enables your computer to render 3D models in real time using a cross between Gouraud and Phong shading. QuickDraw 3D supports texture mapping, reflections, transparency, and colored light sources. The benefits to the 3D designer are obvious. On the modeling side, designers will be able to see what their models look like while under construction without having to take the time to render the scene. On the animation side, the designer will be able to alter and manipulate an animation on the fly. Imagine being able to change the variables in an animation while it is running or move a texture map across the surface of a model in real time.

The primary difference between the image created by QuickDraw 3D and the final rendered animation is image quality. When using QuickDraw 3D the designer has limited lighting preview capabilities, kind of fuzzy texture mapping and reflectivity, and not too much antialiasing but the image is good enough to get an idea of what the finished product will look like.

How do you get QuickDraw 3D? Well it's free for the end user. It's just like QuickTime, you simply drop it into the System Folder and then it's installed. But in order for you to get the most out of the software you'll need some fairly high-end hardware. First of all, you need a PowerPC Mac, the faster the better. Secondly you should consider investing in a QuickDraw 3D accelerator board. With a 3D accelerator board you will be able to display more polygons on a larger monitor at a higher bit depth than on a computer that has no hardware acceleration. Last, invest in a PCI-based rather than a NuBus-based machine.

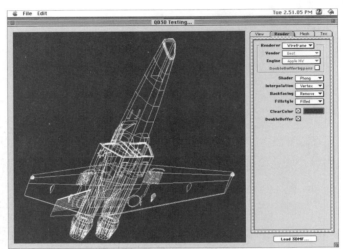

FIGURE *QuickDraw 3D can let you manipulate complex geometry*
3.30 *on screen in wireframe...*

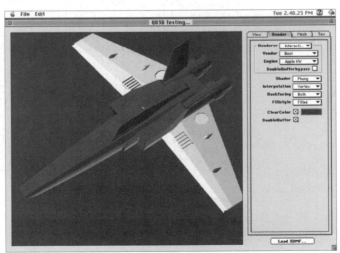

FIGURE *...or in a rendered mode.*
3.31

Storyboarding

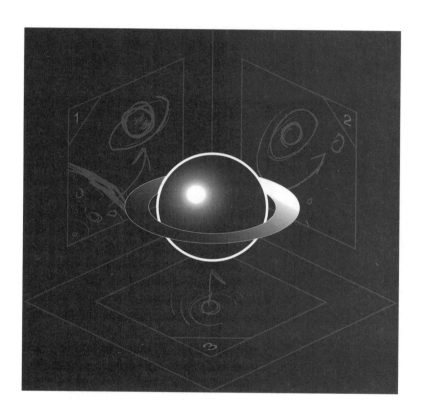

There is a house on the north coast of the island of Jamaica that is laying in ruin today. In the early 1950s a foreign business-man fell in love with a lonely little section of the coastline, overlooking crashing rocks and pounding surf. He decided that he was going to build a mansion so he could sit and brood deep, dark thoughts. Things being the way they were, construction was taking far too long for his tastes; after all he wanted to be alone to brood deep, dark thoughts. Construction material took days to reach his lonely cliff, and basic building materials such as sand and water took even longer. In a fit of misplaced genius, our tragic hero decided to mix saltwater with the concrete so he wouldn't have to truck it in to the site. What he failed to realize was that saltwater and concrete don't mix, and after a few weeks, his grand columns and sweeping arches crumbled away to dust. The ruins of the house are now known as Folly. What's the moral to this story? Patience and foresight can cir-cumvent disaster.

What am I trying to say to you? PLAN AHEAD! This is where the entire concept of storyboarding comes into play. Don't even think about launching your 3D application without first sitting down and doing a brief preliminary sketch of your ideas. You don't start con-struction on an office building without first drawing up a set of blue-prints — imagine what would happen if you did. Construction work-ers would be spending days working on small window trim details that no one except the pigeons would be able to see. You will save yourself hours of wasted work if you just plan wisely.

Everyone needs a storyboard. Hollywood directors, television pro-ducers, multimedia game developers, and even you, the professional 3D animator, need a storyboard. The idea behind a storyboard is to plot the major points in your animation in a graphic manner. A story-board is a series of pictures that illustrates your animation. Underneath the illustration is usually a brief description of the action occurring in the scene. A storyboard puts all of the major scenes into chronological order so that you can plan which models to create and how to plot your animation sequences. It's kind of like a casting list combined with an abbreviated plot line.

SECTION ONE: THE SCRIPT

In this section we discuss writing the story behind our animation and where to find the appropriate source material.

SECTION TWO: CREATING THE STORYBOARD
Once the script is written, we then start our sketches and storyboards.
Find out about traditional storyboarding methods and learn how to
develop your own technique.

SECTION ONE: THE SCRIPT

Start with a story. The story will serve as the script for your storyboard. At this point in the process you should be brainstorming with
your creative department. Try to get all of the basic ideas down, and
then string them together into a logical stream of events. Once you've
done your brainstorming and have gotten a general idea of what you
want to produce, it's time to do a little bit of research.

When you're researching for an animation project you should be
doing two things. Gather as much source material as you can on the
type of models that you want to create, and watch as much television,
movies, and commercials as you can stomach.

When you're researching source material for models try to find as
many detailed pictures as possible. Sure, we are all very creative, but
it's often easier to base our work on the designs of others. For example,
we all know what a castle looks like, but I know for certain that I can
model a far more detailed and interesting castle after looking at a couple of dozen pictures of real ones. Take the time now before you
become frustrated with the project and scrap the whole idea or settle
for a half-baked design. When you're watching all of that television,
try to determine how objects move. For example, if you were doing an
animation of a horse running, it would make sense to try to find as
many slow motion clips as possible on running horses.

Tip. There are also many books on the subject of animal and human
motion. Eadweard Muybridge, a famous nineteenth-century photographer,
compiled thousands of photographs of both humans and a variety of animals in motion. When doing any animation of a moving figure,
Muybridge's work is invaluable.

Now that all of the research is done you need to write your script.
When writing try to describe camera motion, model direction and

speed, and general lighting settings. Be sure to be clear when you write down the sequence of events in your animation so that you or someone else working with you understands the action.

SECTION TWO: CREATING THE STORYBOARD

With your script in hand, start to break down your story into the major scenes. Once the scenes are completed, take out a piece of paper and a pencil and get to work. Using your script as a guide, try to draw the major events in the scene. The level of detail in your illustration is entirely up to you, but I would recommend being very precise if you plan to work in a group environment.

The idea of each individual storyboard is to illustrate all of the important sequences or changes in the scene. For example, if you plan to have a spaceship zoom by the camera, try to give the animator a good idea of how the ship will move through space, how the camera will track the ship, and where it is placed in the scene.

Think of it this way: Each storyboard that you create should correspond to a keyframe in your animation. In the textual caption beneath your illustration, describe factors such as the speed at which the object is moving, the general lighting settings, and atmospheric conditions such as fog, all of which are usually very difficult to illustrate.

I usually try to use SMPTE time code instead of scene numbers and sequential numbers when writing a time down on my storyboards. SMPTE time code is broken down into HOURS:MINUTES:SECONDS:FRAMES. All of my animations start at 00:00:00:00 and then increase per frame number. So if I were creating an animation for television, which has a frame rate of 30 frames per second, and I wanted to create storyboard at two minutes, four and a half seconds I would write 00:02:04:14 at the top of my storyboard. The advantage of using this method is that I can then judge the relative speed of animated objects. When it comes time to animate the project I will then already have a general idea of the timing.

Here's an example of a more traditional sequence of storyboards using a letterbox or cinematic aspect ratio of 2:1.

FIGURE
4.1A
00:00:00:00 Four ships are seen in the distance heading toward the camera, which is stationary. The larger ship is out front, followed by the three smaller vessels. In the background there is a bright starfield. The background color is black and the lighting is coming from an angled overhead parallel light source. Ambient lighting is set to zero.

FIGURE
4.1B
00:00:00:00 Rendered scene from the finished animation.

FIGURE *00:00:01:28 The ships zoom closer to the camera, the camera tracks the larger lead ship, which*
4.2A *appears to be fleeing from the three smaller vessels. The starfield in the background begins to blur as*
the camera continues to track the lead ship.

FIGURE *00:00:01:28 Rendered scene from the finished animation.*
4.2B

FIGURE **4.3A** *00:00:04:15 The lead ship speeds past the camera and the camera pans to follow the fleeing ship. The ship rotates 20° along its lengthwise axis. The stars in the background blur into white lines as the camera tracks the ship. In the lower left corner of the screen a large planet starts to appear, the apparent destination of the fleeing ship.*

FIGURE **4.3B** *00:00:04:15 Rendered scene from the finished animation.*

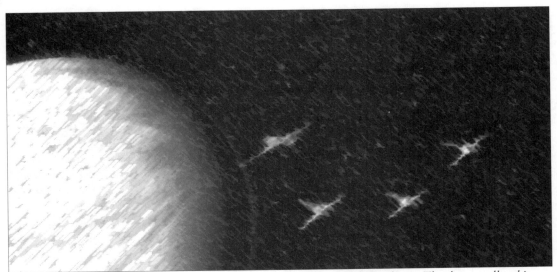

FIGURE 00:00:07.02 *The large ship speeds off into the distance toward the planet. The three smaller ships*
4.4A *fade back into view. The fleeing ship rotates back -20°. The planet begins to fill the screen as the ships fly toward it.*

FIGURE 00:00:07.02 *Rendered scene from the finished animation.*
4.4B

The Nontraditional Storyboard

OK, we can all admit that we don't have the budget of the Hollywood studios and that our company consists of only a few dedicated designers. Your personal position might just be designer, modeler, as well as animator. At that point it might just be a waste of time to create a huge detailed storyboard. If you know what you want to do, why bother going into elaborate detail to explain it to yourself?

Technology is also changing the concept of the storyboard every day. Apple's QuickDraw 3D has made animation more of an interactive process rather than a static one. Camera angles or object movement can now all be changed on the fly and the results can be viewed in real time. But that does not mean that you can skip the storyboarding step entirely.

It's my personal feeling that the storyboard is more for the client rather than the design staff. But with technology taking such huge

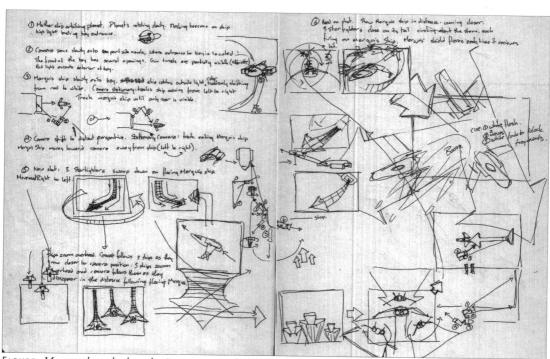

FIGURE
4.5
My storyboards show basic camera angles and position as well as object movement paths.

leaps and bounds, it is now faster to present the client with a rough animation than it is to sketch a traditional storyboard. For example to create a storyboard for a commercial with a dancing cereal box with a pen and piece of paper, you could easily create a rough animation complete with deformations in the same amount of time as it would to sketch the scene. For the client, it might be more convincing to see a quick shaded or wireframe animation than it is to look at a flat piece of cardboard.

So how do you plan an animation for yourself? Whichever process works best for you. I usually just draw a quick sketch of camera position, model movement, and general lighting conditions, and then go directly into sketching the preliminaries for the modeling process.

Casting Call

Once the storyboard's complete, go through each scene and list each model that needs to be created. One of the advantages of storyboarding is that you can get a general idea of how detailed your models will need to be. For example, if a model is either in the distant background or moves very quickly, you do not need to spend unnecessary time creating a detailed model. You also save time by not creating models that will not be used in the animation at all, which is one of my major shortcomings. It's frustrating to spend days on a beautiful model that never appears in the final product.

Now you're ready to go. Turn on your computer and fire up your modeling application. It's time to build something.

5 The Modeling Process

Modeling is perhaps my favorite step of the entire production process. It's at this point that I get to see my ideas take shape from out of nowhere. Traditional artists love to see a pristine white piece of paper or blank canvas, I love looking at an empty modeling window. It's like having a fresh pack of crayons and a brand new coloring book.

SECTION ONE: CONFIGURING YOUR COMPUTER

You've finished your rough sketches and the storyboard, and now it's time to turn on your computer. But before you launch your 3D modeling application, take the time to set up your computer properly.

SECTION TWO: HELPFUL MODELING TIPS

These are some of the cardinal rules of modeling. Try to keep them in mind because they'll save rendering and redraw time as well as reduce the frustration factor.

SECTION THREE: THE MODELING PROCESS

This section contains your very first tutorial. Learn how to finally put what you have learned into action. The Modeling Process will show you how to start to build your first model.

SECTION FOUR: MODELING A ROUGH DRAFT OF A 3D SCENE

How to overcome the first hurdles of creating a model. Learn how to sketch out your model in 3D.

SECTION FIVE: EXPORTING YOUR MODEL

Now that you've built it, how do you get it into another program. The major 3D file formats and how they work are discussed.

SECTION ONE: CONFIGURING YOUR COMPUTER

Unless you're managing ground control for the space shuttle, 3D modeling and rendering is possibly one of the most processor-intensive tasks that you can do on your Macintosh. Your goal in this section is to get your computer running at peak performance to reduce rendering time. Look at it this way: If you can shave off a minute per frame on a 10-second animation, you'll have reduced the rendering time by 5 hours. Remember, every little bit counts. There's nothing more boring than sitting around waiting for your computer to render an animation.

The first issue that needs to be recognized is that you won't be able to multitask while an image is rendering in the background. The CPU's full attention needs to be focused on your 3D application. That's not to say you can't run Photoshop at the same time as your 3D application, but the second you hit the **Render** button, your computer should only be doing one thing and that is rendering. You won't be able to work on a word processing document while your computer's rendering in the background unless you're running a multiple-processor computer such as those offered by Daystar.

Tip. Quit any open applications when you're about to commit to rendering a final animation. You want to dedicate the computer's full attention to rendering.

Freeing RAM

To accurately gauge how well our optimization process is going, we need to do a before and after scenario. Start by finding out how much RAM is available in your computer. Go to the Apple pull-down menu in the **Finder** and select **About This Macintosh**. This will tell you the amount of total memory in your computer, how much is dedicated to your System Folder and how much RAM is left over for you to dedicate to your 3D application. Realistically speaking, I would recommend having at least 16MB of total RAM. If you're serious about 3D, RAM is one of the first things that you should consider purchasing apart from a faster computer. Now make a mental note of how much RAM your System Software is taking up because our goal is to lower this amount.

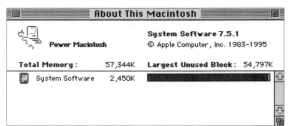

FIGURE   *The Apple Menu's **About This Macintosh**.*
5.1

One of the first steps that you need to do is optimize your System Folder. This process is a good habit to get into, and it should become second nature every time you start to work on a 3D project. The first step is turning off **AppleTalk** in the **Chooser** and then disabling all of the **System Extensions** that you aren't using. Extensions such as fax software, automatic virus detection, or a CD-ROM driver take up valuable RAM, which you will need to dedicate to your 3D application. If you're running System 7.5 or later it comes with a useful control panel named **Extensions Manager**, which allows you to create sets of Extensions that will be launched at startup. I suggest creating a custom set of Extensions that includes only the essentials.

After you've created your Extensions startup list, turn **Virtual Memory** and **RAM Disk** in the **Memory** control panel to Off. If you

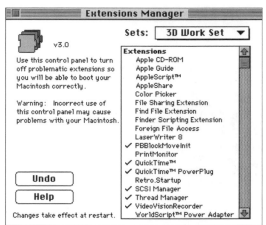

FIGURE   *System 7.5 **Extensions Manager** control*
5.2   *panel.*

have a program such as RAM Doubler running, turn that off as well. Some people do use RAM Doubler in rendering situations, but I've found that it is no substitute for actual RAM. RAM Doubler works by reallocating unused RAM from one application's partition to another program's partition. **Virtual Memory** is another software substitute that fools your computer into thinking it has more RAM than it actually does. **Virtual Memory** spools data that would normally be held in RAM to a hard drive. This read/write process from the hard drive is extremely slow in comparison to the data transfer rate of RAM. Using **Virtual Memory** and programs such as RAM Doubler might actually cause your program to render more slowly, or worse yet crash. The **Use Defaults** button resets the **Disk Cache** size to the recommended factory settings. I usually keep it at around 256K and I haven't notice that much of a performance change when I either increase or decrease the number. Also the **Modern Memory Manager** is a bit of a mystery, and after talking to Apple's technical support line they suggest leaving it on.

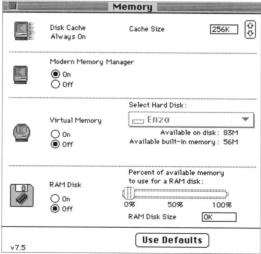

FIGURE *Memory control panel.*
5.3

Once you've resolved the RAM situation, restart your computer and check the amount of available RAM. Hopefully the amount used by the System Software will have decreased and the largest unused block will have increased. Dedicate as much RAM to your application as you can spare. To increase the memory partition of an application, select the application's icon in the **Finder** and then select **Get Info** from the **File** menu. When you allocate RAM to an application, leave at least a megabyte free for the System Folder, because the Mac sometimes has a tendency to crash in low memory situations. Ignore the suggestion to turn **Virtual Memory** on — that advice does not apply to this situation! If your 3D program is broken down into separate applications, you want to dedicate most of your RAM to the rendering engine. For example, the Electric Image Animation System uses the Electric Image application to build a scene, the Camera application to render it, and the Projector application to view the finished product. While it does help to increase the RAM partition to the other parts of the program, the Camera application is the one that should have the largest partition as possible.

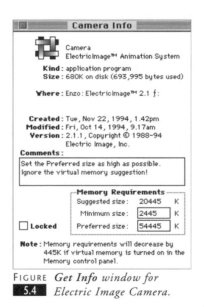

FIGURE *Get Info window for*
5.4 *Electric Image Camera.*

Monitor Depth

Unless you're using a graphics accelerator card it's a good idea to reduce your monitor depth to 8 bit or 256 colors. This can be done in the **Monitors** control panel. Your computer can handle 8-bit graphics faster than it can handle 24-bit. What you're doing here is reducing screen redraw or refresh time; it makes for faster modeling.

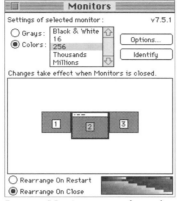

FIGURE *Monitors control panel.*
5.5

Screen Savers and Automatic Programs

One last note, turn off any screen saver programs so they won't interfere with the CPU. Screen savers do very little to prevent CRT burn-in, it's just as easy to turn off your monitor and save a little electricity in the process. If you've been working in your 3D program for a while, or if you've been multitasking with several programs, I would suggest restarting your computer before committing to a long rendering. Sometimes your Macintosh doesn't reallocate RAM back into the system, and the only way to access it is to restart your computer.

Another issue is to turn off any automated function of your computer such as archiving utilities or power savers. The last thing that you want to happen is for your computer to shut itself off in the middle of a rendering and lose the entire project. Also automatic archiving utilities such as Dantz Retrospective can interfere with a rendering in progress, slowing down or crashing the project.

And now your computer's ready to go.

SECTION TWO: HELPFUL MODELING TIPS

These are some of the cardinal rules of modeling. Try to keep them in mind because they'll save rendering and redraw time and reduce the frustration factor.

Perspective

One of the first and foremost things to remember is always model in an orthographic or axonometric mode. In other words, turn the perspective off. You want everything to be as flat as possible. It's easier to judge size and absolute spatial relationships when you work in a *perspectiveless* view.

FIGURE *Two cubes viewed in orthographic mode.*
5.6

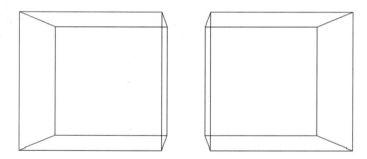

FIGURE *Two cubes viewed in perspective mode.*
5.7

Layers

Make your life easy, model in layers. Keep only the parts of a model on screen that you're working on. The idea is to reduce screen clutter and speed up redraw time. Another reason is because a model can become complicated very quickly. It's easy to get lost in your own model. Another useful tip is to use different colors for various parts of your model to help you to separate the model into workable segments.

Views

Save commonly used views or create multiple cameras. This is a real time saver. When you have a large complicated model and you're trying to set up a certain shot for a rendering, it's best to save the view for a number of reasons. It saves time trying to replicate the exact same shot and more importantly it reduces the frustration factor. I'm basically a very impatient person, and when the screen redraw on a complicated

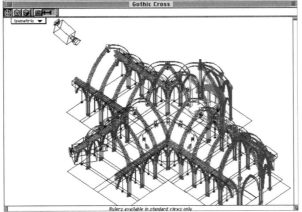

FIGURE
5.8
Multiple cameras placed within a model in Strata StudioPro.

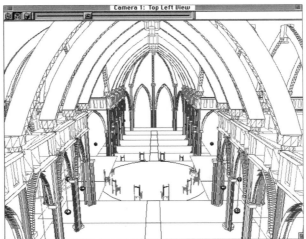

FIGURE
5.9
Camera view of the interior of the model in Strata StudioPro.

model starts to climb over 10 seconds, I start to get a little loopy, especially when it takes a dozen or so adjustments to get the shot right.

Names

Use straightforward naming conventions and try not to be obscure. When you name views, layers, or objects, use names that you, and everyone else that works with you, can easily understand. I know it sounds like common sense but it's easy to get lazy and use the default "Layer One" or "View One" name. If you work in a group environment, and someone else has to animate or texture your model, they're going to be very upset when they have to decipher your cryptic or nonexistent naming structure. On the other hand, if you're eventually going to animate the model, and it has lots of small moving parts, it pays in the long run to name them accordingly.

Model Resolution

Use the least amount of information to create the highest degree of detail. Don't overmodel; keep your polygon count low to reduce rendering and screen redraw time. The less information your computer has to deal with the better. The key is knowing when to use geometry

FIGURE
5.10 *Look closely at the edges of the golf ball and notice how smooth the edge is. That's a sure sign of a bump map.*

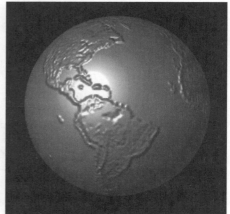

FIGURE
5.11 *Use of a bump map to create the continents saved both modeling and rendering time in this image.*

and when to use mapping. One of the most often cited examples is that of a golf ball. It's entirely possible to use Boolean functions to create the dimples on the surface of a golf ball. But a better solution would be to use a bump map. The drawback is that a bump map doesn't alter the geometry of a model, and the illusion usually falls apart around the edges of the ball. On the other hand if the ball is animated and motion blur is applied to it, no one will notice anyway. The point is knowing when to use geometry, and when to use a texture map.

Another case of overmodeling is lathing an object. Try to keep the number of steps low. It's best to take the time and do a quick render before committing to a lathed shape. Start with a low number of steps and work upward until you're satisfied with the results. Dependent upon how close the camera is to the model in the final rendering, the resolution or number of revolutions have to be increased or decreased. If the camera is close to the model, then you should use a higher number of revolutions; further away, a lower number.

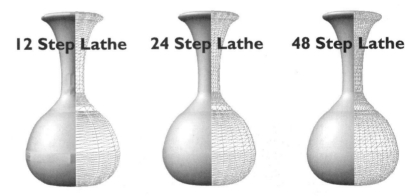

FIGURE
5.12
The vase on the left has too few steps while the vase on the right has too many. The center vase uses the most efficient number of steps.

Overmodeling

Think about what you really need to model. Don't model a background if you can get away with using a scanned image, which is a real modeling time saver in itself. A background can be composited later in post-production, which is another time saver. Also consider whether the backfaces of your models will ever be seen. If you're doing a shot of a house and you never see the back of it, don't create walls or windows for the rear side of the building. Once again, common sense should prevail.

SECTION THREE: THE MODELING PROCESS

I recommend taking out a pencil and a piece of paper and doing a quick sketch of your idea even before turning on your computer. It's easier to work out ideas on paper rather than on a computer. You might think that you've got a solid idea in your head but you actually don't. Proof of this? Close your eyes and imagine what a flock of birds looks like, think really hard. When you reopen your eyes try to recall how many birds were in that flock. Memory's a fickle thing and it's important to have a hard copy of your ideas.

Creating a Model

Launching 3D modeling application for the first time can be an intimidating experience. You've got an idea of what you want your model to look like, but haven't got a clue about how to create it. The tools are all there, but it's easy to become discouraged when the only thing you have on the screen is a bunch of primitives that look nothing like what you had in mind. The key is not to give up; 3D modeling is a blend of both skill and creativity. Once you become proficient in 3D techniques, you'll realize that creativity is the more valuable commodity.

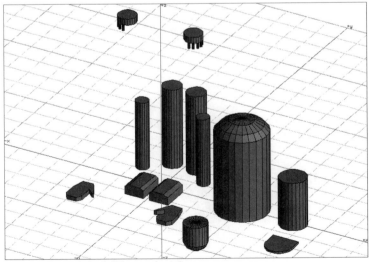

FIGURE *Doesn't look like much right now....*

5.13

A 3D model is simply a collection of geometric shapes. These *shapes* can consist of either primitives or objects that you've created on your own. 3D modeling is like playing with a big bag of building blocks. The advantage is that if one of those blocks isn't the right shape, you have the tools to fix that. All of those dangerous power tools that your parents denied you as a child, such as milling machines, power drills, and band saws, are available in the 3D world, it's just that software developers give them more innocuous names. The entire modeling process consists of putting together all of these small shapes to create one large model.

Tip. Every model in 3D is composed of simple shapes. The trick is being able to break down a model mentally into the component pieces. A snowman is simply three spheres and a cylinder for the hat.

The first step to take in the modeling process is to create the *central object*. This is the main shape or group of shapes around which the model will be based. Once you've created the central object it's very important that you align the central object with the *Origin*. The Origin is where the X, Y, and Z axes intersect and all of the coordinate values equal zero. If you're still a little shaky on the coordinate system, I would suggest going back to your software user's manual for a quick refresher.

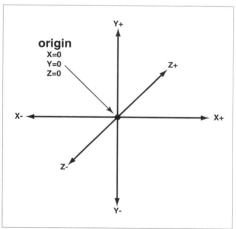

FIGURE *The Origin of the coordinate system.*
5.14

The reason you want to align the central object with the origin is that it will make your calculations easier to compute. Since all of the computations are based on zero you can do most of the math in your head. By starting the project with a central object, we establish the relative scale of the model. In the following tutorial, we're going to create a toy soldier.

**T
U
T
O
R
I
A
L**

TOY SOLDIER TUTORIAL

STEP ONE

Launch your 3D modeling application. The first step is to create the body of the soldier. You can either draw the profile of the body using 2D drawing tools and then lathe the profile or you can just join a cylinder and sphere together.

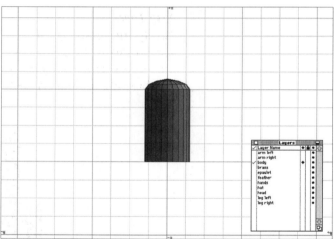

FIGURE
5.15
The body of the soldier is modeled first and centered on the Origin.

STEP TWO

Once we've created a body shape that we're comfortable with, the arms, legs and a head can then be created. It's easier to make proportionate appendages once the core of the model is complete. Use your cylinder and cube primitives to create the appropriate body parts.

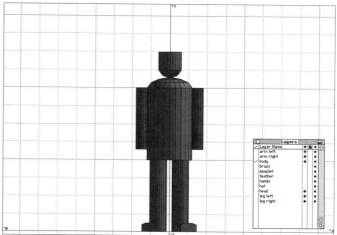

FIGURE *The necessary appendages are added.*
5.16

STEP THREE

Finally the finishing touches such as the hands and the hat are modeled. Creating the small details should be the last step in the process. By this point in the process, you'll realize just how much detail is really needed.

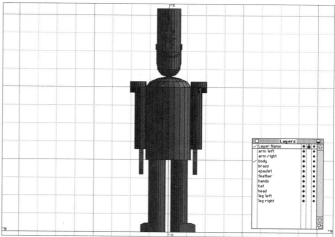

FIGURE *The soldier complete with a nice hat and a pair of hands.*
5.17

FIGURE *What he looks like with a couple of friends and a*
5.18 *little texture mapping.*

The model of the soldier is very simple to create but the same modeling methods can be applied to more complicated projects. The model of the spaceship in Figures 5.19 through 5.22 is composed of a hundred different pieces, but like the model of the soldier it started out as only a few rough shapes.

What you should be doing in the modeling process is working first on the larger parts, trying to get the proper shape, scale, and proportions and then concentrate on the finer details. By using this method, you can get an overall feeling for the composition of the model. If the model seems unbalanced or disproportionate, adding details is not going to help. It's like building a house. The construction teams don't start by installing a bathtub, they start by building a framework on which everything else is hung. If the framework is flawed, the rest of the house is going to look terrible.

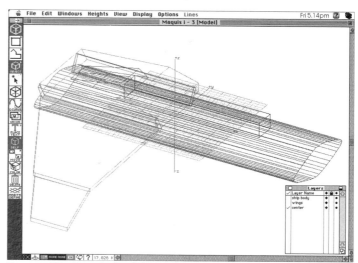

FIGURE
5.19
The first draft of the model composed of the more basic shapes modeled in auto•des•sys from•Z 2.75.

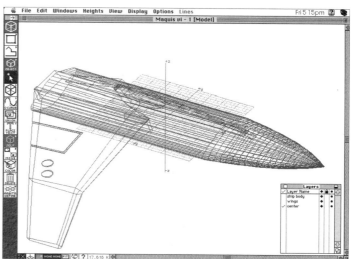

FIGURE
5.20
Primitives are gradually replaced with more complex geometry in auto•des•sys from•Z 2.75.

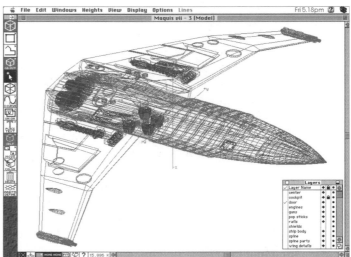

FIGURE
5.21
The finished model in auto•des•sys from•Z 2.75.

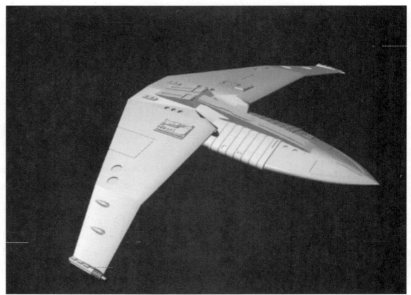

FIGURE
5.22
A rendering of the finished model; we'll add the textures later....

Layers   Although every program handles the modeling process differently as a result of the tools and methods you use, one important theory remains constant. Every model contains a certain hierarchy or parent–child relationship. It's up to you, the modeler, to establish this relationship early on in the modeling process for two primary reasons. The first reason is for texture mapping, and the second reason for animation.

When you're creating a model, you can use a number of methods of grouping or layering your objects depending on your 3D package. On the most basic level, your modeling application will let you place one or more objects on a specific layer. If you're using a separate modeling and animation program, you will need to export the file in order to render the model. By using either the aging DXF or brand new 3DMF format to export your model, layer information is held intact.

Important. Each separate moving part of the same model needs to be on a separate layer when exported from your modeling program if you plan on animating the objects separately.

Tip. Using layers can also simplify the modeling process. By hiding layers that are not in use, you can speed up the screen refresh time as well as making it easier to look at a complex model.

You're probably wondering why layer information is so important. First of all let's cover the animation side of things. For example, let's say that we had a model of an old biplane that we wanted to animate. The model of the biplane consists of separate layers, which include the landing gear, flaps, propeller, and body. If we created the model of the airplane with each part of the model on the same layer, it would be impossible to animate it properly. Each separate moving part of the same model needs to be on a separate layer when exported from your modeling program.

OK, now let's say that you have a model that has no separate moving parts. Then why should you have to save objects on separate layers? The answer is because of texture mapping. If you have a model that consists of several irregular shapes, you wouldn't want to just apply one map to the entire model. You would want to apply several maps to the various parts using a variety of different methods. For example, if you had a model that consisted of a cube and a cylinder, the novice 3D designer would simply slap a map onto the entire object and then be done with it. But you, as the professional, would apply a cubic map to the cube and a cylindrical map to the cylinder. If the model was held on one single layer then it would be impossible to texture separately. Each part of a model that requires its own texture map needs to be on a separate layer when exported from your modeling program.

 Tip. Each separate part of the model that requires its own texture map needs to be on a separate layer when exported from your modeling program.

When you're modeling, you need to keep all of this information in mind. Try to think about which part of your model will need its own texture map and which part will move independent of the rest of the model when animated.

SECTION FOUR: MODELING A ROUGH DRAFT OF A 3D SCENE

Creating a 3D composition or a scene follows many of the same guidelines as creating a model. Like everything else the process should start with a quick sketch. It's easy to get tunnel vision when you're modeling. There's nothing more frustrating than spending hours on a model, and then realizing that it doesn't fit into the overall composition.

FIGURE *A quick sketch of the scene.*
5.23

What you're trying to do when you model a rough draft of a scene is to set up the relative size and placement of the models by creating a sketch in 3D. By using the primitives that come with your modeling package that are close to the shape of the objects that you will eventually model you can create a rough draft. These primitives will serve as *dummy* objects.

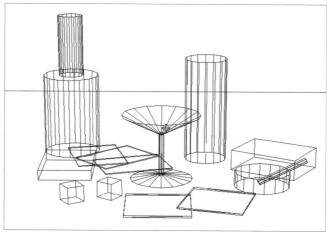

FIGURE *Rough draft created with primitives or* dummy *objects.*
5.24

The use of dummy objects has several advantages. It's easier to move a primitive around on screen than it is to move a more complicated piece of geometry when trying to balance the composition. Screen redraw time is reduced because the computer has to deal with less information. You can also get a pretty good idea on how much detail you have to model. For example, if an object is in the background of a scene you don't have to spend too much time fussing over the level of detail. On the other hand if the object is in the foreground, you'll probably have to spend more time modeling detail because the viewer's attention will be focused on the object.

By using dummy objects it's easier to build in layers and maintain a uniform scale. Once the dummy objects are created, move each object onto a separate layer and then use the primitive as a sizing guide to create the individual models. You'll save time resizing and placing models by using this technique.

FIGURE *The completed scene before rendering...*
5.25

FIGURE *...and after rendering.*
5.26

It's easy to become overwhelmed with a project and, like everything else in this world, it should be taken one step at a time. You shouldn't be overly ambitious for your first project, and it's best to start small and then work your way up to more complicated models. Don't get discouraged, because once you get over the initial learning curve, everything else will fall into place.

Composition

We've all seen paintings of still lives with tables laden with fruit, fish, and all sorts of bric-a-brac. It's always impressive because the composition seems very natural and random, yet at the same time balanced. Composition is one of the hardest skills to master since it's one of those talents that comes naturally to some, yet must be brought out in others. Creating a balanced composition in 3D can be even more challenging since objects are not static such as on a painted canvas but they can be made to move.

One of the best places to look for balanced composition is either in printed magazine ads or television commercials. People spend hours just arranging a bowl of corn flakes next to a spoon and a napkin before even shooting the commercial.

CENTER OF INTEREST

Find the center of interest in your scene. It can be either an object, or just a space on the screen to which the viewer's eye is naturally drawn. An interesting shape or the convergence of overlapping objects can all draw the viewer's interest. Try to balance your composition around this focal point.

If you're doing an animation for a company that sells mouthwash and they want the bottle to dance around in the bathroom, you would want the viewer's attention focused on the bottle rather than on the toothbrush doing the limbo or the singing toilet. Once you've decided on the center of interest, you can do several things to make sure attention stays focused on it. First of all, make sure that the object is well lit within the scene, and that nothing else is larger than your object for an extended period of time. Also try making the objects in the background out of focus using depth of field or fog. Also when animating the scene try to keep the object in the center of the camera's field of view.

BALANCE

The entire concept of balance can be applied to just about every aspect of an animation. The color of objects, the relative size to each other, and the spatial coordinates of each one all affect the balance and thus the composition of a scene. Here is a list of tips that you should consider when setting up your rendering:

- Try to keep your object at different depths to create a foreground and background for the rendering.
- Use point or spotlights that attenuate or fall off rather than a parallel light source. A parallel light offers extremely even lighting, which can look unnatural at times.
- Place one object in front of another, and try to stack multiple objects in a scene. I know you spent a lot of time creating the models but the viewer doesn't need to see every little part of each one. The scene will look more realistic and a sense of depth will be defined.
- Choose the color of your lights carefully. Set the color of the ambient light to be complementary to the primary light source.
- Create objects of varying sizes so the scene will be more interesting to look at and will appear more natural.
- Try using the Figure Ground technique. Render the scene normally but also render the background as an Alpha Channel. The Alpha Channel supplies a silhouette of the scene, which is a great way of judging the composition without being distracted by color or texture.

 Tip. All too often I've spent hours looking at the same scene and my sense of judgment becomes a little clouded and I can't figure out if the scene looks balanced or not. At that point I do one of two things: Either I leave the project and then go back to the rendering after a few hours or I try the mirror trick. I import the rendering into Photoshop and then reverse the entire rendering so that I'm looking at a mirror image of the scene.

SECTION FIVE: EXPORTING YOUR MODEL

It's rare to find a 3D professional on the Mac that uses only one program. Unlike the PC where 3DStudio can handle most of the modeling and animation needs, the Mac has to rely on several applications to get the job done. Many professionals model in one package, ray-trace in another package, and then render animations in yet still another package. As a result, there has to be a common file format that the majority of programs can read.

DXF

Created by Autodesk Inc., the Drawing eXchange Format (DXF) is perhaps the *de facto* 3D file format on the Mac. Just about any 3D program available supports one form or another of DXF. There are three major types of DXF formats available:

- N x M Mesh
- 3D Face
- Polyline

N x M Mesh

The N x M Mesh is perhaps the most widely supported version of DXF, and has the most compact file size. The major limitation of N x M Mesh is that it does not support holes in the mesh. For example you wouldn't be able to export a sphere with a circle cut out of it.

3D Face

3D Face is also another popular DXF format that does support holes in the mesh. It can be a little quirky at times importing individual polygons as separate models, which can create monstrously huge file sizes.

Polyline

Polyline is fairly new on the scene, which means your Mac software may not be able to read it. If you're modeling on the Mac to export to the SGI for rendering, this is the DXF format to use.

The limitations of the DXF format are numerous. While DXF handles polygonal data very well, it is severely handicapped when it comes to spline-based information. Curves and smooth surfaces are affected the most. If you're working with a spline-based modeler for example, the DXF format converts a spline into compound polygons. Also the size of DXF files can be monstrously huge. Apart from geometry, the DXF format also carries both object color and layer information.

RIB

The only way to go if you're using RenderMan is RIB. The RenderMan Interface Bytestream (RIB) format supports lighting, shaders, and spline-based geometry. Since RenderMan is a cross-platform application, the advantages are evident when it comes to exporting in the RIB format to a rendering farm or an SGI rendering station.

Apple's 3D MetaFormat

It's been a long time coming, but with QuickDraw 3D starting to make an impact, Apple's 3D MetaFormat (3DMF) will replace the aging DXF. Lighting information, high-level geometry (NURBS and B-splines), procedural texture maps, and a model's animation are included. The advantage of this format is that it can be accessed directly with QuickDraw 3D. QuickDraw 3D offers drag and drop capabilities, and that means that 3DMF will require no virtually no translation to go from a modeling application to a word processor document. The relative file size and loading time of the 3DMF format is also minuscule when compared to DXF.

CHAPTER

6

Advanced Modeling

CHAPTER REQUIREMENTS
Basic understanding of
Illustrator or FreeHand,
and Photoshop.

Once you become comfortable with your 3D modeling package, you might feel adventurous enough to wander out and see what else is available for the Macintosh. A wide variety of both hardware and software tools are available that can add another dimension to your modeling repertoire.

SECTION ONE: EPS TEMPLATES

There's more to 3D modeling than just one package and programs that are not even remotely related to 3D can be used in a variety of practical 3D applications. Illustration packages such as Adobe's Illustrator and Macromedia's FreeHand can provide the 3D designer with a few more tools to make modeling easier. Illustration programs excel at spline-based 2D line art, which can be imported into just about any 3D application through the Encapsulated PostScript or EPS format. All of the powerful spline-based 2D tools will be at your disposal, including some rather useful text manipulation capabilities.

SECTION TWO: TERRAIN MODELING

Tired of modeling small objects such as coffee pots and armchairs? Is it time to model something big like a mountain range or an entire planet? There are some great push-button 3D terrain programs available that novices and even experienced professionals might find useful. These high-quality, easy-to-use 3D terrain generators are great for creating realistic or surrealistic backgrounds for your animations. On the other hand, if you're looking for a little bit more control in your terrain generation, you can create custom mountains with grayscale bitmaps and import them into your modeling and rendering program with some great shareware applications that are included on the CD-ROM.

SECTION THREE: 3D DIGITIZERS

3D digitizers can take a lot of the work out of creating a 3D model. A variety of digitizers are available to the 3D designer: ultrasonic, mechanical arm, magnetic resonance, and planar lasers.

SECTION FOUR: DEDICATED HUMAN BODY AND TREE GENERATORS

Finally, certain 3D programs are dedicated to creating those hard to construct models such as the human body and trees — yes, trees. While these programs might seem extremely specialized, they're godsends, especially when you're under a deadline and need to create a model in a hurry. Sure you could model these objects on your own, but it would take time — lots of time. Have you ever tried to model the individual leaves on a tree, one at a time? It's definitely better to let the computer take care of those mind-numbing details so you can concentrate on other, more interesting things.

SECTION ONE: EPS TEMPLATES

3D modelers are broken down into two major categories, polygon- or spline-based modelers. And while many of the polygonal modelers claim to support spline tools for creating and editing 2D shapes, those tools are often very primitive or difficult to use, especially when compared to dedicated illustration programs such as Adobe's Illustrator or Macromedia's FreeHand. On the other hand, if you're using a less sophisticated modeler that doesn't support 2D spline modeling, it might seem as if you're out of luck.

Fortunately, both Illustrator and FreeHand can export files under the Encapsulated PostScript or EPS format, allowing you access to the wonderful features of these programs. All of the powerful 2D spline tools and text manipulation capabilities will be at your disposal and just about every 3D program supports the EPS file format. Either FreeHand or Illustrator will definitely be a worthwhile purchase, not only for what they offer for modeling, but for texture mapping as well.

Tip. If your 3D program is able to import Adobe Illustrator files and you're having problems, try saving the Illustrator file as version 3.0. While some 3D programs might support later versions, 3.0 is the most widely compatible version.

Using EPS Templates

There are many usual and unusual applications for EPS files in a 3D modeling program. EPS files are so useful because they give the 3D modeler all of the powerful tools available to the 2D illustrator inside of a 3D environment. The EPS format is simply the means of getting that information from one program to another.

BOOLEAN FUNCTIONS

Only a few high-level modeling programs offer Boolean functions, which are perhaps some of the most essential modeling features required by the 3D designer. Unfortunately, the majority of low-level 3D programs don't support Boolean functions; but by using an illustration program in conjunction with the EPS file format, the designer has a partial solution. The following tutorials require some knowledge of a program such as Illustrator or FreeHand. But don't worry if you are not comfortable with either program; the CD-ROM contains all of the source files for each tutorial as well as a demo version of Illustrator and Freehand.

T
U
T
O
R
I
A
L

SIMPLE BOOLEAN TUTORIAL

It's a simple matter to create a shape in your illustration program and then subtract another shape from it, which is in essence a 2D Boolean function. And although you might not be able to do this task in your modeling package, you can perform this task in Illustrator or FreeHand.

STEP ONE

Launch your copy of Adobe Illustrator. Create a square shape. Go to the **Filter** menu. Select **Create** and then **Star**. Configure your star with as many points as you wish and then click **OK**.

STEP TWO

Center the star shape on top of the square and select both objects. Go to the **Filter** menu and select **Pathfinder** and **Minus Front**. Illustrator then subtracts the shape of the star from the square.

FIGURE
6.1

*By using the **Pathfinder** filter in Adobe Illustrator 5.0, the shape of a star can be subtracted from a square to form a new shape.*

STEP THREE

Save the file as with the EPS format. If you're using the demo version of Illustrator, the EPS file is located on the CD-ROM. Import the EPS file into your 3D application and then extrude the shape. Apply a texture map and then render.

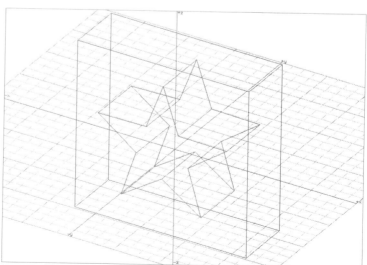

FIGURE
6.2

The 2D template is extruded in form•Z to form a 3D object.

FIGURE *The final shape is textured and*
6.3 *rendered in Strata StudioPro.*

Although not as powerful as integrated Boolean functions, the use of EPS templates offers a partial solution. When you're building a model of a house for example, you can create 2D templates for the walls in your illustration program and cut out the shapes for the windows. After that you can import the shapes into your 3D application and then extrude them to form 3D objects.

T
U
T
O
R
I
A
L

MODELING COMPLEX 2D SHAPES TUTORIAL

I prefer to create most of my 2D shapes in an illustration program simply because the drawing tools are easier to use than anything currently available for 3D packages. But in certain cases, use of an EPS template also saves modeling time and reduces the polygon count.

For the modeler that doesn't have dedicated Boolean functions in his/her 3D package, a model of a gear would be difficult to create. If you wanted to cut the spokes of the gear out of a solid shape, it would be impossible without Boolean tools. Another consideration is that the model wouldn't be very efficient because it would include a tremendous amount of unnecessary geometry.

The picture in Figure 6.4 shows how the bottom faces of the teeth of the gear are below the level of the main wheel. Since these faces would never be visible in any rendering, they are unnecessary. Unwanted geometry increases the file size and adds to rendering time.

Even for the user who does have a package that supports Boolean functions, it's often faster to use an EPS template. A time-consuming Boolean union would have to

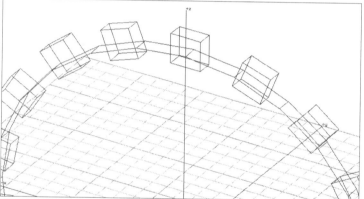

FIGURE 6.4 *The bottom faces of the teeth of the gear would not be visible in a rendering.*

FIGURE 6.5 *2D EPS templates of gears created in Adobe Illustrator 5.0.*

be performed for each tooth when it's joined to the wheel of the gear. In an illustration program, all of the faces can be joined in one step, saving a tremendous amount of time. The 2D shapes that forms the basis of our gears were created in Illustrator by adding and subtracting various shapes from a circle.

T
U
T
O
R
I
A
L

GEARS TUTORIAL

STEP ONE
Import the EPS file into your 3D application.

STEP TWO
Extrude the shapes to the desired depth. It's that easy. If you want to experiment, open the EPS file in Illustrator and play around to see how the shape is created.

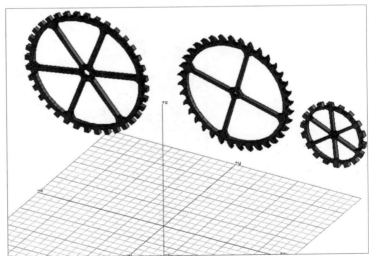

FIGURE *The 2D EPS shapes extruded to form 3D models in form•Z.*

6.6

By using a 2D EPS template, the modeler who doesn't have Boolean functions can create shapes that might have been very difficult or impossible to do in a low-end modeling program. And for any level of modeler, it's usually easier to create 2D shapes in an illustration program, saving both time and effort.

T
U
T
O
R
I
A
L

CREATING 3D TEXT FROM 2D SHAPES TUTORIAL

Another advantage that illustration programs have over 3D modelers is in the field of text manipulation capabilities. While most 3D applications have the basic capacity to handle text, 2D illustration programs excel in this area. Because of the EPS format, 3D applications have full access to a wide range of text manipulation tools. Text can be distorted, stretched, or even squashed with ease.

MACINTOSH3D
PROFESSIONAL

FIGURE *These logos for the Mac 3D Pro*
6.7 *were created in Adobe Illustrator. Since the file can be saved with the EPS format they can be imported into a 3D application and then extruded.*

STEP ONE

Start by launching your copy of Adobe Illustrator. Create two circles of the same size using no fill and a plain black stroke. These two circles will serve as paths on which text will be placed. Don't worry if you're having problems following along, the original Illustrator file is included on the CD-ROM.

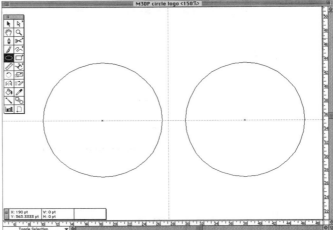

FIGURE *Two circles that will be used as paths for text are created*
6.8 *in Adobe Illustrator 5.0.*

STEP TWO

The next step is placing the text on the paths. For the circle on the right, the baseline shift has to be set to –25 points so that the text will be written below the path rather than on it. Go ahead and write what you want on each circle.

STEP THREE

Once the text is aligned correctly on the paths, the two paths are centered.

STEP FOUR

The last step is optional but a good habit to get into regardless. Some 3D programs might have difficulty reading text or dealing with the baseline shift of the lower set of text. Another problem is that the hollow spaces in a letter might

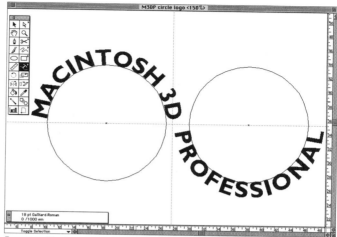

FIGURE
6.9 *Text can be placed directly onto a path, a feature not often found in 3D applications but commonplace in 2D illustration programs.*

FIGURE
6.10 *The two paths are aligned on the same center point.*

be filled. The solution is to convert the text into outlines, which is done by selecting the text to be converted, and then going to the **Text** menu and selecting **Create Outlines**. After that, export the file as an EPS document and then import it into your 3D application. Extrude the shape and then render.

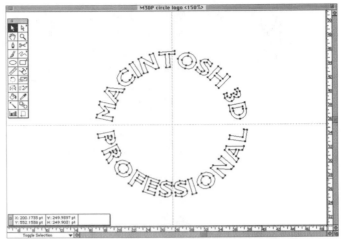

FIGURE **6.11** *The text is converted into outlines by using the* **Create Outlines** *function in the* **Text** *menu of Illustrator.*

FIGURE **6.12** *The text imported into form•Z is then extruded.*

Tip. One drawback to importing EPS files in a 3D application is that the stroke and fill information of a shape or text is not imported. The solution is to convert the shape or text into outlines before exporting the file as an EPS document. Once it's in the 3D application, you will have separate objects that correspond to the stroked areas.

T
U
T
O
R
I
A
L

BOOLEANS AND TEXT TUTORIAL

By mixing and matching what we've learned about Boolean functions and text, we can create a model that incorporates all of these features.

STEP ONE

Convert your logo into outlines in Illustrator. Subtract the outlines from another shape using the **Pathfinder** filter. In this case, the outline of the Macintosh 3D Professional logo is subtracted from a square shape in Illustrator.

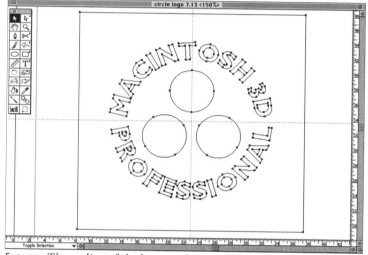

FIGURE **6.13** *The outline of the logo is subtracted from a square shape in Illustrator using the* ***Pathfinder*** *filter.*

STEP TWO

Save the file as an EPS document and import it into a modeling program. Once the EPS template has been extruded, create a cube with the same X, Y dimensions as the extruded shape. Align the two objects, and move the front face of the rear cube flush with the rear face of the extruded shape.

STEP THREE

Group the two shapes and apply a texture map. By using this technique, you have a partial work-around for any absence of Boolean functions.

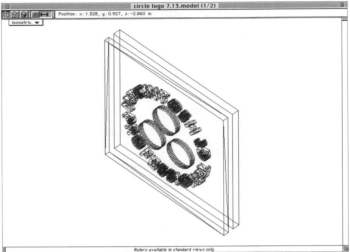

FIGURE *A cube is created with the same X, Y dimensions as the*
6.14 *extruded shape is modeled in Strata StudioPro.*

FIGURE *The final image of the Boolean text rendering in Strata StudioPro.*
6.15

CREATING RIBS WITH EPS TEMPLATES

One of the most difficult tasks in 3D modeling is creating a precisely curved shape such as a airplane fuselage or a boat hull. The user has to create a series of ribs over which a skin will be stretched or lofted. The hard part, of course, is accurately modeling the ribs. There are several ways to create ribs and your most useful tool will be your illustration program.

If you're fortunate enough to have a physical example of the model that you need to create, this is an interesting method. For a model such as an airplane, I've seen a friend take a piece of flexible wire and bend it to fit the contour of the plane's body. He would repeat this task every 2 centimeters down the length of the fuselage with a new piece of wire each time. Once he was finished, he scanned the individual pieces of wire with a flatbed scanner into his computer, and then imported the PICT into Illustrator as a template. He used the template as a guide to create individual ribs. Once the ribs were completed the file was saved as an EPS document and then imported into his 3D modeling program. Each of the ribs was then used to loft the entire fuselage of the airplane.

Another method — and perhaps an easier one — is to use the actual blueprints of an object. Scan the blueprint into the computer and use it as a PICT template in Illustrator.

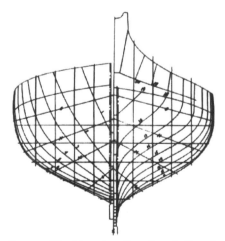

FIGURE **6.16** *The blueprints for a boat hull make an excellent template for creating ribs to be lofted in a 3D application.*

Even if you don't have either a model or blueprints, it's still worthwhile to use an EPS file for lofting templates. The advantage of using Illustrator is that the user has precise control over vertices and direction. It's often easier to manipulate and scale a rib in Illustrator than it is in any dedicated modeling package.

SECTION TWO: TERRAIN MODELING

It's time to look at the big picture. Instead of creating coffee cups and tea pots, it's time to build something big. Terrain modeling gives the user the opportunity to play omnipotent deity and build a world. Mountains, rivers, oceans, and even entire planets can be created in an afternoon.

Dedicated Terrain Modelers

Several software applications are available that can be used for creating a terrain model. The easiest to use are the dedicated terrain modelers such as MetaTools' Bryce and Virtual Reality Lab's Vistapro. Both programs have integrated terrain modeling and rendering capabilities as well as numerous special features. Vistapro, for example, can generate four types of fractal-based trees, create a snow line, has tools for inserting bodies of water, and also has animation capabilities for scripting amazing cinematic fly-throughs. Bryce also has animation capabilities in the works, which include animated cloud and light sources as well as fly-through capabilities.

Many 3D professionals criticize these programs because they fall into the category of push-button 3D. They're extremely simple to use and even the most inexperienced user can produce professional quality results in only a few hours. Personally, I think they are a wonderful way for a novice to get acquainted with the world of 3D modeling. And for the busy professional, both programs are fast and easy means for creating a nice background for an animation. The major problem I do have with both of the programs is that they don't have much in the way of modeling tools or even the option to import DXF models created in another program. But in this case, if Mohammed can't go to the mountain the mountain can go to Mohammed.

FIGURE 6.17 *MetaTools' Bryce offers the user an excellent means for creating dramatic and stunning backgrounds.*

FIGURE 6.18 *This rendering from Virtual Reality Lab's Vistapro shows off some of the excellent features of this program. Vegetation, a snow line, and atmospheric effects can all be added to an animation.*

Grayscale Bitmap Terrain

The second option for creating terrain images is grayscale bitmaps. Several software packagers such as Electric Image, Infini-D, and Strata have integrated bitmap terrain generation capabilities in their programs. But for those of you who aren't using any of these packages, there is an abundance of stand-alone applications that can create terrain. Included on the CD-ROM is a demo version of John Knoll's CyberMesh, which is an amazing Photoshop plug-in that can create not only terrains, but some other interesting shapes as well. Also included on the CD-ROM is a shareware program called Terrainman, which we will be using throughout most of the examples.

Tip. Pay the shareware fee. These guys are creating very practical and useful applications. The only way you'll see more of these programs is if you support these programmers.

T U T O R I A L

CREATING A TERRAIN TUTORIAL
The process of creating a terrain is similar in theory to that of a bump map, but in this case, geometry rather than surface normals is manipulated. The individual pixels of a grayscale image are used as an elevation map. Shades closer to black create polygons lower in the model while shades closer to white will place polygons higher in the model.

STEP ONE
You're going to need a program such as Photoshop or Painter for this tutorial. The first step is to create a new document. Be sure to set the colors to 8 bit and grayscale. The size of the document depends on several factors. Each pixel in a grayscale image used for terrain generation represents approximately one polygon in the model. To get a rough idea of how many polygons will be created from a grayscale image, simply multiply the image height in pixels by the image width in pixels. Most 3D modeling programs have difficulty dealing with a model that's larger than 65,000 polygons so it's a good idea to keep the grayscale map small. For example a 200 x 200 pixel image will result in a model of close to 40,000 polygons. A good technique is to start with a large image and then reduce the size of the map before converting it to a terrain model.

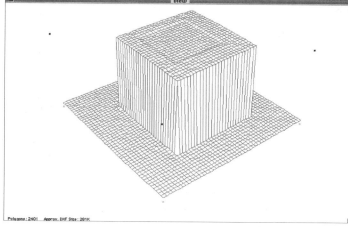

FIGURE
6.19 *2D grayscale bitmap (left) converted into a 3D model (right).*

A good document size to start at is 300 x 300 pixels. For this tutorial we want to create a crater. Start by using the air-brush tool to paint the outside rim of the crater. Go ahead and use whichever method you feel most comfortable with, just remember that the white areas are elevated while the darker areas are lower in the model.

STEP TWO

Reduce the size of your image to around 100 x 100 pixels. Since an 8-bit grayscale image consists of 256 shades of gray, a terrain model only has 256 possible elevation levels. A model's height can be stretched, but in doing so it distorts the polygons. If you don't want the rendered image of the terrain to appear faceted, try to create a gradual transition of shades by blurring the grayscale image of the terrain.

After you have created the terrain bitmap, save the file as a PICT document. The next step is importing the PICT into the terrain program you're using. For the sake of this tutorial we'll be using Terrainman, which is included on the CD-ROM.

Tip. Both Bryce and Infini-D handle only square-shaped terrain bitmaps, so if the image is rectangular the program will distort the image's dimensions to fit those parameters.

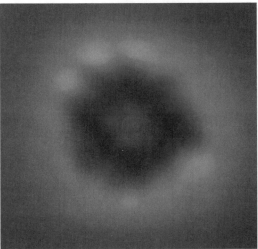

FIGURE 6.20   *This grayscale image will serve as an elevation map for our terrain generation program. The white areas will be elevated whereas the black areas will be lower in the terrain model.*

Tip. Smudging the border of two contrasting shades or applying **Gaussian blur** to the entire image will usually blend the colors enough to provide a gentle transition. The smudge tool also works well for creating erosion lines or crevices. Another useful tip is to use Photoshop's **Noise Filter** on the image before applying **Gaussian blur** to prevent the surface from looking too uniform. A handy hardware tool to have in this process is a drawing tablet. Many software programs feature pressure-sensitive tools such as an airbrush, which is ideal for this type of job.

STEP THREE

Launch the Terrainman application. Go to the **File** menu and select **Open PICT**. Choose the PICT image that you recently completed. The first thing that you should do is adjust the resolution of the model. Under the **Terrain** menu you will see selections for 100%, 50%, and 25% resolution. While manipulating your terrain you should keep the resolution of the model low. Screen redraw time will be faster because the computer will be dealing with less information.

STEP FOUR

Try rotating your model around to see what it looks like. The elevation or the Y-axis scale can also be manipulated in

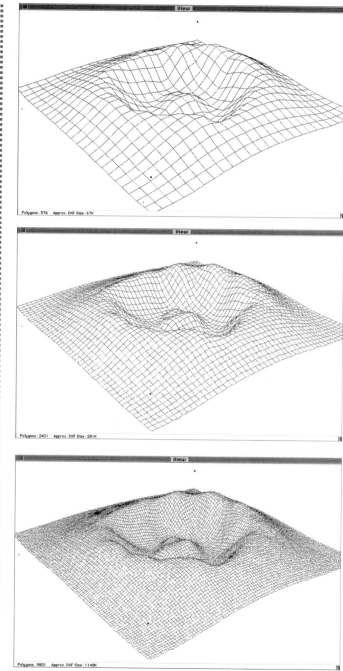

FIGURE *The model of the crater viewed with 25% resolution*
6.21 *(top), 50% resolution (middle), and 100% resolution in*
Terrainman (bottom).

Terrainman by clicking and dragging on the top set of anchor points on the corners of the model.

Try not to stretch the height of the model too much. The terrain modeling program has only a finite number of polygons. When you stretch the height of a terrain model, you're stretching the height of the polygons. If the polygons become too distorted, the object will appear to be faceted when rendered. If that's the effect that you're trying to achieve, swell; but if it isn't, try to add more intermediate shades in the grayscale map.

Terrainman also allows you to crop the bottom of the model by clicking and dragging on the lower set of anchor points. If you intend to obscure the foundation or the lower parts of the terrain with another plane or terrain model, it's a good idea to crop any polygons that won't be visible. Once again it's maximizing all of your available resources.

STEP FIVE

Turn the resolution back up to 100% and then save the file as a DXF model. After that import the model into your 3D application and there you go — instant terrain.

**T
U
T
O
R
I
A
L**

CANYON TUTORIAL

Perhaps one of the most famous cinematic finales in history is the Death Star trench scene from *Star Wars*. Now you too can create your own cinematic masterpiece along the same lines. But instead of the trench of the Death Star, we're going for a more natural feel so we'll use a desert canyon.

STEP ONE

The first step is to create a grayscale PICT to use as our elevation map. Start with a rectangular-shaped file using a 2:1 ratio. Remember that the white areas in the map will be the highest part of the terrain model, and the black areas will be on the canyon floor. Notice the white spots in Figure 6.22 in the center of the canyon; they will end up as columns. Feel free to change the bitmap to suit your own tastes — after all it's your planet. Reduce the size of the image to around 200 x 100 pixels. Save the image as a PICT.

FIGURE 6.22 *The white blobs in the center of the canyon elevation map will turn into columns when imported into Terrainman.*

STEP TWO

Import the PICT into Terrainman. Tweak the elevation so that you're satisfied with the results. Save the model as a DXF file and import it into your modeling program.

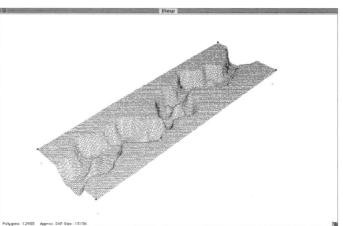

FIGURE 6.23 *Our 2D grayscale image has been converted into a 3D model in Terrainman.*

STEP THREE

The tricky thing about terrains is creating and then applying an appropriate texture map. In Figure 6.24, two maps are applied to the canyon. One map is a planar projection map applied directly on top of the canyon. The second map, which displays the stratification of the rock, is another planar projection applied to the side of the canyon. If your program does not support multiple maps on an object, you can either split the model up into individual pieces or create separate grayscale maps for each part of the model.

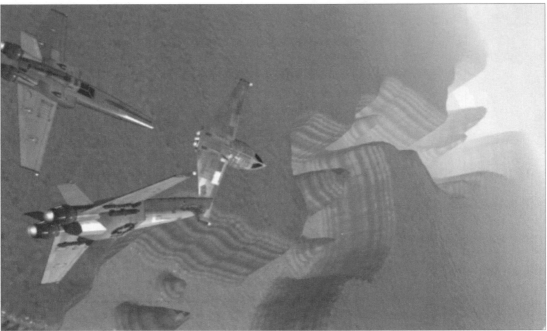

Figure
6.24 *Two color maps were applied to the model of the canyon. One for the ground coloration and the second map for the stratification in the rock.*

Fog or depth of field is used in this image to fade the foreground into the background. This feature is especially useful in landscape situations for two reasons. First, it gives the viewer a sense of scale and, second, it saves time because you don't have to create and then render a background image.

T
U
T
O
R
I
A
L

Cave Tutorial

In this project we're going to add another element to our model and that is water. In the real world, not our computer-generated one, water is usually level and flat, hence the term *water table*. With a little foresight in the creation of the grayscale PICT, we can add the illusion of water. The image that we're trying to create is that of a long ovoid chamber with sides that slope down to the center to an underground sea. In the center of the body of water we'll want a couple of islands to break up the monotony.

STEP ONE

The first step is to create the PICT images that we will use for the cave ceiling and floor. Make the dimensions of the image roughly rectangular. Start with a 400 x 200 pixel file. When we start to draw the grayscale image for the floor, you need to paint a black channel down the center. This is the canal the water will flow through. In the middle of the channel, create a few white islands that will poke up through the water. The grayscale map should be lightest at the sides and then darkest in the center. Once you're satisfied with your cave floor, reduce the image size to 200 x 100 pixels and then save the file as a PICT (Figure 6.25).

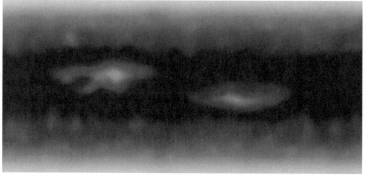

FIGURE 6.25 *Grayscale image of the cave floor. Notice the black canal for the water and the white blobs for the islands.*

STEP TWO

For the roof of the cave make the dimensions of the file identical to the cave floor. When drawing the cave ceiling we want the sides of the wall to slope downward and the top to be studded with stalactites. Create little white dots for your stalactites and a dark gray border to make the walls slope down. Once you're satisfied with your cave roof, reduce the image size to 200 x 100 pixels and then save the file as a PICT (Figure 6.26).

STEP THREE

Open the PICT for the cave floor in Terrainman. Set the elevation of the map to where it looks acceptable. Both Terrainman and CyberMesh offer the ability to crop the mesh. In Terrainman the user can shift a cropping plane

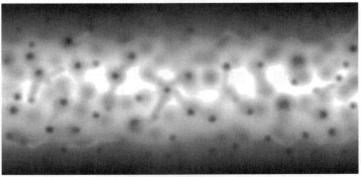

FIGURE 6.26 *Grayscale image of the top of the cave. The white dots are stalactites.*

upward by moving the lower set of anchor points to remove unwanted polygons. In CyberMesh the user has the option of not creating polygons for black pixels. In either case it's a good idea to use this feature to reduce the size of the model. Save the file as a DXF model (Figure 6.27).

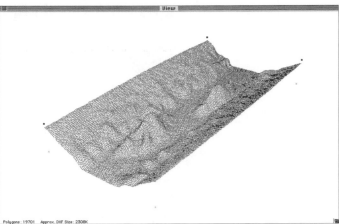

FIGURE 6.27 *The 3D model of the cave floor in Terrainman. Notice the channel in the center of the model and the small islands that will peek out of the water.*

STEP FOUR

Open the PICT for the cave ceiling in Terrainman. Set the elevation of the map to where it looks acceptable. Save the file as a DXF model (Figure 6.28).

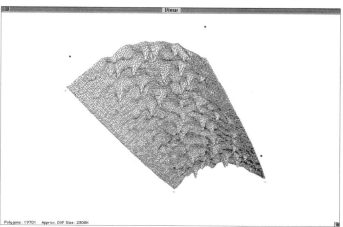

FIGURE *The 3D model of the cave ceiling will sit directly on top of*
6.28 *the first model of the floor.*

STEP FIVE

Once we've created all of the models, we can import them
into a rendering application. You will need to locate the
models in roughly the same positions as in Figure 6.29. Place
the models directly on top of the other with just a small section of each model overlapping.

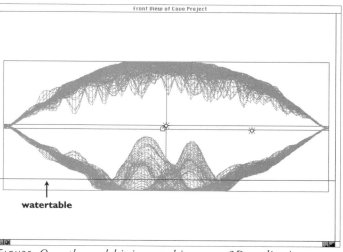

FIGURE *Once the model is imported into your 3D application, create*
6.29 *a plane to serve as the water table.*

The last step is to create a plane that will intersect the lower part of the cave. This plane will serve as our water table. Remember that anything below the level of the plane will be obscured.

STEP SIX

Time to apply texture maps to your model. The cave walls use a speckled bump map, which was created in Photoshop by applying the filter **Add Noise** to a white background with a little **Gaussian Blur**. The surface of the water is partially reflective material, with a very subtle bump map for a rippling effect. For lighting there is a primary light in the distance and a secondary fill light to the right and behind the camera. Atmospheric depth was also added with fog starting a little bit in front of the camera and then fading out to the background color in the distance.

FIGURE 6.30 *The final rendering of the model from Electric Image. Notice that fog was used to create atmospheric depth of field in this scene.*

OTHER USES FOR TERRAIN MODELING

Don't feel restricted to creating mountains and valleys with your terrain generation program. By carefully manipulating your grayscale elevation maps, you can actually create nonplanar geometric shapes and models.

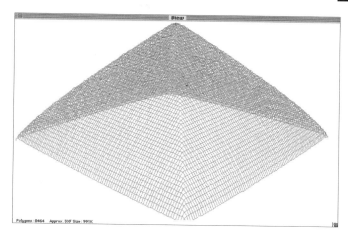

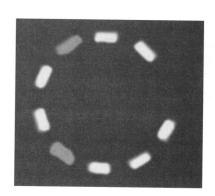

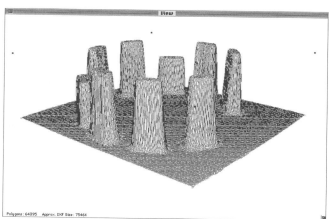

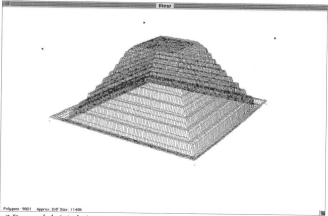

FIGURE 6.31 *Grayscale PICT (left) and resulting 3D model (right).*

CyberMesh

Knoll Software's CyberMesh is another terrain generating program. In addition to planar meshes, CyberMesh can wrap a mesh into a cylindrical or spherical shape. You can create the surface of an asteroid or the continents of a planet with a grayscale bitmap wrapped in a spherical manner. The primary advantage of CyberMesh is that it is relatively inexpensive and it works as a plug-in for Photoshop. Once the grayscale image is created, you can apply the plug-in and then pop directly into the CyberMesh application.

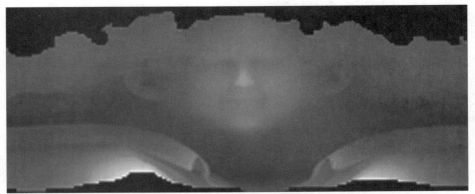

FIGURE *Grayscale image of John Knoll's head.*
6.32

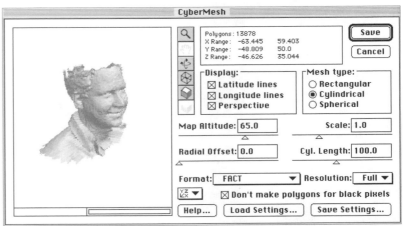

FIGURE *Cylindrical mesh created from grayscale image of John Knoll's head*
6.33 *created in CyberMesh.*

SECTION THREE: 3D DIGITIZERS

In section two we discussed using EPS templates to create ribs with which we could loft the shape of an airplane fuselage. The process involved bending wires around a plastic model of an airplane and then scanning the individual wires. Does that sound like a long and complicated process? It is.

3D digitizers can take a lot of the work out of the modeling process. Point entry 3D digitizers are peripherals that allow the user to input real-world X, Y, Z coordinates into their computer. The object that the user wishes to digitize is securely fastened in a stationary position, and a stylus is moved over the surface of the object. When the user needs to enter a point, a foot pedal, trigger, or keystroke registers the spatial coordinates at the tip of the stylus. These points can then be used to create lines, polygons, or patches to compose the surface of the 3D model. The process is simple, yet it does require some advanced planning.

The major advantages of 3D digitizers are realized in two areas. The first is creating an accurate computer model of an already existing physical object. The second benefit comes in the area of creating organic shapes. I find it far easier to create a character, for example, out of modeling clay than it is to use any spline-based computer modeling program. Once the character is completed, I can digitize the model into the computer.

The best digitizing method is to draw a grid on the surface of the physical model to serve as reference points. By using this technique, the polygons will be evenly spaced, forming a uniform surface. Remember, the goal in creating any 3D model is to use the least amount of information to capture the highest degree of detail.

There are four major categories of 3D digitizers:

- Mechanical arm
- Ultrasonic
- Magnetic
- Laser

Mechanical Arm Digitizers

Mechanical arm units usually consist of triple-jointed armatures with a sharply pointed stylus on the end. The user holds the stylus in his/her hand and moves the tip over the surface of the object being digitized.

The mechanical arm is fastened to a digitizing table, which roughly defines the total digitizing area. The digitizer calculates real-world X, Y, Z coordinates at the tip of the stylus from high-resolution sensors in the joints of the armature.

One of the drawbacks of a mechanical arm system is that the armature can be restrictive at times, making it difficult to reach certain places on an object. Also the digitizing area of the unit is limited to the length or reach of the arm, yet it is possible to digitize objects larger than the reach of the arm by dividing the object into segments.

The primary benefit of mechanical arm units is the low cost and ease of use. Several manufacturers offer units just under $1200 with digitizing software included.

Ultrasonic Digitizers

Ultrasonic digitizers work on the principle that sound will travel at a constant rate of speed. A digitizing stylus emits ultrasonic transmissions, which are received by a separate array unit. The digitizing hardware calculates the time it takes for the sound to reach the array from the digitizing probe, and extrapolates the X, Y, Z coordinates.

Since the digitizing probe is only attached to the rest of the hardware by a thin cable, the user is given almost total freedom of movement to reach just about every angle on the object. The primary advantage of this type of system is the ability to digitize large objects. Sizable physical models can be digitized in one session instead of having to move the object and realign the software. Many ultrasonic units have the capacity to digitize volumes of 8 x 8 x 6 cubic feet.

There are a few limitations inherent to ultrasonic digitizers. One of the main problems is that the digitizing probe needs to be within line of sight of the detector array. If the operator or model obscures either end of the system, it cannot register accurately. A solution to this is to suspend the detector array from the ceiling, making the physical installation of the unit somewhat of a challenge. Another issue that has plagued ultrasonic digitizers is atmospheric conditions. Humidity, temperature, and air density all affect the accuracy of the readings. To quote one major manufacturer response to the accuracy of their unit: "We make digitizers, not air."

Magnetic Digitizers

Magnetic digitizers look a lot like drawing tablets, except for the thin wire attached to the digitizing probe. A low-intensity magnetic field is generated by the tablet and a receiver located within the stylus transmits the coordinates to the hardware. Objects to be digitized are placed on the surface of the tablet and then the stylus is used to select points on the model. The operator has total freedom of movement to access virtually all segments of the model that can fit on the top of the digitizing tablet.

The advantage of magnetic units is that the operator is neither restricted by a mechanical arm or line of sight transmission, which makes this unit the most flexible in terms of user input.

On the other hand, electromagnetic digitizers have one major limitation. The primary handicap is that they cannot digitize or be operated close to metal objects. If you're only going to digitize clay figures there's no need to be concerned. But if you're a 3D service bureau, you might want to think again.

Laser Digitizers

These units are generally at the high end of the spectrum. They're usually extremely accurate as well as extremely expensive. Film studios as well as professional 3D animation houses use this type of equipment.

The digitizing process is fairly automated and the size of the object being digitized can range from a paper clip up to the entire human body. CyberWare, a Monterey, California, company specializes in human body scanners that not only capture geometry, but color information as well. The drawback to laser scanners? Apart from a six-digit price, laser scanners are notorious for being too good, digitizing too much information. But then again, nothing short of a workstation is able to run these digitizers, and if you have one of those, you can certainly handle the information.

SECTION FOUR: DEDICATED HUMAN BODY AND TREE MODELERS

We all know that if we put the time and effort into a project, we could create just about anything in 3D. The problem of course is finding the time for the project. Wouldn't it be nice if we could simply push a button and let the computer spit out a completed model? Inexpensive parametric modelers for both the human body and for trees are available for the Mac and are definitely a worthwhile investment. You're probably wondering what a parametric modeler is and why you need one? A parametric modeler is a 3D program that supports user input for specific parameters that correspond to various modeling features.

The primary advantage of a parametric modeler is that the user does not have to create a single polygon, since the program takes care of all of that for you. Sure, you could model a tree or a human body from scratch, but it would take time — lots of time.

Fractal Design's Poser

Have you ever tried to draw an accurate illustration of the human body without a model? Worse yet, have you ever tried to create a 3D model of the human form in a 3D application? As anyone who has tried to do either would tell you, it's not easy. Fortunately, for all of those budding artists and designers that don't have the time to create a complex 3D model or the budget to hire a human model to pose for hours on end, Fractal Design has developed Poser.

CONTORTIONISTS FOR HIRE

The primary advantage of using a parametric modeler such as Poser is that the user can manipulate a human figure with a minimum of fuss. You can choose either a male or female figure, and each body part can be scaled along the X Y Z axes. The interface is remarkably simple and easy to use. In the main window a 3D model of either a male or female figure is displayed. The model can be viewed in a number of different ways ranging from bounding boxes to a unique lit wireframe mode. All of the various parts of the human figure can be scaled or tapered on the three axes by either clicking and dragging on the individual segments

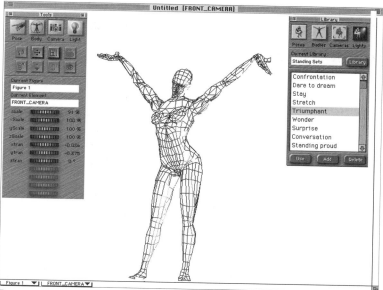

FIGURE
6.34
You can create either an adult or child, male or female figure with Fractal Design's Poser.

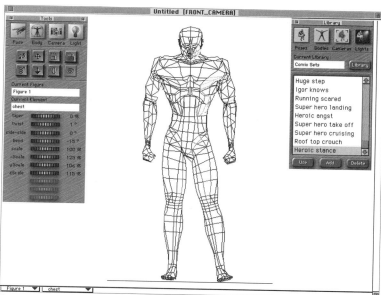

FIGURE
6.35
A model can be manipulated by either dragging the appropriate body part, or by tweaking the corresponding dial

or by manipulating parametric dials. The user can also rotate and position body parts using the same method.

Dynamic links are preestablished between the body parts so, for example, if you moved the hand downward, the arm, shoulder, and chest would gradually follow along. If you're having a hard time striking that perfect pose, Poser comes with a variety of different poses that can be applied to the models. The sets of poses range from athletes in midjump to comic book superheros flying through the air. Several figures can be added to the same scene, making it easy to plan the interaction between models. Basic primitives or Props such as spheres and cubes can also be added to scene.

Although Poser does have its own internal rendering engine, I would actually recommend importing the files into your own 3D application. You will have more control over textures as well as animation capabilities. Models can be exported from Poser by using the DXF or RIB format. Unfortunately, this is where some 3D users might become a little disappointed with the program. Poser only exports the various pieces of the model on one layer. In other words, all of the various body parts are all on the same layer when exported with the DXF or RIB file format. What this means for 3D animators is that animating a Poser model in a third-party software package is next to impossible unless the model is split up into individual pieces. As a whole, this program is still very useful. I like being able to create a human figure in Poser and then integrate it into a larger model. The amount of time that this program will save you is immeasurable.

Onyx's Tree Professional

While it might not have a flashy name like all of the other programs, Tree Professional is definitely one of the workhorses of the 3D world. Tree Pro is a parametric modeler for trees and some varieties of shrubs. Yes, many people might scoff at such a limited range of modeling capabilities, but if the need ever arises for you to create an accurate looking tree, any tree, you will need this program.

The user can create a tree by tweaking slider bars that correspond to virtually every aspect of a tree ranging from height, trunk width, the length of branches and twigs, to the color of the leaves. There are three types of trees from which to choose: broadleaf, palm, and conifers. The level of detail available is absolutely mind-boggling. Tree

FIGURE *Onyx Tree Pro lets the user choose a variety of different leaf types for*
6.36 *different types of trees ranging from broadleafs to conifers to palms.*

Pro creates models that are accurate down to the individual pine needles on a Douglas fir and the swaying fronds on a palm!

When creating a tree, the process is a lot like how Mother Nature
grows one in reality. You start with the trunk, setting the height, width,
texture, and curvature. Once the trunk's created, the branches, twigs,
and leaves are added. The user has absolute control over the spread,
crown, and density of both the branches and twigs. Once the skeleton
of the tree is complete, several different types of leaves can be selected
ranging from red and gold maple leaves to long slender green palm
fronds. Since Tree Pro can export the file as either a PICT or DXF file,
the color information applied to the model layers is retained.

It is important to note that you are going to need a serious 3D
application that can handle the large DXF files generated by Tree Pro.
Electric Image, for example, has no problems with large DXF files but
lower end applications might choke on the glut of polygons. You can
control the level of resolution when exporting a model, but for a
highly detailed model expect the polygon count to skyrocket into the
50K to 60K range. Most 3D programs have difficulty handling files
larger than 65K polygons but Tree Pro does have several options for
reducing the polygon count.

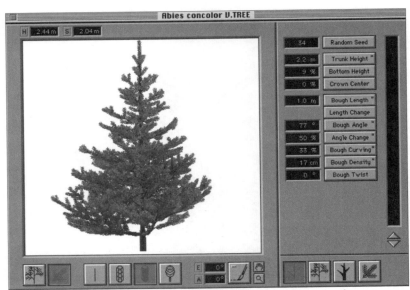

FIGURE *The amount of detail on the conifers is accurate down to the*
6.37   *individual needles in Onyx Tree Pro.*

Tree Tricks

If you're a little tight on cash and you can't afford to buy yet still another program, or if your 3D application can't handle the monstrously huge files created by Tree Pro, don't despair. There are a couple of quick and easy work-arounds to create trees in 3D.

T
U
T
O
R
I
A
L

METHOD ONE

The first method involves a trick with texture mapping. Start by figuring out what type of tree you want to create. The next step is to create a primitive that corresponds to the shape of the tree. If, for example, you wanted a pine tree or conifer, you would create a elongated cone and then texture map foliage to the cone. If you wanted to create a broadleaf type of tree, then you should use an Easter egg shape. You will need to use two different types of maps, a color map for the leaves and a transparency map for the space between the leaves. An additional ambient and diffuse map will be necessary depending on the nature of your 3D application.

FIGURE *Color map for a broadleaf tree.*
6.38

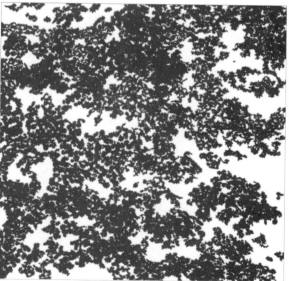

FIGURE *Transparency map for a broadleaf tree. The*
6.39 *white areas will be transparent and the black*
areas will be opaque.

By mapping both a color map and a transparency map to a primitive shape, you can create a fairly nice tree. You can also model a trunk using a sweep on path in combination with a taper function.

T U T O R I A L

METHOD TWO

auto•des•sys's modeling and rendering application form•Z RenderZone suggests another alternative method for creating trees. This method can be applied to just about any 3D application. form•Z is bundled with a CD-ROM that includes several photorealistic tree textures and is also included on the Mac 3D Pro CD-ROM as well.

FIGURE   *The tree texture included with form•Z RenderZone 2.7 is also*
6.40   *on our CD-ROM.*

STEP ONE

Instead of mapping our tree texture onto a 3D shape, auto•des•sys recommends using two 2D shapes. Start by creating two 2D rectangular planes, which are perpendicular to each other. You can then create the structure for the tree color maps.

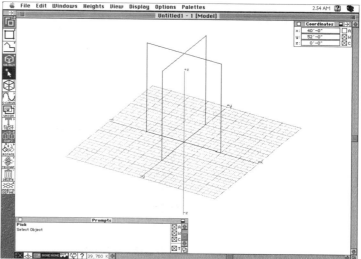

FIGURE *Illustration of the tree model in auto•des•sys's form•Z 2.75.*
6.41

STEP TWO

Apply a color map to each of the rectangular planes.

STEP THREE

Make the black areas of the color map transparent. If your program does not have that function, create a transparency map. See the section on Alpha channels in Chapter 16 for directions on creating a transparency map. The tree is complete.

FIGURE **6.42** *The color maps are applied to each 2D plane.*

FIGURE **6.43** *Rendering of the finished tree in form•Z RenderZone.*

CHAPTER

7

Materials and Texture Mapping

CHAPTER REQUIREMENTS

Basic understanding of Photoshop.

I remember when I used to build plastic model kits. I painstakingly glued together small bits and pieces of plastic and skin. Then I spent hours sanding the rough edges of the model until I finally finished assembling my masterpiece. Yet the model still only looked like a lump of plastic, nothing like the ultrarealistic Phantom F-4 on the front of the box. Due to my impatient adolescent nature, I had a hard time realizing that the model was only half finished. After glancing back and forth between the picture on the box and my still sticky model, I realized that the model on the box was painted. In a flash of revelation I understood that's how they made it look so real and I could do that too. So I took out my can of spray paint and covered the model with a coat of matte battleship gray. The model still didn't look anything like the one on the box.

OK — so I gave up after that — but ironically enough the same painting problems came back to haunt me when I first started 3D modeling. I would create amazing models yet they never looked realistic when they were rendered. I should have persisted when I was younger. Lessons that I could have learned back then would have saved me time and frustration now.

This is where the magic of texture mapping comes into play. The term *texture mapping* can be used as a catch-all phrase to describe the creation and application of materials and maps to a 3D model. Texturing a 3D model is a lot like painting a plastic model kit. A plastic model must first be primed, painted, detailed, and then decals are added. The 3D designer follows many of the same steps but uses slightly different terminology.

While modeling is a definite skill, texturing a model is an art. Good texture mapping skills are essential to the professional 3D designer. A well-crafted material or texture map can add depth, scale, and realism to a model, transforming a dull, flat rendering into an eye-catching 3D masterpiece.

SECTION ONE: MATERIALS — THE VIRTUAL ALCHEMIST

Most 3D programs come complete with a library of materials such as glass, aluminum, and gold. Yet when you try to create your own material, it just somehow doesn't look quite right. Have you ever wondered how a material's specular color or index of refraction influences a surface? In Section One we learn how to tweak our materials to get that added degree of reality in our renderings as well as finding out what each of those mysterious material properties does.

SECTION TWO: MAPPING BASICS

Before you start to create your own color and texture maps, you have to plan how they will be applied to the surface of a model. In this section we discuss the four different ways in which a map can be applied to a model: planar, cubic, cylindrical, and spherical. We also learn how to create seamless or tilable textures and when and when not to use them.

SECTION THREE: CREATING CUSTOM MAPS

Once we figure out how to apply a map to a model, we have to calculate the size, dimensions, proportion, and bit depth of the map based on the type of model and final size of the finished rendering.

SECTION FOUR: CREATING AND ALIGNING A BITMAP

Finally, we look at a practical application for all that we have learned about mapping: a step-by-step guide to creating a color map and aligning it precisely to the surface of a model. Some simple techniques are discussed that take a lot of the guesswork out of the entire process.

SECTION ONE: MATERIALS — THE VIRTUAL ALCHEMIST

For the Hollywood miniature model maker, the first step in the painting process of a model is to sand and then prime the surface. The goal is to create a uniform surface over which the primer and final coat of paint can be applied. For the 3D designer, the process is somewhat the same. We don't have to sand our models of course, but we do have to prime and then apply a base coat of paint. Instead of thinking in terms of paint, think of the process as actually creating the substance or material of which the object will be composed.

While the model maker paints a surface to look like aluminum, the 3D designer creates a material with all of the physical characteristics of aluminum. When the model maker paints a model, all he's really doing is changing the color of the surface. When we create a material for a model, we are setting the physical characteristics of the surface. We have absolute control over how shiny, reflective, or even how hard a material appears. By manipulating all of these factors and a few others, we can create materials that look like glass, metal, wood, plastic, or whatever we need.

Material Color Theory

Just about every 3D application has the option to create your own custom materials. What is a material? A material is a user-defined substance such as gold, glass, or marble. Generally speaking, it does not involve a color map. A material is created by tweaking a variety of different attributes such as specularity and transparency, both of which will be covered in the latter half of this chapter.

When it comes to creating a material, it's usually best to have a real-world example of the substance handy. I understand that a bar of gold or a rod of plutonium is hard to come by, but try to substitute with something close to it in terms of physical characteristics. The first step in creating a custom material is setting the color of the material. A material's color can be broken down into three separate components:

- Ambient color
- Diffuse color
- Specular color

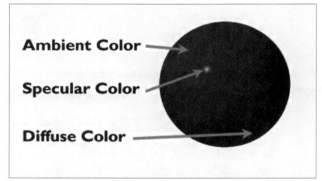

FIGURE *Chart of ambient, diffuse and specular colors.*
7.1

DIFFUSE COLOR

The diffuse color of a material is the easiest to identify. Diffuse color is what we usually refer to when we describe the color of a material. For example, if you were looking at a red ball that is illuminated by a single light source, the central part of the ball that is completely lit would be red and the part near the edges would be a dark gray. The red color, which would be most visible in the illuminated area of the ball, is the diffuse color. If an object is completely lit by a pure white light with no part of the object in shadow, the only color your eye would perceive is the diffuse color of the object.

When you're setting the diffuse color of your material, try to keep in mind how it looks when it is fully illuminated. Another consideration is that very few materials in this world are fully saturated. In other words when you play with the **Apple Color Picker** don't set the material's color to the most extreme settings. For example, even the purest white surfaces have small amounts of other colors such as yellow. And in reality, black is very rarely completely black, it's more of a mixture of very dark blues.

SPECULAR COLOR

Before we discuss specular color, you should understand specular reflection. Specular reflection is the reflection of specular light off of the surface of an object and is often referred to as either highlight or glint. Specular color is the color of the specular reflection. If you're having a hard time visualizing this, refer back to the diagram in Figure 7.1.

Specular color is a blend of both a material's diffuse color and the color of the object's light source. When it comes to setting the specular color of a material, it's important to recognize what type of material you're trying to create. Metals tend to have specular colors close to the color of the light source. Steel and aluminum for example have specular colors close to white when illuminated by a white light. But be careful, the specular color of other metals tends to rely more on the diffuse color of the material rather than on the color of the light source. The specular color of gold and brass, for example, is a rich yellow, regardless of the color of the light source.

Tip. A good way to set the specular color of a metallic material is to copy the settings from the diffuse color, and then increase the brightness or luminance value. For a metal such as aluminum, increase the luminance value more than you would for a metal such as gold.

Once again, it's a good idea to have a sample of the substance that you're trying to duplicate. Materials such as glass, plastic, lacquered woods, and highly reflective materials all tend to have specular colors close to that of the primary light source. If you're unsure, leave the specular color at white.

AMBIENT COLOR

The ambient color of a material is the color of the material when it is in shadow. When you're first starting out, it's a good idea to use the same settings for the ambient color that you used for the diffuse. Very few materials have different ambient and diffuse colors. The reason the ambient color appears darker is simply because there is a reduction in illumination on the surface of an object. Very few materials in the real world have ambient colors that are different from their diffuse colors. Materials that tend to glow or emit their own light is an example. Many programs don't even have the option of changing the ambient color of a material but offer the option of glow instead.

Physical Properties

Color is only one of the attributes that makes a material look realistic. Now that we've established the color of a material, we can apply the physical characteristics of the material's real-world counterpart. By juggling the following attributes, we can make a material seem hard, soft, metallic, or even fragile.

- Ambient value
- Diffuse value
- Specular value
- Reflectivity
- Transparency
- Index of refraction
- Glow

This is where the real power of 3D comes into play. The physical modeler can apply a glossy coat of paint to make the surface of the object shinier, but we can go a step further to make a surface transparent, reflective, or even glow.

AMBIENT VALUE

The ambient value of a material determines the amount of ambient light that a material will reflect. Think of the ambient value as the brightness control of a material's shaded regions. Higher ambient values result in less contrast between the ambient and diffuse colors of an object. On the other hand, if the ambient value of a material is lower, the area of a material that is in shadow will be closer to black.

Tip. Setting the ambient value of a material depends on the type of material you're trying to create. For example, some materials such as a piece of white paper look very bright in shadow. On the other hand, a black sweater would be lost in a dark room.

FIGURE 7.2 *Notice how the shaded areas in the object move closer to black as the ambient value is reduced. The sphere on the left has a high ambient value, the center sphere a medium value, and the right a low value.*

DIFFUSE VALUE

The diffuse value of a material controls the amount of diffuse light a surface reflects. When the diffuse value of a material is higher, it tends to be brighter, and when the value is decreased, a material will appear to be darker. On the sphere at the far right in Figure 7.3, the diffuse value is so low, the surface appears to be in total shade. The object seems to be entirely the same color as the ambient light color since there is no diffuse light being reflected from the surface. Materials that have lower diffuse values tend to be more evenly lit with less of a sharp transition from highlight to shadow.

Tip. The diffuse value of a material affects how dull the surface will appear. Higher values give the material more of a matte finish. It's important to set the diffuse value of a material in relation to the Specular value because they are inversely proportional. As the diffuse value is increased, the specular value should be decreased. It's rare to have a material with both a high diffuse and high specular value.

FIGURE 7.3 *The diffuse value controls the relative brightness of a material. The sphere on the left has a high diffuse value, the middle sphere a medium value, and the sphere on the right a low diffuse value.*

SPECULAR VALUE

The specular value controls how much specular light a surface reflects, and is associated with how shiny or glossy a material appears. The average 3D program breaks down the specular reflection of a material into two distinct parts: the highlight and the halo that surrounds it. The size of the highlight belies the nature of the material. For example, a smaller concentrated highlight usually occurs on machined surfaces, whereas a broader highlight in combination with a large halo indicates a glossy surface. Generally speaking, a small concentrated highlight is usually an indication of a hard material.

Tip. By increasing the specular value of a material, a surface appears to become more glossy. A high specular value, used in conjunction with an equal degree of reflectivity, will result in a material that looks both smooth and hard.

When the specular value of a material is increased, the diffuse and ambient value of a material should be decreased. High diffuse and ambient values tend to wash out or overexpose a surface which would obscure the more subtle specular highlight.

FIGURE *A material appears glossier with higher specular values. The*
7.4 *sphere on the left has a high specular level, the middle a medium value, and the right a low specular value.*

REFLECTIVITY

When the specular light being reflected off of the surface of a material has very little diffuse value, and is equal to the intensity of the surrounding light, we call this *reflectivity.* It sounds complicated, but it really isn't. Just think of reflectivity in terms of how much of its surroundings the material tends to reflect.

When it comes to creating a reflective surface, several considerations need to be made. First of all, how reflective will the surface be? Shiny metals such as chrome are more reflective than brushed aluminum, and polished wood is much more reflective than an ordinary two by four. Another consideration is that as a surface becomes more reflective, it creates the illusion that it is composed of a very smooth, hard material.

Tip. Don't arbitrarily increase the reflective value of material. There aren't that many materials in the world that have highly reflective surfaces. Many novices usually increase this value just because they think that it will make the rendering more realistic. Polished wood, for example, rarely has a mirror-like finish.

As a material is made more reflective, the ambient and diffuse values of a material should be reduced for the same reasons that they were lowered for high specular values. High ambient and diffuse values will tend to obscure the reflection of an object. As a material becomes more reflective, the less the ambient and diffuse values matter anyway. Several programs automatically compensate for an increased reflective value, but if it doesn't and your material is not reflective, try reducing the ambient and diffuse values.

In Figure 7.5, as a material approaches perfect reflectivity, it loses more of its diffuse color. A perfect mirror, which is impossible in the real world but entirely possible in a 3D environment, reflects all light and has no diffuse or ambient color at all.

FIGURE 7.5   *As a material becomes more reflective, less ambient and diffuse light is reflected from the surface of the object. The sphere on the left has a high reflective value, the middle a medium value, and the right sphere a low reflective value.*

TRANSPARENCY

The transparency level of a material controls the amount of light that is able to pass through a material. Lower values will create an opaque material; higher levels will produce fully transparent objects. As with both reflectivity and specular values, reduce the level of both the ambient and diffuse values as you increase the transparency value. If the ambient and diffuse values are too high, the surface of the object will be opaque because the material will reflect too much ambient and diffuse light.

When you're setting the transparency of a material, it's best not to set the field to its maximum setting. In reality a fully transparent material is physically impossible, because at that point it would be invisible.

FIGURE 7.6   *The sphere on the left has a high transparency setting, the middle a medium setting, and the right a low transparency setting.*

INDEX OF REFRACTION

The index of refraction controls the amount of refraction or distortion that occurs through a transparent material. Glass and water are good examples of materials that distort light. The refraction index of air is around 1.0, which is no distortion, while water is around 1.3 and glass can be anywhere from 1.5 to 1.6.

When you're setting the index of refraction for a material such as glass, it's a good idea to consider the relative thickness of the model. A thick pane of glass usually has a higher index of refraction than would a thin pane. The ceiling for the index of refraction is around 2.0. Once you've crossed this threshold, there aren't any real-world materials that exceed this level.

Tip. When you're creating a model that will be transparent, such as a wine bottle or a martini glass, remember to model the inside wall of the object. Many novices model only the outside wall, which results in a very unnatural looking object when rendered.

Tip. Due to the physical nature of refraction, only raytracers can mimic this optical aberration. Very few people use raytracing as an animation algorithm on the Mac because of the long rendering times involved.

FIGURE
7.7
As the index of refraction increases, so does the distortion. The sphere on the left has a high index of refraction, the middle sphere a medium value, and the right sphere has a low index of refraction.

GLOW

This attribute is used to create materials that are self-illuminating. Light bulbs, radioactive materials, and neon signage are all examples of materials that produce their own light. When the glow value of a material is increased, the luminance value of the diffuse color of a material is also increased slightly. When glow is applied, the amount of diffuse light that a material reflects is uniformly increased over the entire surface of the material. As a result, the amount of ambient light that a material reflects is decreased.

Be careful when increasing the glow factor of a material. Surface detail becomes obscured with higher glow values since the entire object will be covered by only one uniform color. It's also important to note that a glowing object casts no light of its own nor does it add to the overall illumination of a scene. Remember that a glowing object cannot be used as a light source!

Tip. It's a good idea to locate a light source in or near a glowing object to create the illusion that the material is actually casting light. Another alternative is to use a glow or illumination map — we'll cover that in the next chapter.

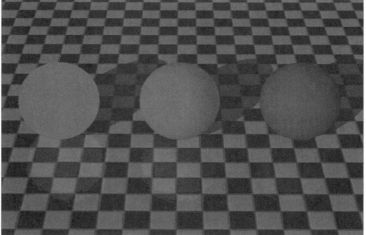

FIGURE *Notice how surface detail decreases as the glow factor increases.*
7.8 *The sphere on the left has a high glow value, the middle sphere a medium value, and the sphere on the right has a low glow value.*

Putting It All Together

It takes a practiced eye and a lot of experience to combine all of these factors to create an authentic looking material. When the right color is combined with the proper physical properties, you can create just about any material imaginable.

If you're having problems creating your own material, a good place to begin is with the textures that come with your 3D program. Change just a few values at a time and do a quick rendering. It's important to spend some time getting familiar with your 3D application before you start to texture a large model. Each program handles materials differently, and the same setting in one program will yield different results in another. Experiment on models of spheres because they render quickly and the curved surface gives you a good idea of what a material looks like from all perspectives.

Tip. Many 3D programs use a bump map in combination with a metallic material to accurately recreate a substance. Be sure to check and see what materials are included with your 3D application.

Creating a material is only the first step in texturing a model. If you're wondering why materials and their physical properties are so important, bear with me for only a moment. For example, you need to know what the specular value of a material does in order to fully utilize a specular texture map. The physical properties of materials are keys that will unlock the secrets of texture mapping. How can you use a diffuse texture map, for example, if you don't know what the diffuse color of a material controls?

If you're still feeling a little fuzzy, I'd suggest going back and reading this chapter again. Don't use the excuse that you're only going to cover the entire surface of your model with a color or texture map anyway. To create custom texture maps, you need a solid understanding of how each physical characteristic affects the surface of a material.

T U T O R I A L

SPACESHIP TUTORIAL
Now it's time for a practical application of what we just covered.

STEP ONE
Launch your 3D application and then import the DXF file for the spaceship. Select the entire model and then clear any color or texture that has been applied to it. Think of it as priming the surface of a model in order to prepare it for painting. Remember that DXF files carry both layer as well as color information. The color information for all of the pieces of the model needs to be set to your program's default color. Do a quick rendering of the model. It should look like the image in Figure 7.9.

FIGURE 7.9 *Rendering of the spaceship without materials or textures applied.*

STEP TWO

The image looks extremely flat. At this point, it doesn't even look plastic, which would be a welcome improvement. Materials that will add a little more realism to the rendering need to be created and applied to the individual pieces of the model. First start with the main body and the wings, which will be made of the same material. The material that we're going to try to create for those parts is kind of like aluminum. Your program should have some way of setting the following parameters for a material:

Diffuse color:	Red-232, Green-252, Blue-255
Ambient color:	Red-232, Green-252, Blue-255
Specular color:	Red-255, Green-255, Blue-255
Ambient value:	60%
Diffuse value:	60%
Reflectivity:	33%
Specularity:	100%
Highlight:	Small to medium size
Halo:	Medium to large size

The hardest part of creating aluminum will be in dealing with the specular reflection. You should be able to edit the size of both the specular highlight and halo. Some programs let you set the hardness of the material, which in turn influences the size of the highlight. Once again the best thing to do is to play around with the program until you get it right.

STEP THREE

For the rest of the smaller pieces of the model it's up to you to create your own elemental recipes. Experiment on your own to create whichever materials you wish. Here's what I did in case you're not sure.

For the cockpit windows I wanted a glassy type of substance with a dark glossy color. The diffuse color was set to a very dark blue, close to black. The specular value was set high, with a very small highlight and large halo. The diffuse and ambient values were set considerably lower.

For the guns and the detailing, I wanted a matte finish. Diffuse values were set moderately high, and specular values were close to zero.

FIGURE *Rendering of spaceship with material applied.*
7.10

Not bad, but we can do better. What we need to do is a quick critique of our work. What's wrong with this picture?

- The surface is too clean and uniform. In reality the surface of a spaceship would be smudged, dirty, maybe even a little bit rusty. Even the most well taken care of spaceships look a little bit used.
- The entire body of the spaceship seems to be made out of one piece of metal. The surface of the spaceship would look more realistic if it were made up of individual panels of metal. For pieces such as the guns and the cockpit window, it's fine to leave the materials as they are because they're relatively small in comparison to the rest of the ship.
- The model kind of looks like a toy. There's no sense of scale or proportion in this model. It could be fifty feet or five inches in length — there are no visual clues to the size of the model.

So what do we do? Settle for a mediocre rendering? No, we forge ahead into the world of texture mapping.

SECTION TWO: MAPPING BASICS

A lot of different terminology is used when it comes to describing mapping and there's no real clear-cut consensus on which term is right or wrong. Some of the more common terms and definitions associated with them are given here. Maps that are used as pictures or images are referred to as *color maps*. You could use a color map to create the illusion of wood grain panels, brick walls, or a billboard. But maps don't have to be just images, they can also be used to describe or alter the surface of a material. These types of maps fall into the category of *texture* or *surface maps*. We use texture maps to add roughness, bumps, and even a sparkle to the surface of a material.

Part of the reason we use mapping is because it would be next to impossible to model everything in a 3D environment. For example, if we were creating a model of a bathroom with a tile floor, we could model each tile individually and add unwanted megabytes to the model. Instead, we can use a bitmap image of tiles and *map* it onto the polygon that is used to represent the floor. This bitmap image can be either a scanned picture, an image that you've created in Photoshop, or from any number of third-party vendors that market royalty-free textures. By using texture maps we not only save on modeling time, but on rendering time as well. When we use a texture map in a rendering, the computer does not have to deal with any additional geometry.

Regardless of what we call them, the key to realistic looking results is using both color and texture maps in conjunction. In the case of a brick wall, for example, we would use a color map to define the color of the bricks and a bump map to create the illusion of mortar. But before we go rushing ahead and create a map that doesn't fit on the surface of our model, we need to learn a little bit more about the method for applying a map.

How It Works

Applying a map is a lot like wrapping a birthday present. You start with a flat sheet of wrapping paper and cover a 3D object. In 3D modeling, you're performing the same task, yet your tools are much more sophisticated. The problem with wrapping a present is that you must cut and fold the paper in order to make it fit around the box. Folds, creases, and mismatched paper patterns are always obvious on any wrapped package. In 3D, we have the means to apply a map so that we can avoid all of those problems.

In our 3D application we can't cut our map, but we can stretch our map infinitely in all three dimensions without ever having to worry about tearing the image. Remember to think of your map as magic rubber wallpaper that can be stretched to cover any type of surface. This wallpaper can be stretched along all three axes.

Another option available when mapping a model is the ability to scale the size of the map relative to the surface of the object. If the map is too large or small, the user can simply reduce or enlarge the dimensions of the map, something you obviously can't do with wrapping paper. If the map isn't large enough to cover the entire surface, and you don't want to stretch the map, there is the option of repeating or tiling the map, which works well in certain circumstances.

Types of Mapping

A map can be applied to the surface of an object in four different ways:

- Planar
- Cubic
- Cylindrical
- Spherical

When it comes to choosing which method to use to apply a map, the easiest process is to choose a method that corresponds to the shape of the object. For example, use spherical mapping for spheres and cubic mapping for cubes. But make sure that you experiment — it's often a better idea to use cubic mapping on a sphere to minimize distortion.

PLANAR MAPPING

Planar mapping is probably the most commonly used and easiest to comprehend method of mapping. Applying a planar map to an object is like pasting a postage stamp on an envelope. The only difference is that with planar mapping, the stamp or map will show through on the other side of the envelope. It's like drawing on a sheet of paper with a magic marker — the mirror image bleeds through to the other side. The other interesting feature of planar mapping is that the map conforms itself to the surface of the object. For example, if you're applying a map to a surface with a lot of indentations, the map will automatically fill all of the crevices as well as the side walls of the crevices.

Planar mapping works best on large flat surfaces. The advantage of using planar mapping is that it offers the least amount of distortion when applied to an object. Use planar mapping when the majority of the faces of an object are all close to being coplanar. It's fine if there is a little variation in the surface such as a slight curve or wave. But if

FIGURE
7.11
Planar mapping applies a map to an object by projecting the image onto the surface a model.

there's a sharp transition or if some faces on the object are perpendicular to each other, cubic mapping might be a better choice.

CUBIC MAPPING

Cubic mapping applies a map in a cubic fashion to the surface of an object. In other words a map will be applied relative to each of the six faces of an imaginary cube that surrounds the object that you wish to be mapped. Cubic mapping should be used with any shape that is roughly rectangular. Cubic mapping also works well with a seamless texture on spherical objects when you want to avoid the pinching of the map at the two poles.

FIGURE **7.12** *Cubic mapping applies a map to each of the six faces of an imaginary cube that surrounds a model.*

CYLINDRICAL MAPPING

This type of modeling is best used when you're applying a map to something like a tree trunk or wine bottle or any object that is roughly cylindrical. The map will be wrapped around the circumference of the object like a Tootsie Roll wrapper. Be careful when applying a map in a cylindrical fashion because the map can become distorted at the end caps of the object.

FIGURE
7.13
Cylindrical mapping wraps a map around the circumference of a model.

SPHERICAL MAPPING

Spherical mapping applies a map much in the same way that we would apply a flat 2D map of the surface of a globe. The top and bottom of the map where the North and South poles are located is pinched while all of the countries along the equator are stretched.

FIGURE
7.14
Spherical mapping wraps a map around the entire surface of a model, pinching the map at the two poles and stretching the map at the equator.

Creating a spherical map that compensates for polar distortion is extremely difficult. For example, look at the bump map in Figure 7.15 that we used to create a golf ball, it had to be stretched at the top and bottom to compensate for polar distortion.

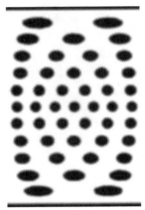

FIGURE *Bump map for a*
7.15 *golf ball.*

Tiling Maps

Why bother to create huge texture maps when you can have the computer repeat the same one over and over again? The process is like tiling your bathroom floor. When you're laying square ceramic tiles, you lay them down so that each side of a tile is adjacent to the next. This process can be performed virtually the same way with color and texture maps, except that it can be done over a 3D surface. Tiling allows the user to repeat a map across the surface of an object by duplicating the map in both horizontal and vertical directions. The advantage of using tiling is that if there is a naturally occurring pattern in the map, such as a brick wall or tile floor, the user only has to create a small portion of the map, and then use the tiling options to repeat the pattern.

There are a few considerations when it comes to creating a map that will be repeated. A *tilable* or *seamless map* will need to be created. When a map is repeated on both the horizontal and vertical axes, the top of the map has to match the bottom, and the right side of the map has to match the left. A seamless texture is necessary because if the map does not match on all of its sides, there will be a seam or a break in the pattern where two tiles meet.

TEXTURE CREATION APPLICATIONS

Some 3D programs offer a feature to mirror a map along the X and Y coordinates to reduce seams. Maps will be flipped so that the right side of one tile will be next to the right side of the next tile. While this method is partially effective, it is not a total solution. There are several dedicated texture applications that make the creation of seamless texture maps a breeze. Here's a list of a few companies that offer seamless texture creation programs:

- Adobe   TextureMaker
- Specular   TextureScape
- Virtus   Alien Skin Textureshop

Another option is to use a wide range of Photoshop plug-ins that cater in part to the 3D designer. MetaTools' Kai's Power Tools are a great assortment of plug-ins that aid in the creation of everything from fractal-based gradient fills to their own custom seamless texture generating engine. Another useful tool is the Seamless Welder filter, which can create tilable maps from your own images. Another Photoshop plug-in is Xaos Tools' Terrazzo, which creates tilable *kaleidoscopic* types of tiles. Terrazzo works well for creating a texture for a Persian rug or nifty floral wallpaper.

Several third party vendors such as Artbeats and Form & Function also offer CD-ROMs full of photo-grade tilable images which are well worth looking into.

Tip. If you don't have any of these tools there is still hope. By using the clone tool in Photoshop, or any other application that supports this feature, you can create a seamless texture with a modicum of effort. By carefully cloning the border of one side of a texture map to the other, you should be able to create a seamless image.

WHEN AND WHEN NOT TO USE SEAMLESS MAPS

One of the most common mistakes of the novice 3D designer is to use a tilable texture map in the wrong circumstance. The best time to use a tilable map is when you're trying to achieve the look of a repeated pattern. Wallpaper, wood panels, and brick walls are good examples.

When shouldn't you use tilable maps? When the surface of an object has random features such as the surface of the ocean, the leaves on a tree, stars in the sky, or pebbles in the bottom of a stream. When used in these *natural settings,* the major drawback to tilable surfaces is that they tend to create an easily definable pattern that the human brain is very adept at perceiving. It's unusual for nature to create a pattern in any of these cases.

For a map such as for a brick wall, a repeating pattern is entirely acceptable and expected. But it's important to note that the color pattern of the bricks will eventually repeat itself, cuing the viewer into the fact that the image is computer generated. If the amount of detail in a map is reduced, or if the number of repetitions of a map is low, it's harder to notice a repeating pattern.

There are a few ways of handling the situation with the brick wall which can be applied to just about any map. The first is to make all of the bricks the same color when we create the tilable color map. With the proper lighting and shadows, we might be able to get away with it. But in reality things are rarely so uniform, brick walls are often composed of various colored bricks. So the best option is to create one large color map for the entire wall, and create random color patterns of bricks on your own. It is much more work, and it will increase rendering time slightly, but the results are worth it.

If time is an issue, and you still want to create a tilable map, keep in mind a few things. The larger the map — in terms of the number of bricks that you draw — the less of a chance the viewer will be able to perceive a pattern. If you try to keep the number of repetitions of the map low as well, the better your chances at not creating a recognizable pattern.

SECTION THREE: CREATING CUSTOM MAPS

The first consideration that we must deal with when it comes to creating our own color and texture maps is the size of the image. When I mention size I'm referring to both the horizontal and vertical dimensions as well as the map's file size and bit depth.

Size

Starting with the physical size of the map, it is important to perform a rough estimate of the approximate size of a rendered map. For example, if we were to use a color map that is 320 × 320 pixels and apply it to the face of a cube, we would not want the rendered size of the face of the cube to exceed 320 x 320 pixels. If the size of the rendered face of the cube exceeds those dimension, the color map will be pixelated or blocky when rendered because the program has to extrapolate for information that is not there.

Tip. Having problems visualizing this concept? Think about it this way. If you look at your color map in a program such as Photoshop at normal magnification, it appears fine. But when you use the magnifying glass tool to zoom into the image, it appears pixelated. The same thing occurs when you move a color map too close to the camera in your 3D application.

A good rule of thumb is to create a map slightly larger than what will be seen in the rendering. You should give yourself a comfortable 20% margin of error. It's often not easy to judge how large a map has to be, especially when you're doing an animation rather than a still image. The best method is to use the point in time at which the camera is closest to the model to determine the size of the map.

Bit Depth

Another consideration is the bit depth of a map. It's a good idea to reduce the bit depth of a color map to the lowest possible level while maintaining the highest degree of image quality. Don't fool yourself into thinking that you need a 24-bit color map all of the time. You can get the same results using an 8- or 16-bit map as you would with a 24-bit map in many cases. For example, the color maps on the space station created by Foundation Imaging for Babylon 5 are mostly in 8 bit. There will be times when you will need a full 24- or 32-bit color map, such as with subtle shade gradations like dirt, rust, or smudges, but for most applications, keep it small.

Tip. Keep your texture maps at a full 8 bit! Don't reduce texture maps to 4- or 2-bit images. All of the information is vital since each shade of gray corresponds to a specific level. More on that later.

Why should you bother with reducing the size and bit depth of your maps? The program can easily scale a map to fit an object and the more colors the better, right? Not entirely true. The entire idea of reducing file size is to conserve your available resources. Most programs have to either load maps into RAM or spool them from a hard drive. In the case of loading it from RAM you have better things to keep in there such as object geometry. And you don't want to have to spool anything from your hard drive because the effect on performance will be staggering. Also the less information that your CPU has to deal with the better. CPU time that is spent on mapping can be better allocated to rendering. The bottom line is increasing rendering speed.

Proportions of Maps

Now that we've nailed down the relative size of a map, we have to work on the actual dimensions of a map. The horizontal and vertical dimensions of a map depend on both the method that you are using (i.e., planar or cubic) and the shape of the object that you are mapping. You can always let your 3D program automatically scale any sized map to fit around any object, but in doing so it probably would distort the map. What we can do is resort to our high school geometry lessons to get it done right.

CYLINDRICAL MAPPING

Let's say we have to create a label for a wine bottle or a soda can and we need to calculate the horizontal dimension of the map. The vertical dimension of the label is dependent solely on how high you want it to be, but the width of the label is directly related to the circumference of the can. We want the label to fit around the entire circumference of the can. Think back to high school geometry for the formula. The formula for calculating the circumference of a cylinder is:

$$\text{circumference} = 2\pi r \text{ (where } r \text{ is equal to the radius of the cylinder)}$$

or

$$\text{circumference} = \pi d \text{ (where } d \text{ is equal to the diameter of the cylinder)}$$

The diameter or radius of an object is usually easy to determine in a 3D program. Just about every program allows the user to call up the X-axis dimensions of an object. These dimensions are equal to either the radius or diameter of the cylinder, depending on how your program displays this information.

Just in case you didn't understand this, we'll do a quick example. If we had a model of a can that was 4.5 inches in height with a diameter of 3 inches, our equation would be:

$$\text{circumference} = \pi d$$
$$\text{circumference} = \pi \ (3 \text{ inches})$$
$$\text{circumference} = 9.4377 \text{ inches}$$

The horizontal value of the map would be close to 9.5 inches and the vertical value a little bit less than 4.5 inches, so the top and bottom lip of the can would be seen.

CUBIC MAPPING

Cubic mapping is fairly straightforward and no real rules apply. But here's a common mistake that hopefully you won't fall into. Many beginners think that since the object they're mapping is roughly cubic in shape, they should automatically choose cubic mapping. This is only true part of the time. For example, if we wanted to texture something very un-politically correct such as a cigarette box, we could drive ourselves crazy trying to use cubic mapping to get the job done.

Instead we should use planar mapping to apply a separate map to the individual faces of the box. When it comes to calculating the dimensions of each map, they should correspond exactly to the dimensions of each face of the box. If your program doesn't support multiple surface maps, break the faces of the box up into individual objects and then apply a map to each face.

SPHERICAL MAPPING

There's no easy way to map a 2D image onto a sphere without distortion. The top and bottom of the image will always become pinched in a polar fashion. If you are using only one map with no tiling to cover the entire surface of a sphere, use a width to height ratio of 2:1, where the horizontal dimension of your map is twice as large as the vertical dimension. When using spherical mapping, the maximum area of vertical coverage on a sphere is 180° while the maximum area of horizontal coverage is 360°.

Planar Mapping

A planar map is probably the easiest type of map to size. It's a simple matter to get the horizontal and vertical proportions of an object. Since a planar map is applied to the surface of an object head on, the Z axis is not important. The width and height of our map would be directly proportional to the X and Y dimensions of the object. The problem is that not everything you model will be perfectly rectangular. In the next section we'll cover how to create a color map for an oddly shaped object.

Section Four: Creating and Aligning a Bitmap

We're going to kill three birds with one stone in this section. We're going to do the following all at the same time:

- Create a color map.
- Determine how large our color map will need to be.
- Align the color map to a model.

First of all, what is a color map? In the simplest terms, a color map is an image used to add color to the surface of a model. It's just like applying wallpaper to a room or decals to a toy car. In a sense it's kind of like painting your model, except that you're using 2D images. When we apply a color map to an object, the color map usually overrides the diffuse color of any material that is applied to the object. For example, if you create a material that has a diffuse color of green and apply it to the surface of an object, and then apply a color map that is yellow to that same object, the object would most likely be yellow once it is rendered.

One of our primary goals in 3D is trying to make our images look more realistic, not as if they had been created by a computer. Ahh, the irony of it all. Anyway, what we're trying to do with color maps is break up a uniform surface by adding dimension and depth to an image.

To complete this section, you are going to need a program such as Photoshop, Painter, or Collage. I highly recommend either Photoshop or Collage because of the layering features. These layering features will make your life much easier I promise. You'll see what I mean in a moment.

T
U
T
O
R
I
A
L

SPACESHIP COLOR MAPPING TUTORIAL

STEP ONE

The first step is to import the DXF model of the spaceship into your 3D program if you haven't already done so. Clear the model of any materials or textures that you might have applied to it from the previous lessons. Or leave the colors as they are; it sometimes helps if the different parts of a model are colored differently because it is often easier to determine the grouping or object structure.

STEP TWO

The next step in the process is to place the camera directly above the spaceship. The camera should be absolutely perpendicular to the X, Y plane of the model. Turn off perspective, or make sure the camera is in the orthographic mode.

STEP THREE

Now you have to make a careful decision. Think about how large the model will appear on the screen in the final animation. Zoom into the model until you feel that the model is scaled appropriately. Then zoom in another 15% to 20% just to give yourself a good margin of safety.

Tip. If you're having problems visualizing the size of the eventual rendering, use a 640 x 480 pixel window as a default for both multimedia as well as broadcast quality animations. Even if you are doing an animation for multimedia where the average screen size is only 320 x 240 pixels, it's best to use a larger window as a sizing guide. Chances are you might have to do some editing and special effects in postproduction and it's better to use a larger screen size animation rather than a smaller one. Also you're probably going to have to render stills at a higher resolution for promotional pieces.

STEP FOUR

You now have a few choices. The first is to perform a screen capture by pressing **Command Shift 3**, the second is to render the model out with wireframe or hidden line, and the third is to render out the model normally. The choice is entirely up to you. Sometimes it is easier to be more exact with a wireframe or screen capture than it is to use a rendering because you can see all aspects of the object's geometry. In our case we're going to render the image with Phong.

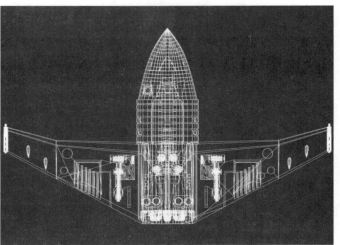

Figure **7.16** *A wireframe rendering of the spaceship is sometimes easier to use in the mapping process.*

Figure **7.17** *A Phong rendering of the spaceship will be used to create our color map.*

STEP FIVE

Open the rendering of the spaceship in your graphics program. For the sake of this tutorial we're going to use Photoshop 3.0 and a lot of its layering features. The theory behind what we're going to do is the same in any program so if you don't have Photoshop, you can still follow along by varying the lesson slightly.

If you've had a chance to look at the hierarchy or grouping structure of the spaceship, you would have noticed that the wing section is separate from the rest of the body. We're going to texture the wing first. Crop the image so that only the wing is visible as in Figure 7.18. Try to be as precise as possible, down to the closest pixel. This image is going to serve as the foundation of the wing's color map.

FIGURE **7.18** *The rendering of the spaceship is cropped so that only the wing is visible.*

STEP SIX

Create a new empty layer over the background. The cropped image of the wing should be on the background layer. On the new layer, draw an evenly spaced grid with a highly visible color. We're going to use this grid as a reference guide to align the color map to features on the model.

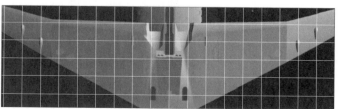

FIGURE **7.19** *A grid is created in a separate layer over the background image of the wing.*

Create a new layer between the grid and the background. Fill the layer with a neutral color such as white. Save the file with the name "Wing Texture Master." Flatten the image and then save it as another document with a name like "Wing Texture." We don't want to overwrite the original file!

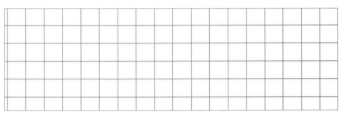

FIGURE
7.20
Create a new layer between the grid and the background and fill it with white. Flatten the image and save it as "Wing Texture."

STEP SEVEN

Open your 3D application and then apply "Wing Texture" to the wing using planar mapping. Keep the scale or the coverage of the map to 100% in both the horizontal and vertical directions. If you created your map properly, it should fit

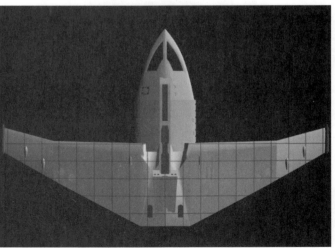

FIGURE
7.21
The rendering of the spaceship with "Wing Texture" applied to the wing section.

precisely. If you have to stretch the map to fit in either direction it will end up being distorted once it is rendered. Render the image.

STEP EIGHT

This step requires the most patience out of the entire process because you're going to have to do it several times. Multiple monitors will definitely come in handy here. Open the rendering in Photoshop. It should look like the image in Figure 7.21. Open the file "Wing Texture Master" (remember this is the one that has all of the layered information). Hide the white background layer and then create a new layer over the grid. It's on this layer that we're going to create our actual color map.

By using both the grid as well as the image of the wing in the background layer, it's easy to line up our panels. In Figure 7.22 you'll notice that we started the process by lining up panels with specific features on the wing. We're not going to finish the color map yet, because we need to make sure that the panels are aligned with the surface features.

We only need to do one side of the wing because the map is going to be symmetrical, once we get everything lined up and colored we can just copy a mirror image to the other side of the map. Now save any changes that we've made so far.

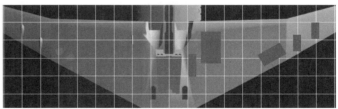

FIGURE
7.22 *Colored panels are aligned to features on the rendering of the wing in Photoshop on a separate layer.*

Make the white layer visible, and then flatten the image. Save the file once again as "Wing Texture." You'll now need to repeat Step 7.

STEP NINE

If you've aligned all of your panels correctly, the rendering should look like the image in Figure 7.23. If it doesn't, go back and fiddle with the file "Wing Texture Master" and try to align the panels. You will need to repeat Step Eight again. Fortunately, since all of the information for the color map is held in separate layers, it makes it easy to perform revisions.

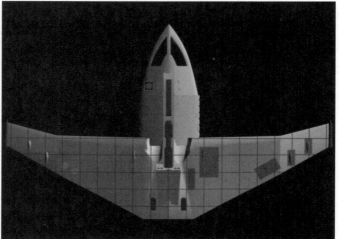

FIGURE **7.23** *Rendering of the "Wing Texture" applied to the surface of the wing and aligned correctly.*

Once you've gotten the preliminary panels aligned, go ahead and finish the rest of the color map. Remember that you have to construct only one side of a map because we can mirror the image. In Figure 7.24 you can see what the completed color map should look like. Notice that the outline of the map

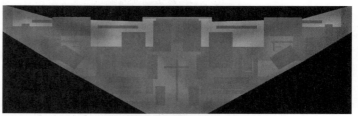

FIGURE **7.24** *The completed color map for the wing section.*

is slightly larger than the actual size of the wing. This is just to give us a little bit of leeway in case we've miscalculated.

STEP TEN
Once you're satisfied with the wing's color map, go ahead and reapply it to the model and then render away. It should look like the image in Figure 7.25.

FIGURE
7.25
Rendering of the completed color map applied to the wing section.

Tip. There are a few things that you can do to your color maps to add a little bit more realism. It's rare in reality to see a surface that is completely uniform. Add a little bit of dirt, grime, or rust to a map with Photoshop's airbrush tool. On the color map of the wing put burn marks near the air intakes and smudge some dirt on the leading edge of the wing. It is important when you apply your rust and grime to do it all on a separate layer or in a copy of the original file! Don't do anything that you can't undo. We're going to need to use these color maps later in the texture map section, and we don't want any smudges on the texture.

STEP ELEVEN
Repeat the entire process for the body and the other parts of the spaceship. Hey, no one ever said this was easy. Well, if

you want a shortcut all of the textures are included on the CD-ROM. Once you've gotten all of the color maps finished, your model should look like the image in Figure 7.26.

FIGURE
7.26   *The spaceship fully color mapped and rendered.*

This technique of using multiple layers and grids can be applied to just about any object to which you need to add a color or texture map. Although the grid did not seem to be extremely useful in this exercise, it comes in handy when you are creating maps that will be applied in a spherical or cylindrical fashion or to any nonplanar surface. When you get a little bit more proficient in mapping, you'll be able to skip many of the intermediate steps. Stick with it though, it gets easier.

Congratulations on making it this far. Everything else involved in mapping will be easy. We do need to finish mapping the model of the spaceship. We have only one more step, which we'll do in the next chapter on texture mapping.

8

Advanced Texture Mapping

CHAPTER REQUIREMENTS
Basic understanding of either Premiere or After Effects, Illustrator or FreeHand, and Photoshop.

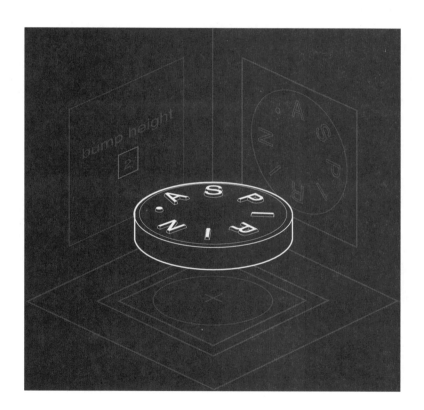

This is where the magic of 3D begins. You have already started to create the illusion of reality with color maps, and now you need to build on what you already know. Texture or surface mapping can be used to create a variety of effects that make it easier to mimic reality in 3D. In this chapter we're going to learn about each type of texture map and experiment with practical examples for each one. It's important to have a good grasp of what the physical properties of materials are and how they work. For example, you should know what specular reflection is and how glow works before proceeding with this chapter.

What is a texture map? Simply put, a texture map is used to alter the surface of a material to produce a variety of results. When we create a 3D material such as gold or aluminum, we set the physical characteristics of the object. Those surface characteristics dictate how shiny, reflective or transparent the material will appear when rendered. When a texture map is applied to a material, it is used to control the intensity and location of specific physical characteristics. For example, a transparency map can be used to control *where* and, more importantly, *how* transparent the surface of an object will appear when rendered.

Tip. In more general terms, a color map paired with several different types of maps such as a glow, specular, or transparency map can also be cumulatively referred to as a texture map.

The majority of 3D applications offer the user a variety of choices when it comes to texture maps. Each of the most common types of texture or surface maps is covered in its own individual section of this chapter.

SECTION ONE: SPECULAR MAPS

Add a shine to the surface of a model. Specular maps are my favorite type of map. Learn why these maps can add realism to your model with very little effort.

SECTION TWO: TRANSPARENCY MAPS

Save yourself some modeling time and use transparency maps. You can use the more practical applications for these maps such as masking parts of a model and use also them in conjunction with ambient and diffuse maps.

SECTION THREE: DIFFUSE MAPS

Believe it or not, there is a practical application for diffuse maps. You will have to read it to believe it.

SECTION FOUR: BUMP MAPS

In this section, we discuss how to add texture, detail, and text to the surface of a model without modeling. Bump maps are another excellent means to add realism to a rendering.

SECTION FIVE: GLOW MAPS

Tiger, tiger, burning bright in the forest of the night. Use glow maps to create windows on a building or simulate a backlit neon sign.

SECTION SIX: REFLECTIVITY MAPS

Some of the best kept secrets in the world of 3D. We discuss how to use reflective maps to add realism to your flying logos.

SECTION SEVEN: ANIMATED MAPS

Perhaps the coolest of all of the maps, these actually move on the surface of your model. A description is given of each of the aforementioned maps along with instructions on how to make them move.

You have probably noticed that the majority of the maps just listed correspond to a specific type of physical characteristic. By using all of these maps, usually in conjunction with a color map, we can achieve some very realistic or interesting results. Most 3D programs can link or assign multiple texture maps to a single color map. For example, it is common practice to assign transparency, ambient, and diffuse texture maps to a single color map.

All of the preceding maps, with the exception of animated maps, are 8-bit grayscale images. Either a color or a texture map can be animated over time and we will cover this topic in Section Seven of this chapter.

A Mapping Background

Most programs work under the same premise that the darker shades of gray or black in a texture map have less of a value than the lighter shades of white. For example, with a transparency map, any area that is black will be completely transparent and any area that is white will be completely opaque. This is why it is important to keep a texture map at 8 bits! You will need all 256 shades of gray with which to work.

Tip. If any of your maps does not provide the results you're looking for, try using the negative of the map. For example, one program might use the white areas on a map as the transparent area while another might render it as opaque. Be sure to check with your software manual if you're uncertain.

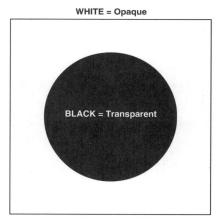

WHITE = Opaque

BLACK = Transparent

FIGURE *When using a transparency*
8.1 *map, the black areas will*
render as opaque and the
white areas will be
transparent.

FIGURE
8.2 *A rendering of the transparency map applied in a cubic fashion to a 3D object.*

An easy way to comprehend how texture maps work is to think of them as either masks or as stencils. When you create a stencil for spray painting, you cut shapes out of a piece of cardboard. The remaining pieces of cardboard shield the surface from the spray paint while the holes allow the paint to pass through. A texture map works in the same way except that you use color to define where the *paint* can pass through a map. The color white allows the largest amount of paint to pass through and the black areas allow the least. In reference to a specular map for example, the white areas of a texture map will reflect the most specular light and the black areas will reflect none at all.

The advantage of using grayscale texture maps is all of the shades between black and white. The intermediate shades of gray allow certain percentages of *paint* to pass through relative to the lightness or darkness of the shade of gray. Now instead of thinking in terms of *paint*, think of texture maps as controlling the values of the physical properties of a material.

Important. Whenever we use a texture map in conjunction with a color map, it is extremely important that both maps be correctly aligned down to the pixel! In some cases you can simply convert your color map to grayscale and then use that image. This method is highly recommended because you can save on time and you'll be guaranteed that the image will be aligned properly.

One last thing to remember before you get started with this chapter. The same rule of scale applies to texture maps as it does to color maps. Be sure that when you create your texture map you keep in mind how large the map will appear when it is rendered. If the texture map is rendered larger than it actually is, the map will appear pixelated since the computer has to interpolate for information that is not there!

SECTION ONE: SPECULAR MAPS

Specular maps are my favorite type of texture map. They can be used to create many subtle effects that add to the overall realism of a model. Specular maps control how much and, more importantly, *where* specular light is reflected from a surface.

A specular reflection on the surface of an object is often the same shape as the light source. For example, if you wanted to create a specular reflection that corresponds to sunlight streaming through a four-paned window, you could do any number of things. The first method is to create a gobo for the light source to filter through or apply a gel to the light source itself. The problem with this technique is that all of the elements of the rendering need to be set up with a high degree of precision. The light's intensity, direction, and spatial position as well as the object's specular value and placement all have to be arranged correctly. In order to get the specular reflection placed properly on the surface of the model, several variables have to be coordinated in a very accurate manner.

A much easier solution is to use a specular map, which will produce the same results with far less effort. Another benefit to using a specular map is that the user can assign a specific color to the specular reflection. For a more realistic rendering, try matching the color of the specular reflection to that of the primary light source.

T
U
T
O
R
I
A
L

SPECULAR WINDOW TUTORIAL

In this tutorial we're going to apply a specular map to the surface of a sphere to mimic the specular reflection of a paned window.

STEP ONE

Start by creating a specular map in Photoshop. You want four squares of white on top of a black background. Apply a slight degree of Gaussian blur to the image before saving the file. The specular reflection when rendered will be more realistic since the light in reality probably would not create a sharp-edged reflection.

FIGURE *Grayscale specular map for the*
8.3 *window. Notice that the edges of the white areas, which represent the frames of glass, are slightly blurry.*

STEP TWO

Apply the specular map to the surface of a sphere in your 3D application. Make sure that the specular value of the material is turned on and set to a fairly high number. The correct specular value for the object depends on the application and will require some trial and error. Be sure to use spherical mapping when applying the specular map.

STEP THREE

Render the image. It should look like the picture of the sphere in Figure 8.4.

FIGURE *Notice how the specular map controls where*
8.4 *specular light is reflected from the surface of the object.*

Tip. By using a window-shaped gel or gobo in addition to the window-shaped specular map, a window-shaped shadow can also be cast.

T
U
T
O
R
I
A
L

SPECULAR SPACESHIP TUTORIAL

Another use of specular mapping is creating the illusion of scale. Remember the model of the spaceship that we worked on in the last chapter? It's time to finish it. We applied a color map to the model yet it still didn't look quite real enough. Even though the color map broke up the solid surface color of the model, the spaceship still looked a little flat. By using a specular map we can add the finishing touches to our model.

What we're going to do in this tutorial is make the surface of the spaceship look as if it is constructed of small individual panels. By using two different types of maps in unison, both a color and a specular map, we can make each panel look as

FIGURE
8.5
Rendering of the spaceship with only a color map applied to the surface.

if it is made of a slightly different material. Remember when we created the color map for the spaceship and I stressed how important it was to save a copy that wasn't smudged or dirty? We're going to use that clean copy now.

To create a specular map that will align itself precisely with a color map you can use a copy of the color map. You could try to create an exact duplicate of the color map in grayscale but it is far easier to convert the color map into a grayscale image in Photoshop. By using this method you're guaranteed that both the color and specular maps will be perfectly aligned.

STEP ONE
The first step in the process is to convert all of the color map for the spaceship to grayscale images. Remember to keep a copy of the original color maps because you'll still need to apply them to the model.

STEP TWO
The next step in the process is to adjust the brightness and contrast of the recently created specular maps. The relative

brightness or darkness of the map depends on how glossy you want the surface of the model to appear. The darker areas on the map will not reflect as much specular light as the lighter areas. The key to a realistic rendering when using a specular map is a subtle contrast between the shades of gray.

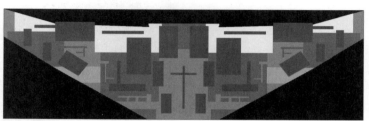

FIGURE
8.6
The specular map for the wing section was created by converting the color map into a grayscale image and adjusting the brightness and contrast of the file.

STEP THREE

Once you've created your grayscale specular map, import both the specular and color maps into your 3D application. Link the specular map to the color map and apply it to the wing of the spaceship.

3D programs handle texture maps differently and you should check your user's manual. If you have to apply the specular map to the model separately from the color map, be sure to use the same mapping technique and dimensions as the color map. In this case, both maps need to be applied in a planar fashion.

STEP FOUR

Increase the specular value for either the specular map or for the wing material itself. Once again it depends on the software package that you are using. If you're not sure, check with your manual. Go ahead and render the image.

STEP FIVE

Repeat Steps One through Four for the remaining color maps for the model.

FIGURE *The final rendering of the spaceship with both a color and a*
8.7 *specular map applied to the surface of the model.*

A specular map produces a very subtle effect that adds a tremendous amount of realism to an image. Be sure to look at the animation of the rotating spaceship on the CD-ROM. You'll be able to see what the specular map looks like in an animation.

SECTION TWO: TRANSPARENCY MAPS

In this section we're going to learn how to use transparency maps and also be introduced to both ambient and diffuse maps. For starters, here are a few reasons why we use transparency maps:

- To create shapes that would be very difficult to model.
- To create transparent areas on color maps.
- To save on modeling time.

By using a transparency map, we can create objects that would have otherwise been very difficult to model. For example, if your modeling program doesn't support Boolean functions you can use transparency maps as a partial work-around. Another useful feature of transparency maps is to create a transparent area on a color map. In the following tutorial we will create a color map and then apply it to a model of a glass bottle. By using a transparency map, the glass material can be seen through the designated areas of the color map.

Using a transparency map is fairly straightforward. For most programs, the areas on the map that are closer to white will be opaque and the areas on the map that are black will be transparent. But some applications such as StudioPro work on the completely opposite principle, where white is transparent and black is opaque. In this case just use the negative image of the transparency maps.

T
U
T
O
R
I
A
L

TRANSPARENCY TUTORIAL
In Figure 8.8 we have a grayscale transparency map. We're going to use it to create a shape that would have been difficult to model.

FIGURE *In this transparency map, the areas in*
8.8 *black will be completely transparent and the areas in white will be opaque.*

STEP ONE
Launch your 3D application. Create a sphere and apply the transparency map to the sphere using spherical mapping.

STEP TWO
Depending on which 3D application you're using, you have to set the level of transparency of the map to either 0% or 99%. Experiment to see which one is the correct value. Once again, setting the value is a trial-and-error process.

Render the image.

FIGURE *The transparency map applied to a*
8.9 *sphere.*

Important. Whenever you use a transparency map, you might need to use a diffuse and ambient map as well!

If your image doesn't look like the one in Figure 8.9, I'm not surprised. I've intentionally left out a key step in the process. Depending on your 3D application and the rendering algorithm that you used, the program probably rendered both the diffuse and ambient light reflected off of the transparent parts of the model. In other words even though some parts of the model were transparent the application probably accounted for the invisible areas. If you didn't have this problem, then feel free to ignore the next few steps in this tutorial on diffuse and ambient mapping, and consider yourself lucky that your 3D application is fairly smart!

Important. Texture mapping does *not* change the geometry of an object. Transparency mapping does *not* create actual holes in the surface of a model, it only creates the illusion that parts of a model are transparent.

To fix the problem with the invisible areas, you will need to create an ambient and diffuse map that will mask the transparent areas of the model. Ambient and diffuse light is still being reflected from the transparent parts of the model, which in this case causes the transparent areas to look slightly opaque. We want the visible parts of the model to reflect ambient and diffuse light, whereas the invisible parts of the model should reflect none at all. In this case the ambient and diffuse maps are identical to the transparency map.

FIGURE *The ambient and diffuse*
8.10 *map is identical to the*
transparency map.

STEP FOUR
Apply the ambient and diffuse map to the model of the sphere. Render the image again and you should get the same results as the image in Figure 8.9.

Tip. If the inside wall of the sphere is invisible, there might be another reason. Some programs only render the outside polygonal faces of objects in order to conserve on rendering resources. Check your 3D application's manual on how to convert a model into double-sided polygons or a double-sided object.

In this case it would have been very difficult to model the geometry seen in the rendered image in Figure 8.9. An interesting experiment for you to try is to apply various types of transparency maps to several shapes using different mapping methods.

Another application for transparency maps is simulating Boolean functions. If you're using a modeler that does not support Booleans, you can use a transparency map to subtract areas on the surface of a model. The problem with this method, of course, is that the surface of the object would not have any depth since the walls of the model would appear to have holes cut into them.

T
U
T
O
R
I
A
L

BOTTLE LABEL TUTORIAL

For this tutorial, we're going to combine what we know about transparency maps with both ambient and diffuse maps. We're going to create a transparent window in a color map so that the underlying material of the model can be seen.

STEP ONE

The first step is to import the DXF model of the bottle into your 3D application. Examine the model of the bottle carefully. You will notice that the inside wall of the bottle is on a separate layer than the outside wall of the bottle. The model is created in this way because if both walls were on the same layer, and you applied a texture map to the model, the texture would be mapped onto both the inside and outside walls of the bottle.

STEP TWO

You will need to create a material that resembles glass. If your 3D application does not already have a glass material and you have to create one from scratch, try using the following parameters:

Diffuse color:	Red-255, Green-255, Blue-255
Ambient color:	Red-255, Green-255, Blue-255
Specular color:	Red-255, Green-255, Blue-255
Ambient value:	1%
Diffuse value:	1%
Reflectivity:	25%
Transparency:	98%
Index of refraction	1.4
Specularity:	100%
Highlight:	Small
Halo:	Small

Notice that both the ambient and diffuse values of the glass material are set very low. If they were higher, the material would appear to be overexposed when rendered. Also our index of refraction setting means that we're going to have to use a raytracing algorithm when we render the image. Remember that only raytracing algorithms are able to render transparent images with refraction.

STEP THREE

Apply the glass material to both the inside and outside wall of the model.

STEP FOUR

In the next few steps we're going to link ambient, diffuse, and transparency maps to the color map of the bottle label. Check with your 3D application's manual to see how your program handles linking these maps.

Start the process by importing the image pictured in Figure 8.11 as a color map.

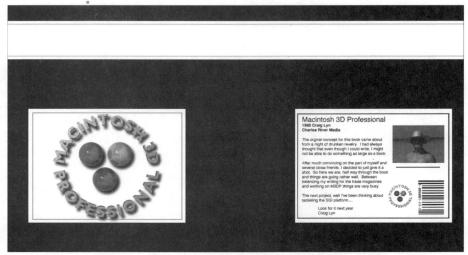

FIGURE *Color map for the outside wall of the bottle. Only the labels will be visible in the*
8.11 *final rendering.*

STEP FIVE

Now we need to create a transparency map so that the glass material shows up underneath the color map. Only the label itself should be visible in the final rendering. When creating a transparency map for this model remember that the area covered by the label should be white so that it will be opaque when rendered. The areas not covered by the label should be black so that it will be completely transparent when rendered. Apply the transparency map to the outside wall of the bottle.

Tip. A good technique for creating a transparency map from scratch is to use the actual color map as a guide so that you can be precise down to the pixel.

FIGURE *The transparency map for the outside wall of the bottle has*
8.12 *transparent areas as black, and opaque areas as white.*

STEP SIX

In this step, we have to create an ambient and diffuse map for the color map of the label. Since the label is made of paper, it would not have the same ambient and diffuse values as glass.

By using a map, we can specify exactly which areas on the label will reflect ambient and diffuse light. We want only the label to reflect ambient and diffuse light; the glass material should not reflect any at all. The ambient and diffuse map is identical to the transparency map. Apply the ambient and diffuse map to the outside wall of the bottle using cylindrical mapping.

FIGURE   *The ambient and diffuse map for the outside wall of the bottle*
8.13   *is identical to the transparency map.*

STEP SEVEN

Make sure that you use the cylindrical mapping method to apply the color and texture maps to the outside wall of the bottle. If you want more realistic results, try using the same map that you used for the transparency map as a specular and reflectivity map. In this case only the bottle will reflect both specular and surrounding light, whereas the label will appear to have more of a matte finish.

Tip. If the label appears to be totally black in the rendering, try increasing the ambient and diffuse values of the outside glass material to 100%.

FIGURE   *Completed rendering of the bottle.*
8.14

SECTION THREE: DIFFUSE MAPS

Diffuse maps are one of the most infrequently discussed topics in the field of 3D. Many 3D professionals only use diffuse maps in conjunction with ambient and transparency maps such as in the previous tutorial. Technically speaking, diffuse maps control the location and amount of diffuse light reflected off of the surface of a model.

Tip. As for ambient maps, I really haven't found anything particularly useful about them. Feel free to e-mail me if you find anything interesting.

T
U
T
O
R
I
A
L

DIFFUSE SPACESHIP TUTORIAL

Here's one use for a diffuse map that very few people know about. On its own, a diffuse map can alter the color of the underlying material to create a pattern. Once again we're going to use the model of the spaceship, but instead of using a color map, we're going to use a diffuse map to create the same paneled effect.

STEP ONE

The first thing we need to do is convert the color maps that we used on the spaceship in the previous chapter to grayscale images.

STEP TWO

Once you have converted the color maps to grayscale images, apply them to the surface of the model as diffuse maps. Set the physical characteristics of the material to match a hard metallic substance such as aluminum. The diffuse map will control the amount of diffuse light being reflected from the surface of the model.

By changing the color of the material, the entire color of the model can be altered. The advantage of using a diffuse map is that if you change your mind about the color of the spaceship, you can simply change the color of the material instead of having to recreate a new color map. Another benefit is that all of the colors will be varying shades of the base material, which creates a more uniform and subtle color effect. The drawback of course is that you can't have multiple colors such as red and green on the same map since everything will be a derivative of the material's color.

FIGURE 8.15 *Diffuse maps are used instead of color maps to produce the paneled effect on the surface of the spaceship.*

SECTION FOUR: BUMP MAPS

Bump maps are the most frequently used and most commonly misunderstood of all of the texture maps. A bump map works by tricking the rendering engine into thinking that a surface has actual depressions or indentations. Bump maps come in handy when it is necessary to add texture or detail to the surface of an object without modeling.

Important. A bump map does not alter the geometry of an object! It merely creates the illusion that a surface has depressions.

How Bump Maps Work

Bump maps work by distorting the surface normals of an object, which are usually perpendicular to a surface. The white spaces of a bump map define the high areas and the black spaces define the low areas. Any intermediate shades of gray cause the normals to point at an angle to the surface. In Figure 8.16 the surface normals are all aligned perpendicular to the surface of the object. Since there is no bump map applied to the object and the surface normals are all aligned, the rendering engine would render the surface as completely flat or smooth.

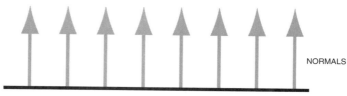

FIGURE **8.16** *Without a bump map applied, the surface normals of an object are perpendicular to the surface.*

By applying a bump map, you can fool the rendering engine into thinking that the surface has more than one layer. In Figure 8.17 a bump map distorts the normals so that it appears as if there is an indentation on the surface.

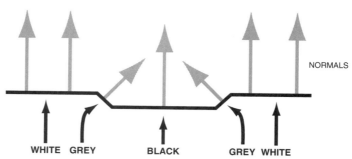

FIGURE **8.17** *The gray areas of a bump map distort the surface normals so the rendering engine thinks that they are angled to the surface. The black and white areas of the bump map do not distort the surface normals at all.*

In Figure 8.17 only the gray areas of a bump map distort the surface normals. If you have a bump map with a sharp transition from white to black, the surface normals will all remain perpendicular and the entire surface will appear flat when rendered as in Figure 8.18.

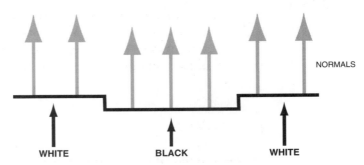

FIGURE *Notice that no normals are disturbed when the bump map has*
8.18 *only black and white areas.*

Tip. The best method for creating a bump map is to start with a black and white image and then apply **Gaussian blur** to it in Photoshop.

Using a Bump Map

Now that you understand how a bump map works, it's time to discuss several uses for a bump map. Bump maps can add a tremendous amount of dimension and reality to an image. The more common uses for bump maps are:

• Making a surface appear rough or textured
• Adding surface detail to a model
• Engraving text

Bump maps are very useful in breaking up large uniform surfaces. They add texture, realism, and depth to an area and prevent objects from appearing flat or plastic. Ordinary flat surfaces can be made to look pitted or weathered or specific surface details can be added to a model that would have been difficult or time consuming to create.

Tip. A bump map should be thought of as a subtle way to add reality to an image. You shouldn't rely on bump maps too much to take the place of modeling because the illusion of a bump map falls apart at close range.

BRICK WALL TUTORIAL

In this tutorial we're going apply both a color and a bump map to the same object to create the illusion of a brick wall. The color map will serve to define the red bricks and the white mortar while the bump map will be used to create the illusion of depth of the recessed area for the mortar as well as adding texture or roughness to the surface.

STEP ONE

We're going to start by first creating a color map for the bricks. The bricks will be a shade of red and the mortar between the bricks will be white. Once you've created the bricks, try applying the **Add Noise** filter to the image so that the color does not appear to be too uniform.

Tip. On occasion it is far easier and faster to create a color or texture map in Illustrator than in Photoshop. Illustrator offers more precise control over aligning and duplicating shapes. Once an image is completed in Illustrator it can be imported and rasterized in Photoshop.

FIGURE
8.19 *The color map for the brick wall was created in Photoshop. By using the filter* **Add Noise** *you can make the image more rough.*

STEP TWO

The next step is to create a bump map for the texture. Remember that you need to align the bump map precisely to the color map. In this case, the white lines of the mortar in the color map need to match the black lines of the bump map. In Figure 8.20, which shows the bump map, you can see that the white areas define the raised area of the bricks while the black areas define the recessed mortar. Be sure to convert the image to grayscale before saving the bump map.

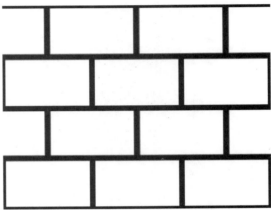

FIGURE 8.20 *The bump map for the brick wall has the recessed area for the mortar defined in black and the area for the brick in white.*

If we went ahead and used the image in Figure 8.20 as a bump map it would look pretty good, but we can do better. We need to add a little bit more roughness to the surface of the bricks so that they look more realistic. By applying the **Add Noise** filter in Photoshop to the image we can make the surface appear uneven.

Important. Remember that most texture maps are 8-bit grayscale images! If you are working in a 24-bit color mode, be sure to convert your files to 8-bit grayscale before saving them.

STEP THREE
Launch your 3D application. Apply both the color and bump map to the surface of a model. Render away.

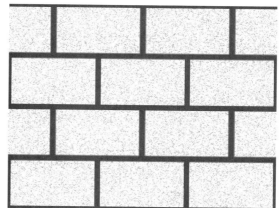

FIGURE *The bump map for the wall texture.*
8.21

FIGURE *The brick wall texture with a color and bump map rendered in*
8.22 *Strata StudioPro.*

TILES TUTORIAL

In this tutorial we're going to create another texture map that uses both color and bump maps. Once again, it is extremely important to make sure that the color and bump map are precisely aligned. In some cases it's easier to create a bump map by converting the color map to grayscale and then inverting the colors.

STEP ONE

Start by creating a color map in Photoshop. We want to create the illusion of tiles. Figure 8.23 shows our final tilable color map.

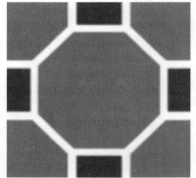

FIGURE *The color map for the tiles texture*
8.23 *was created in Photoshop.*

STEP TWO

Use the color map as a guide to create the bump map. The white areas in the color map need to be inverted to black. Notice how the octagonal part of the bump map tile has smudges of white in Figure 8.24. When the map was created I used the airbrush tool in Photoshop to apply a subtle amount of white to the gray areas so that the surface would appear distorted. This type of bump map produces a surface that appears uneven rather than pitted.

When you create your own bump map, consider first how the finished surface should look when it is rendered. Sharp transitions on a bump map give the surface a hard-edged look while softer transitions offer a more distorted surface.

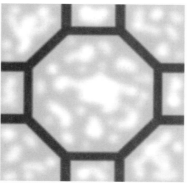

FIGURE
8.24
The bump map for the tiles uses a smudged white bump map which produces an uneven or wavy surface when rendered.

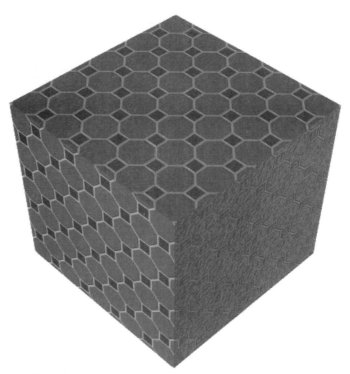

FIGURE
8.25
Completed rendering of the color and bump map in Strata StudioPro.

STEP THREE
Go ahead and apply both the color and bump maps to an object in your 3D application.

Tip. When it comes time to create your own bump maps, remember to apply a little bit of **Gaussian blur** to both the color and bump maps before saving them. You need a gradual transition from black to white in order for a bump map to be effective.

T
U
T
O
R
I
A
L

TEXT-SHAPED BUMP MAP TUTORIAL
Here's another application for bump maps. Try not to limit yourself to thinking that a bump map is only for creating surface texture. They can also be used to add surface detail. In this tutorial we're going to use a bump map to simulate an engraved surface.

STEP ONE
Start by creating a logo in a program such as Illustrator. Then import the file into Photoshop so that we can save the image as a PICT.

FIGURE *The Macintosh 3D Professional logo*
8.26 *was first created in Illustrator 5.0.*

Tip. It's a real time saver to use the **Clipboard** features of the Mac OS when working with line art. Copy the logo created in Illustrator to the clipboard by pressing **Command-C** on the keyboard. Then switch over to Photoshop and create a new document. Paste the Illustrator logo into the new document, Photoshop will then automatically rasterize the logo into a bitmap format.

STEP TWO

Once the logo is imported into Photoshop, apply Gaussian blur to the image to soften the edges. Remember that one of the keys to a successful bump map is to make the transitions from black to white gradual. If you want to make the surface appear rough when rendered, apply a little bit of noise to the map to give it more texture.

FIGURE **8.27** *The bump map for the logo has a little bit of Gaussian blur and Noise applied to the image in Photoshop.*

STEP THREE

Save your bump map as a PICT file and import it into your 3D application. Apply the texture map using cubic mapping. Render the image. (Figure 8.28.)

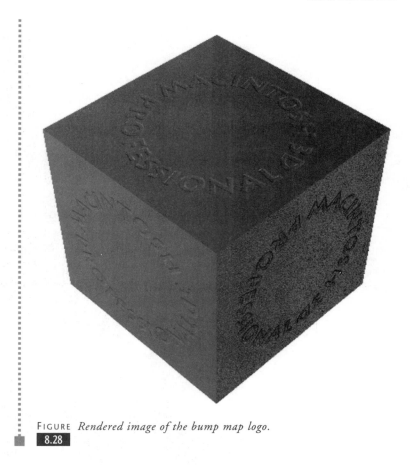

FIGURE *Rendered image of the bump map logo.*
8.28

MORE BUMP MAP EXAMPLES

By now you should have a pretty good grasp of bump maps. Here are a few examples of grayscale bump maps and what they look like when paired with a color map and then rendered.

Tip. A subset of bump mapping is displacement mapping. In this case a grayscale image can be used to actually alter the surface geometry of a model when it is rendered. To date, there is only one program capable of true displacement mapping on the Macintosh. Pixar's MacRenderMan offers perhaps the most realistic rendering engine, with features such as motion blur, procedural texture mapping, and displacement mapping.

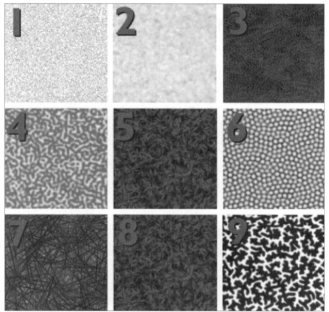

FIGURE *Examples of bump maps.*
8.29

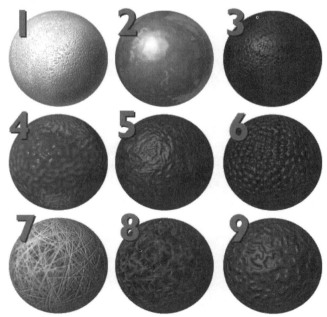

FIGURE *Rendered bump maps paired with color maps*
8.30

SECTION FIVE: GLOW MAPS

Glow maps control the location and amount of illumination that a surface emits. Practical applications of glow maps range from creating the illusion of windows on a building at night to mimicking the reflected glow of a neon sign off a brick wall. When working with either glow maps or glowing objects, it is important to remember that neither casts light of its own. If you created a model of a light bulb and then increased the glow factor of the bulb's material, and then placed it next to another object, the model of the bulb would not illuminate nor light the other object.

To create the illusion of an object casting light, we would use a glow map. You're probably wondering why not just use an actual light source to do the same job? There are a number of reasons why a glow map is more efficient. Aligning a map on an object is often faster than trying to accurately align a light source, and many programs don't support shaped light sources or gels. Rendering speed is also lowered when using a glow map rather than an actual light source. Last, it saves on modeling time. Imagine having to create a light source for each and every window in a model of a skyscraper, when it would be faster and easier to use a glow map instead.

**T
U
T
O
R
I
A
L**

GLOWING SIGN TUTORIAL

In this example we're going to create a scene with a sign that appears to be backlit. By using a glow map on the wall behind the model of the sign, it can be made to appear as if there are several lights located directly behind the model. This technique also works well for mimicking the glow of self-illuminated objects such as neon or fluorescent light bulbs.

STEP ONE

Import the model of the scene into your 3D application. Apply a metallic texture to the signs, and a texture of your own choosing for the floor and ceiling.

STEP TWO

The tricky part in this entire process is creating a glow map that precisely matches the dimensions of the wall. In fact, not only do the dimensions of the map have to be identical, but the placement of the illuminated areas located behind the sign have to match as well. By doing a screen capture of each wall of the model you can create a map from which to plan where the illuminated areas need to be placed.

Tip. Pressing the **Command-Shift-3** keys will capture the current screen. The resulting PICT will appear in the window of your startup hard drive.

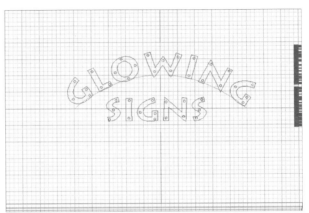

FIGURE **8.31** *By using a screen capture of the model we can plan where to place the glowing areas in the glow map.*

STEP THREE

Import both of the screen captures for each of the model's walls into Photoshop. Crop the image down to the pixel so that only the wall is visible as in Figure 8.31. Now you have an accurate guide with which to create your glow map.

Make the background area black and the area directly behind the sign white. Use the airbrush tool so that the glowing areas behind the sign appear partially fuzzy. Repeat this process for the second wall.

STEP FOUR

Import the glow maps for the scene into your 3D application. Apply each glow map to the corresponding wall using planar mapping. The maps should fit precisely on the surface of the model. Set the Glow Factor for each wall to either 1%

FIGURE *Glow map for one of the walls. The white areas will be*
8.32 *glowing in the final rendering of the scene.*

or 99% — once again, it depends entirely on your 3D application. Finally set the main light source to be around 20% or less. If it is set higher it might obscure the glowing walls.

Now render the scene, which should look like the image in Figure 8.33.

FIGURE *By using a glow map, we can create the illusion that the signs*
8.33 *are backlit.*

SPACE STATION EXAMPLE

Like specular maps, glow maps are a wonderful means of adding a sense of scale to your model. For this section it would be a good idea to have a copy of a program such as either Illustrator or FreeHand to create some of the color and glow maps that we are going to use in the tutorial. If you don't feel like creating these maps, don't worry because they're already done for you and included on the CD-ROM.

In this tutorial, we're going to use a glow map to create windows on a model of a space station. Using glow maps in this fashion definitely gives this model a great sense of scale. Without the glow map the station looks kind of small and dinky. More like a toy rather than a massive station floating above a planet. Figure 8.34 shows the model without a glow map.

FIGURE **8.34** *Space station with no textures applied to the surface. Notice that it looks kind of naked.*

STEP ONE

First of all, import the DXF file of the station into your 3D application. Get accustomed to the various layers of the model. The first part of the model that we'll deal with is the saucer section. Do a screen capture or rendering of the space station from directly above. You'll be using the resulting image as a guide or map to create your glow map for the windows.

STEP TWO

Since the saucer section is circular, the dimensions of the map will be 1:1 or square shaped. The screen capture should be used as a guide for the placement of the windows on the map. The idea is not to place any windows where they might conflict with any surface detail.

We're going to start by creating the color map for the saucer in an illustration program such as Illustrator or FreeHand. In order to align the map correctly to the surface of the model, you can either import the screen capture into your illustration program or make an educated guess. I highly recommend importing the screen capture into your program and using it as a template to create your color map.

Once you have the screen capture imported into your illustration program, use it as a guide to create a series of concentric circles that correspond to the surface details on the model. These circles will be your guides for placing the windows. If you're not sure whether the circles on the map are aligned correctly, convert the file into a bitmap image in Photoshop. Then map that image onto your model in your 3D application and do a quick rendering. This is a good

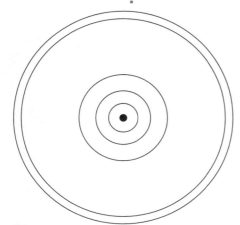

FIGURE 8.35 *The series of concentric circles created in Illustrator corresponds to surface details on the model of the space station. We will use these circles as our guide to creating the color map.*

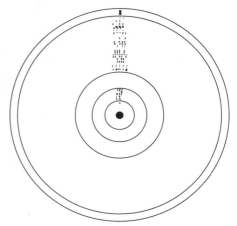

FIGURE 8.36 *Create a column of windows in Illustrator. Try to create a random pattern and then rotate copy the windows around the central axis of the image.*

habit to get into, because it will save you time in the long run. There's nothing more frustrating than completing a texture map and realizing that it doesn't fit or isn't aligned properly with the model (Figure 8.35).

STEP THREE

Create a column of various sized windows in Illustrator and place them in a random fashion. Select all of the windows and then rotate copies of the windows around the central axis of the map (Figure 8.36).

STEP FOUR

This is going to be the most time-consuming step. Once you have rotated and copied the windows around the central axis, randomly select and delete individual windows. The idea is to make the map look more random, but at the same time retain a pattern. Save the file. This image will be used to create the color map in Photoshop (Figure 8.37).

STEP FIVE

Make a copy of the Illustrator file that you are using for the color map. You will use this copy to create a glow map. Be sure to use a copy of the file and not the original.

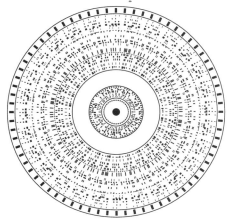

FIGURE
8.37 *Once all of the windows have been created, delete individual windows to make the pattern appear more random.*

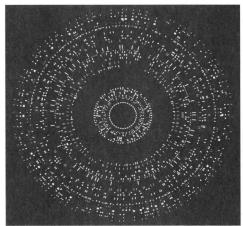

FIGURE
8.38 *The illumination or glow map for the saucer section was created in Illustrator. The black areas are dark while the white areas will glow.*

Once again, randomly select and delete individual windows. Try to keep to the original pattern that you created in Step Four. The reason that we're not making all of the windows glow is because it would look unnatural. Take an office building at night for example. It would be rare to see all of the lights on inside at any one given time. Once you're satisfied with your map, you will need to invert the colors. Remember the windows need to be white and the background black. You can either do this in your illustration program or in Photoshop (Figure 8.38).

STEP SIX

Import your Illustrator files for the color and illumination map into Photoshop. Once the images have been rasterized, save the images as PICTs and then import the maps into your 3D application. If you want to go a step further, experiment with the color map in Photoshop. Try adding a little bit more detail to the map.

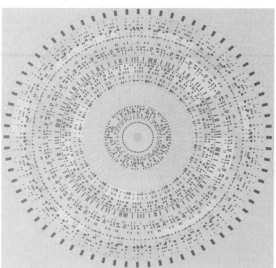

FIGURE *Add more detail to the color map in*
8.39 *Photoshop using the windows as your guide.*

STEP SEVEN

In your 3D application, apply the color and glow map to the saucer from above using planar mapping. Be sure to turn on the glow factor for your map. Do a quick rendering of the space station. If all of the maps are lined up, repeat the process for the rest of the model.

Add some lights to the underside of the model so that it illuminates the saucer section. You'll notice that there is also a specular map applied to the saucer; this map is included on the CD-ROM.

FIGURE *The space station with glow maps applied. The glow maps create the illusion of windows*
8.40 *on the surface of the model.*

SECTION SIX: REFLECTIVITY MAPS

Reflectivity maps control how and where a map reflects other objects. Like the other types of maps in this chapter, the white areas reflect more light, whereas the shades closer to black do not reflect light at all. One of the more obvious uses of reflective maps was briefly mentioned in the section on transparency maps. By using the masking features of a map, areas on a model can be made to be nonreflective while other areas become very reflective.

But don't just limit yourself to thinking in terms of masks. You can create many interesting effects with a reflectivity map. One of the most practical uses of a reflectivity map is controlling the amount of light reflected off of the surface of a model. 3D professionals that create flying logos use reflectivity maps in almost all of their projects. The effects are subtle at times, but their absence is always noticeable.

T
U
T
O
R
I
A
L

FLASH OF LIGHT TUTORIAL

In this tutorial we're going to create a logo that has a flash of light crossing the front surface of the model. We can use several methods to create the light flashing over the model. The first and possibly the hardest method to use to create this effect is to animate two tube shaped lights moving from one end of the model to the other. There are a few problems inherent with this method:

- Over-illumination of the scene
- Coordinating the movement of lights over a period of time
- Finding a program that supports tube lights

Perhaps the best method of creating this flash of light is to use an animated reflectivity map. No matter where the camera or lights are placed in the scene, the flash of light will appear perfect 100% of the time. In the following section, we cover how to create an animated reflectivity map. For now, we create a static map.

Tip. Try beveling the text of the model so that there are more surface areas to catch light.

STEP ONE

Import the model of the logo into your 3D application. Apply or create a brassy material to the model. Apply a bump map to the model if you want to add a little bit of texture to the image.

STEP TWO

Take a screen capture of the model from the front. Import the screen capture into Photoshop and then crop the image to the exact dimension of the model. You want the map to fit the dimensions of the model exactly so that it does not become distorted when mapped on the model. Use the resulting image as your template to create the reflectivity map.

STEP THREE

Fill the background of the template with black. Draw two wide white lines diagonally across the image. Apply a little bit of Gaussian blur to the image until it looks like the map in Figure 8.41. The white lines will reflect the most light on the surface of the text so that it looks like there is a gleam on the front of the model.

FIGURE *The reflectivity map for the logo precisely matches the shape of*
8.41 *the model. The white areas of the map will be the glint or*
reflection on the model.

STEP FOUR

Import the reflectivity map into your 3D application. Apply the reflectivity map to the logo using the planar mapping method. Set the reflectivity of the model or map to around 25%. Render the image.

STEP FIVE

A flash of light should be in the center of the model. If it isn't there, try setting the reflectivity of the model or map to a higher setting. If you were going to animate this model, you would have used an animated texture map so that the flash of light would travel across the surface of the model. The background of Figure 8.42 shows a still from an animated color map produced by VCE on their Pyromania 2 CD-ROM. Be sure to look at the animation of this project, which is included on this book's CD-ROM.

FIGURE
8.42   *Rendering of the logo with a flash of light*

T
U
T
O
R
I
A
L

RIPPLING REFLECTION TUTORIAL

In this example we're going to do somewhat the same thing as in the previous example. But instead of creating a flash of light, we're going to create the illusion that rippling water is being reflected on the surface of the model.

STEP ONE

Import the model of the logo into your 3D application. Apply a brassy material to the model or create one.

STEP TWO

Take a screen capture of the model from the front. Import the screen capture into Photoshop and then crop the image to the exact dimension of the model. You want the map to fit the dimensions of the model exactly so that it does not become distorted when mapped on the model. Use the resulting image as your template to create the reflectivity map.

STEP THREE

In this example the reflectivity map and background were created in Adobe's TextureMaker. Use the textures included on the CD-ROM. When the original texture was created, the dimensions of the map were calculated from the dimensions of the screen capture in Step Two.

STEP FOUR

Import the reflectivity map pictured in Figure 8.43 into your 3D application. Apply the reflectivity map to the logo using

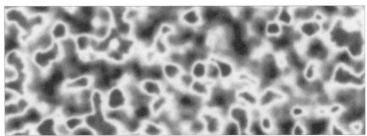

FIGURE *The reflectivity map was created in Adobe TextureMaker and*
8.43 *mimics the reflection of sparkling water on the surface of the model.*

the planar mapping method. Set the reflectivity of the model or map to around 25%. Render the image.

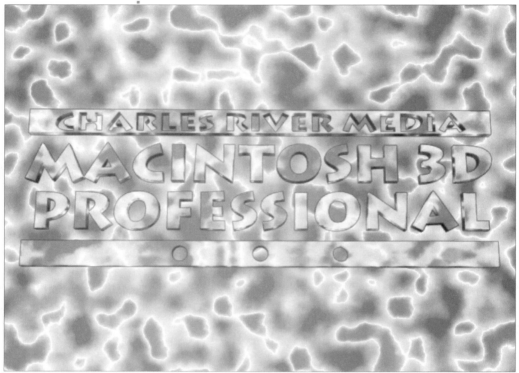

FIGURE *Rendering of the logo with a rippling reflectivity map.*
8.44

SECTION SEVEN: ANIMATED MAPS

In Chapter 7 and in this chapter, we've discussed how to apply and use both color and texture maps. In this section we're going to add a little bit more dimension to our work and animate our maps. But before you get excited about using animated maps, make sure that your software package supports this feature. Some programs only support animated color maps while others can animate texture maps as well.

Once you've figured out if your program can handle animated maps you need to know how to create them. Apart from your 3D application there are a few software packages that will be necessary to create your own animated maps. Here's a list of possible applications that you could use to create animated maps:

- Adobe After Effects
- Adobe Premiere
- Equilibrium DeBabelizer
- Adobe TextureMaker
- Specular TextureScape

It's not necessary to run out and buy all of these packages at once, but plan to include either a copy of After Effects or Premiere in your software budget. When it comes time to do postproduction work, you will need access to at least one of these programs.

Video Sources

Animated maps can be created from a variety of sources. If you're fortunate to have a high-end Macintosh AV system, you can capture video signals directly into your computer. On the other hand, if you're using either a Radius Video Vision Studio Card or Media100 Suite you have the option of using hardware compression to capture your video.

Tip. When capturing video, make sure that you're capturing directly to your fastest hard drive. Also be sure to optimize your drive so that you reduce the chance of dropping frames. It also helps to know the maximum space and also reduce the chance of dropping a frame if the screen size is playback size of the captured video in the animation. You can save storage space and also reduce the chance of dropping a frame if the screen size is smaller. It's easier to capture a 320 x 240 screen than a 640 x 480 screen. Also before you start to capture video calculate what the final frame rate will be of your final animation so that you can capture your video at the same speed.

If you don't have access to either of these hardware options you can always use one of your own animations as an animated color map. Finally, if all else fails, companies such as Visual Concepts Engineering and other third-party vendors make great CD-ROMs with precaptured imagery.

Important. Remember, the same rule is true for animated maps as it is for both color and texture maps: Make sure that the final rendered size of the map does not exceed the actual size of the file. If it does, the image will be pixelated!

Software Sources

If you are trying to create an animated color or texture map from scratch, a few software-based solutions are available. First of all, several dedicated applications such as Adobe's TextureMaker and Specular's TextureScape allow the user to create a color map from scratch and then change the parameters of the texture over time. These changes can then be animated to produce a variety of results. The animated color map that we used to create the background in the Rippling Reflection tutorial was created in TextureMaker.

After Effects, Premiere, and DeBabelizer also can be used to create animated color maps. Since all three programs recognize Adobe Photoshop plug-ins they all have access to virtually the same filters. When using any of these programs you can either apply a filter to a QuickTime movie or apply a filter over time to a still image to create an animated map.

Tip. The Ripple, Zig Zag, and Pinch filters, which are standard with both After Effects and Premiere, can all be applied over time. The Ripple filter can be used to create a series of concentric rings as the movie progresses. The advantage of this feature is that the user does not need to use animated files in order to create an animated texture.

Animated Color Maps

Animated color maps can be used in a variety of situations. For example you could map captured video onto the screen of a model of a television or create your own drive in theater by mapping old movies onto a model of a movie screen. The possibilities are endless. Even your own previously rendered animations can be imported into your 3D program and used as a color map.

Here are a few suggestions for animated color maps:

- If you don't have particle effects in your 3D program and you want to create a waterfall or a rushing stream, try using an animated color map instead. See Chapter 14, Animation Special Effects, for more information on how to do this.
- Try mapping footage of fire onto a semitransparent plane. If you also synchronize a flickering projection light with the same color map, you can create a convincing illusion of a camp fire or hearth.
- Looking for the perfect explosion? Try using VCE's Pyromania CD-ROM. You can map an animated shock wave onto a plane and then position it anywhere in your animation.

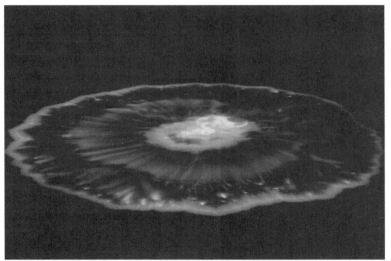

FIGURE   *Still from an animated shock wave on VCE's Pyromania 2 CD-ROM.*
8.45

Animated color maps can be used for just about anything. The trick of course is knowing when or where to use them. I usually turn to animated color maps when I find that I can't accomplish a certain effect in 3D. Fire, smoke, and explosions are all examples of very difficult effects to recreate in 3D. On higher level platforms such as the SGI, particle groups can be used to recreate these effects. Unfortunately, for the Mac user, they just aren't available. So the best alternative is animated color maps. Be sure to read Chapter 14 Animation Special Effects for more information on this subject.

Animated Reflectivity Maps

In Section Six of this chapter we introduced the use of reflectivity maps. Reflectivity maps can add that missing element to an animation. It's that feeling you get when you watch an animation and you think that something is not quite right.

The reflectivity map in the Flash of Light tutorial provides a very subtle effect, and without it the animation appears flat or lifeless. The hardest part about creating the Flash of Light animation is creating the animated reflectivity map.

T
U
T
O
R
I
A
L

ANIMATED FLASH OF LIGHT TUTORIAL
In this example we're going to create an animated reflectivity map. The effect that we're trying to achieve in the final rendering is a flash of light or glint crossing the surface of the model, which in this case is the Macintosh 3D Professional logo. You will need a program such as After Effects or Premiere to create this map. There is a demo version of Premiere included on the CD-ROM if you would like to follow along. The Premiere project file is also included.

STEP ONE
Import the model into your 3D program. Take a screen capture of the model and import the image into Photoshop. Crop the image to the exact dimensions of the model. Scale the image to whatever size you feel the image will be rendered at, but be sure to keep the ratio of the horizontal to vertical dimensions the same.

STEP TWO
We're going to use the screen capture as the basis for the background of the animated reflectivity map. Fill the image with black and then save the file as a PICT and name the file "Black Background."

STEP THREE
Create a new document that is roughly twice as long as it is high. Make the vertical dimension of the new file roughly equal to the vertical dimensions of "Black Background."

Draw two thick white lines horizontally and then apply Gaussian blur to the image. The resulting image should look like the picture in Figure 8.46. Save the file as a PICT and name it "Flash."

FIGURE *The reflectivity map for the Flash of Light animated map has*
8.46 *two white lines that correspond to the reflective area.*

STEP FOUR

Import both "Flash" and "Black Background" into either Premiere or After Effects. When the program prompts you to enter the frame size of the project use the same dimensions as "Black Background." For the sake of this tutorial we'll use Premiere.

STEP FIVE

Set the duration of both clips to 3 seconds. Place "Black Background" into track **A** and "Flash" into track **S1** (Figure 8.47).

STEP SIX

Select the Flash clip and then choose **Motion** from the clip menu. When the **Motion Settings** window pops up, set the rotation at the start and end of the clip to 45°. Also move the position anchor points for both the start and end clip closer to the visible area. Click the OK button. Figure 8.48 and Figure 8.49 both illustrate the motions settings.

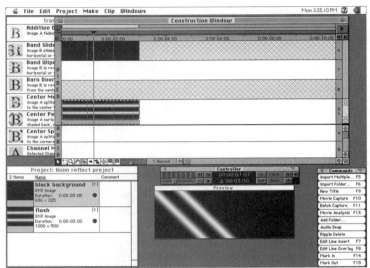

FIGURE
8.47
By using Adobe Premiere 4.0 we can create an animated reflectivity map. The "Black Background" clip has to be placed into track A and the "Flash" clip into track S1.

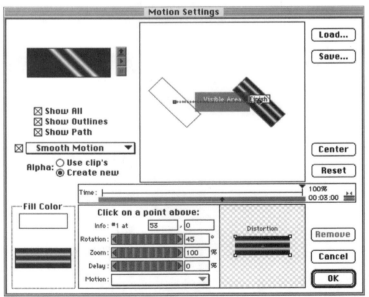

FIGURE
8.48
*The **Motion Settings** window in Adobe Premiere 4.0 lets the user rotate a clip and move a clip over time.*

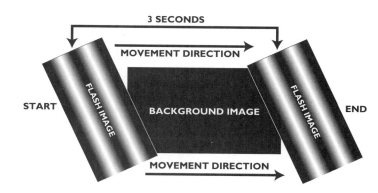

FIGURE *The clip of the flash moves from left to right over three seconds.*
8.49

STEP SEVEN

Render the movie and then import the animated texture into your 3D program. Use the animated texture as a reflectivity map. Take a look on the CD-ROM for an animation of the completed project.

Animated Bump Maps	Animated bump maps can be used to create a variety of various effects, ranging from rippling water to text spontaneously emerging from the surface of a material. Included on the CD-ROM is a rippling water animated color map used in Section Six of this chapter. The map was created in Adobe's TextureMaker and is used as both a color and a reflectivity map. To use the animation as a bump map it needs to be converted to grayscale, which can be done in a program such as Equilibrium's DeBabelizer, which is included on the CD-ROM. If you're interested in creating a rippling water effect, use the animated bump map on a planar surface that has high specular, reflective, and transparent qualities.

With a little bit of time and creativity, you can create an animated bump map that has detail moving all over the surface of an object. In this section we're going to create an animated bump map of text emerging from the surface of an object. The project file for this tutorial is included on the CD-ROM.

ANIMATED BUMP TEXT TUTORIAL

In this tutorial we're going to create the illusion of our logo emerging from the surface of an object with an animated bump map.

STEP ONE

Create a logo either in your illustration package or in Photoshop. The background of the logo needs to be black while the logo itself needs to be white. Save the image as a grayscale PICT file.

FIGURE
8.50   *Grayscale image of logo to be used as an animated bump map.*

STEP TWO

Import the logo into Premiere. Set the frame size of the animation window to equal the dimensions of the logo. Set the duration of the image of the logo to be around 3 seconds.

STEP THREE

This is the key step in the procedure. Select the logo clip. Go to the Clip menu and select **Filters**. Apply the **Brightness and Contrast** filter to the logo clip. Under the **Settings** selections choose the **Start** button. Set the Brightness slider bar to –255. Click **OK**. Under the **Settings** selections choose the **End** button. Set the **Brightness** slider bar to 0. Click **OK** and then click once more.

STEP FOUR

Render your animated map. By adjusting the **Brightness** of the image over time, the movie shows the logo fading in from black. When rendered as an animated bump map, the logo will appear to become embossed on the surface of an object over time.

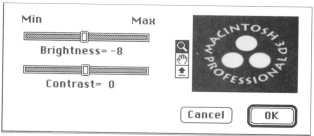

FIGURE **8.51A** *The Brightness and Contrast filter can be applied to a clip over time in Premiere 4.0.*

FIGURE **8.51B** *This image is a color map that is used in conjunction with the animated bump map.*

STEP FIVE

Import the rendered map into your 3D application and then apply the movie to an object as an animated bump map.

FRAME 0   FRAME 45   FRAME 90

FIGURE *Rendering of the animated bump map of the logo.*
8.52

Animated Transparency Maps

You can use animated transparency maps to create some very interesting effects. A ghostly mist or fog can be created by mapping a partially transparent moving image on several parallel planes. By creating two or three infinite planes that are located close to each other on the Y axis, and mapping a different transparency map onto each plane, you can create the illusion of a swirling mist.

In this section we're going to create an animated transparency map that creates the illusion of an object dissolving into thin air. We'll be using Premiere for this tutorial and the project file is included on the CD-ROM.

Tip. If you want to create an animated map for either a bump map or transparency map, try using the **Ripple** filter included with either After Effects or Premiere.

T
U
T
O
R
I
A
L

FADING CUBE TUTORIAL
We want to create an animated map that starts out completely white and then fades to black. In addition we want to create a swirling effect throughout the entire animation.

STEP ONE
The key to creating any type of animated map is scale. You have to first calculate the dimensions of your finished product before you even launch Premiere. Once you've figured out the desired size of your map, you need to scale up the dimensions of the source image by around 50%. If you want your animated map to be 200 x 200 pixels after it has been rendered in Premiere, the size of your source image should be 300 x 300 pixels.

STEP TWO

Create your still image using the scaled up dimensions. We want the final output from Premiere to be 200 x 200 pixels so our still image size should be 300 x 300 pixels. The still was created in Adobe Photoshop using the **Render Clouds** filter.

STEP THREE

Launch Premiere. Set the dimensions of the project to 200 x 200 pixels then import the still image of the clouds. Set the duration of the still to 3 seconds and drag the clip into the **Construction** window, select the clip and then select **Motion...** from the **Clip** menu.

STEP FOUR

Remove any motion settings that Premiere has applied by default. The next step is to scale up the dimensions of the image at both the start and end keyframes. This is accomplished by dragging the four anchor points to the furthest corners in the distortion window. This needs to be performed twice for both the start and end point of the clip. The reason that this step needs to be done is so that the screen will be completely filled when we apply a filter or rotation to the still.

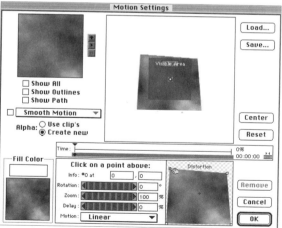

FIGURE 8.53 *Be sure to remove any motion settings that Adobe Premiere has applied to the clip. Then use the distort anchor points to scale up the image of the clouds.*

If the still was set to the exact dimension of the final rendered product, the background color would show through!

STEP FIVE

Set the time index of the clip to the end keyframe and then type in 360° in the Rotation field. This will make the still image spin over the duration of the clip.

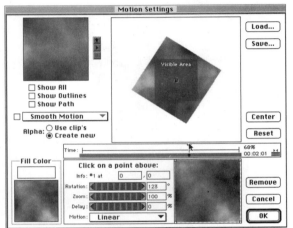

FIGURE 8.54 *Set the rotation of the image to 360° for the duration of the clip in the Motion Settings window in Adobe Premiere.*

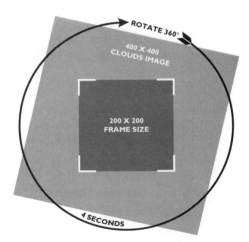

FIGURE 8.55 *The motion settings for the clip.*

STEP SIX

The previous steps set the scale and movement to the clip. Now you can add a few special effects. Select the clip in the **Construction** window and then select **Filters** from the **Clip** pull-down menu. Apply the **Ripple** filter to the clip. Notice that the white background shows through underneath the rippling edges of the image. But since we have already increased the scale of the image in Step Four we do not need to be concerned.

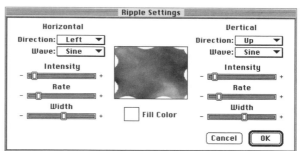

FIGURE *The Ripple filter adds another level of distortion*
8.56   *to our animated texture in Adobe Premiere.*

STEP SEVEN

Apply a second filter to the clip. In this case we're going to use the **Brightness and Contrast** filter. The effect that we're trying to achieve is an image that starts as completely opaque and then gradually changes to entirely transparent. By using the **Brightness and Contrast** filter over time, we can make the clip start as completely white and fade to black. Under the **Settings** selections choose the **Start** button. Set the **Brightness** slider bar to 255. Click **OK**. Under the **Settings** selections choose the **End** button. Set the **Brightness** slider bar to –255. Click **OK** and then click it once more.

STEP EIGHT

Render your animated texture map and then import it into your 3D application. Apply the clip to your object as a transparency map.

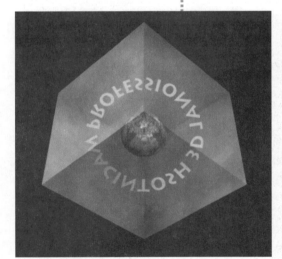

FIGURE   *The animated transparency map applied to an object and then rendered in Electric Image: (top)*
8.57   *start, (bottom left) middle, and (bottom right) end.*

 Lighting

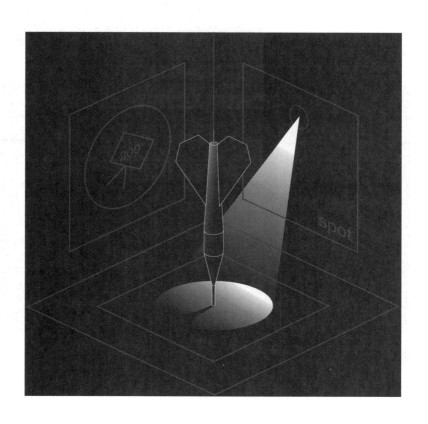

The modeling is finally completed and all of the texture maps have been applied. The scene is now set to add the lighting. Don't dismiss the importance of lighting. In Hollywood and on Broadway, the lighting technician's job is paramount for creating mood and feeling within a scene. Just think of the dark shadows and pools of light in the movie *The Godfather*. Even before Marlon Brando started to speak you could sense a feeling of power and foreboding emanating from the dimly lit figure. Movie directors spend hours setting up the lighting of a scene before the cameras start to roll. Before hitting that render button you should do the same. Fortunately you won't have to climb on top of rickety scaffolding balancing 100-pound spotlights to set the mood for your rendering. Also you'll have an arsenal of tools that the movie director can only dream about.

SECTION ONE: BASIC LIGHTING AND COLOR THEORY

We start off with how light and color interact: the RGB and HSL color models, complementary colors and how to choose them, and the moods colors can evoke.

SECTION TWO: TYPES OF LIGHT SOURCES

We next discuss the various types of light sources offered by your 3D application and what they are and how they work. Descriptions and definitions of point, parallel, and spot lights are given.

SECTION THREE: ANGLE OF INCIDENCE, LIGHT ATTENUATION, AND SHADOWS

We learn how to mimic the way that light works in reality. Concepts such as falloff, shadow flare, and angle of incidence are discussed and defined.

SECTION FOUR: LIGHTING A SCENE

Learn how professional photographers videographers, and cinematographers light their studio sets. A description of primary, fill, accent, back, grazed, and ambient lights.

SECTION ONE: BASIC LIGHTING AND COLOR THEORY

Red, Yellow, Blue Color Model

It's time to forget all you learned in kindergarten about color. Think back to when you used to eat the paste and play with fingerpaints. When you added yellow and blue, you got green, and when you mixed yellow and red you would get orange. And when you mixed them all together, you would end up with a dark gray sludge. This entire process is a subtractive or pigment-based system of color. The more colors you add to the mixture, the darker the resulting hue. Light does not work this way!

RGB, CMYK, and HSL Color Models

When you mix light it is an additive process and when you add more colors to a pool of light the whiter the resulting hue. Why is this? Think back to Physics 101 when your instructor told you that white light is composed of all of the colors of the spectrum. To prove this your teacher probably shone a beam of white light through a prism, which split the light up into a brightly colored rainbow of its component colors.

In most Mac programs you have a choice of using the RGB (red, green blue), CMYK (cyan, magenta, yellow, black), or HSL (hue, saturation, luminance or lightness) color models. The CMYK color model is primarily used in print based applications, while most people working in video, multimedia, or 3D usually use the RGB or HSL color models.

RGB COLOR MODEL

By mixing various amount of red, green, and blue light, you can produce any color that is visible to the human eye. Just think of the RGB color model as your original pots of fingerpaint with each pot being a primary color. The most important thing to remember about the RGB model is that when a fully saturated red, green, and blue light are all combined in equal quantities the resulting color is white.

Color on the computer is calculated in terms of bit depth, with 24 bits being the highest or most amount of color on the screen at one time. 24-bit color is the equivalent to millions of colors, 16 bit for thousands of colors, 8 bit for 256 colors, and so on down the line. In 24-bit color, 8 bits are allocated for the color red, 8 bits for

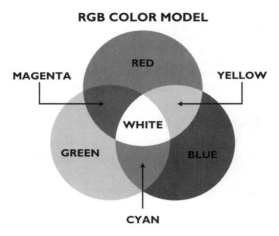

FIGURE *RGB color model.*
9.1

green, and 8 bits for blue, which adds up to 24 bits. By mixing various values for red, green, and blue, you can create any color in the visible spectrum.

When creating a color based on the RGB color model, you can set the RGB fields in one of two ways. The first is by setting the percentage of the color, between 0% and 100%. The second and more accurate way is by giving the numerical value between 0 and 255 that corresponds to a specific bit depth of the individual color. The RGB Apple Color Picker works in this way.

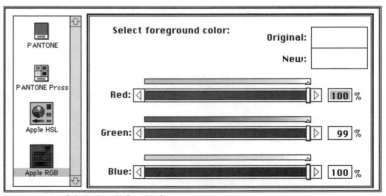

FIGURE *Apple's RGB Color Picker.*
9.2

Tip. Try this yourself in your 3D program. Turn off any ambient light sources. Create three spotlights with overlapping beams. Each spotlight should be a fully saturated red, green, and blue. In the area that has all three beams overlapping the light should be white.

HSL COLOR MODEL

The HSL color model operates on a somewhat different principle than the RGB. Instead of mixing various amounts or red, green, and blue in order to produce the desired results, the user starts with a color wheel. The color wheel shows a rough representation all of the colors that are available to the user.

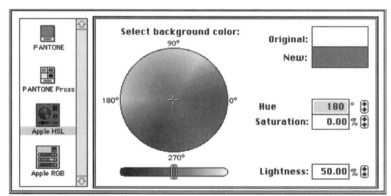

FIGURE *Apple's HSL Color Picker.*
9.3

Hue

By selecting a color on the wheel you're setting the hue of a color. *Hue* is what most people commonly refer to as *color*. When using Apple's **HSL Color Picker** the hue of a color can be input in a numeric field ranging from 0° to 360° or by simply dragging the cursor over the appropriate hue.

Saturation

Saturation controls the purity or amount by which the selection is mixed with other colors. On the outside rim of the color wheel, colors are completely saturated, more so than the colors closer to the center of the wheel. In the direct center of the wheel the resulting color should be completely white since it's a combination of all colors. If a color is completely saturated it is pure. Therefore any color located on the outside of the wheel is 100% saturated while any color in the center is 0% saturated.

Tip. When it comes to setting the hue of either a light source, material, or even a background keep this fact in mind. In nature it is extremely rare for a color to be completely saturated. Gray usually has a touch of white or blue and black is never completely black. Don't make a light source completely white, try adding a little blue or yellow to the color for a more natural feel. A good example is that of a circus spotlight; in reality, it always has a small amount of blue in the cone.

Luminance

Finally luminance controls how bright or illuminated a color appears. As the luminance of a color increases, the selection will appear to become more washed out, and as the luminance decreases, the color will appear more dim or dark. A color is considered to be pure when the luminance is equal to 50% since it is neither being lightened or darkened.

Fortunately for the 3D user the Apple OS makes the **RGB** and **HSL Color Picker** standard in most programs. Since the interface is standardized, you only need to learn it once rather than a multitude of times.

Complimentary Colors

By using the HSL color model it is fairly easy to calculate the complementary color of a selection. Strictly speaking, a complementary color is the opposite color in the spectrum necessary to return a color to white. By using the RGB color model this is fairly hard to judge, but by using the HSL model's color wheel it's a simple matter. The complementary color is directly opposite the original color on the other side of the color wheel. By adding 180° to the **Hue** field in Apple's **HSL Color Picker** the complementary color of the selection can be immediate set.

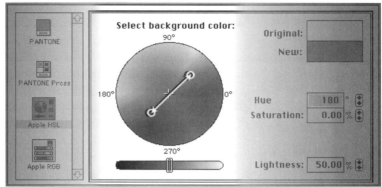

FIGURE *A complimentary color is directly opposite the original color on the*
9.4 *HSL color wheel.*

COLOR AND MOOD

Now that you've gotten a bit of a grasp on how to create your own color from scratch, this section describes the feelings that color evokes. When lighting a model, both the color of the direct and ambient light play an important role in creating the mood or the feeling of a scene. Light blue or white light can convey feelings of cool of cold climates or clinical or sterile surroundings. A bright yellowish green light can convey feelings of a hot tropical atmosphere while a purplish blue color can convey a damp subterranean underground feeling. The mood set by lighting also has a direct correlation to the temperature of the light.

COLOR TEMPERATURE

The color of light and the level of illumination can be described in terms of temperature. For example, a scene that is lit by candlelight or firelight is illuminated by warm orange and muted red tones. On the other hand, a winter scene that is lit by bright, almost harsh white light is described as being cold and intense. Brighter lights that are closer to white are best described as being cool or cold, while colored lights closer to red, orange, and violet are best described as being warm or hot.

When it comes to setting the intensity of a light or how much illumination a light will cast, it is usually calculated in terms of the actual color of the light. As a light's color is set closer to white, the illumination level of the light should be set closer to 100%. In other words a light's color is a direct indication of how much light it should cast. For example, a blue light would rarely have an intensity close to 100%; it would be closer to 50% to 60%. On the other hand a brighter color such as white or light green would warrant a higher intensity.

Tip. When setting both the color and intensity of a light source in your 3D program try using this method. Use the hue and saturation controls to set the color of the light source and use the luminance value to control the level of illumination. Leave the light's illumination level set to the program's default, which should be 100%.

DISTANCE AND COLOR

As an object or background recedes into the distance, the colors further away from the camera become more subdued or muted. Keep this fact in mind when applying either depth of field or fog to a rendering. The images in the foreground will tend to have warmer tones while the objects in the background will appear cooler. In this case, make sure that the relative illumination of the foreground objects is not higher than the objects in the background. This concept is extremely important to remember when you're either compositing a background in postproduction or using a precaptured image for the background during rendering. It's also good to consider this concept before setting the color of the fog when trying to mimic the illusion of depth of field.

SECTION TWO: TYPES OF LIGHT SOURCES

Gone are the days of having to set up miles of cables and lug around 100-pound canister lights. In 3D we can simply drag and drop our lights with a click of a button. We also don't have to erect towering scaffolds to mount our lights, we can simply hang them in virtual space.

Light sources are the means with which you'll be illuminating your scenes. The best way to become familiar with how each type of light works is to experiment with them in your 3D program. Start by creating a plane and then place a few primitives on the surface. Add the various types of light sources to the scene and observe the rendered results. It's important to understand how to set the falloff, intensity, color, and shadow casting capabilities of each type of light source. Configuring light sources varies from program to program, but they all behave in exactly the same manner. It's best to become familiar with how to work with your lights in your application before starting this section. For those of you who are not too comfortable with your 3D application this means a trip back to the manual for you.

The average 3D program has the following types of lights at it's disposal:

- Parallel or global
- Spot
- Point or radial

Some of the more sophisticated programs offer:

- Ambient
- Tube
- Black or negative

PARALLEL LIGHTS

Parallel or global lights are the closest 3D light source to natural sunlight. All of the rays of light cast from a parallel light source are parallel. Parallel lights provide the most even lighting in a scene, illuminating a model in a uniform manner. The trick is knowing when to use a parallel light.

You should use a parallel light when illuminating a scene that is set outdoors since most natural lighting from the sun is fairly even. You wouldn't use a parallel light to illuminate a scene set indoors or to mimic the light cast from a source such as a lightbulb or a spotlight.

An easy way to visualize how parallel lights work is to imagine an infinite plane that is centered on the parallel light. The plane itself is perpendicular to the light rays emitted from the light source. Now envision the plane as being one large light ray. Since the plane is infinite the entire area beneath the plane is illuminated in a completely even fashion.

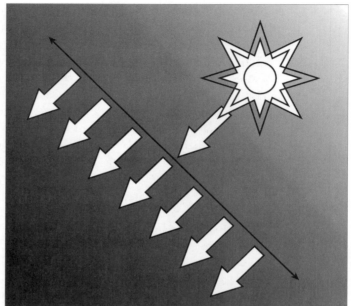

FIGURE 9.5 *A parallel light source illuminates a scene in a completely even manner since all of the light rays cast by the source are parallel.*

FIGURE 9.6 *Rendering of a scene lit by a parallel light source, notice that the scene is evenly lit and the shadow not distorted.*

SPOTLIGHTS

Spotlights offer the user the most control over light in a 3D environment. On an average, most users will probably use spotlights more than any other type of light source. The primary advantage of using spotlights in 3D is the amount of control over shadow, direction, location, and orientation that they afford the user.

The best way to understand how a spotlight works is to visualize a pointed cone. The bulb is located at the tip of the cone with the light rays traveling in the direction of the base of the cone. The rays of light that comprise the spotlight are confined within the volume of the cone itself. Many 3D programs allow the user to define an inner and outer cone for a spotlight.

The intensity of the light is uniform up to the boundary of the inner cone and then falls off to a predefined intensity at the perimeter of the outer cone.

Tip. Electric Image affords the user the additional luxury of setting the color for both the inside and outside cone of a spotlight as well as creating a visual glow. If you don't have the option of visible light sources or glowing lights, be sure to read Chapter 11, Lighting Special Effects.

FIGURE 9.7 *Light cast from a spotlight travels in one direction springing from the tip of an imaginary cone toward the base.*

FIGURE
9.8
Rendering of a scene lit by a spotlight, notice how the light cast by the light source is concentrated in the center and then immediately falls off to form a circle of light.

POINT OR RADIAL LIGHTS

Point or radial lights are most like real-world lightbulbs. Light is cast in a spherical fashion outward from the center of a point light source.

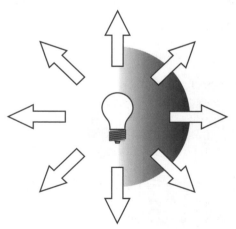

FIGURE
9.9
The light cast from a point light source is cast in a spherical manner. A point light is most like a real-world lightbulb.

Point lights are especially useful for brightening shadows or to increase the general illumination in darker areas of your 3D scene.

Since the light cast by a point light is emitted in a radial or spherical fashion, the illumination provided by this light source is uneven. The light is most intense directly beneath the center of the point light, and then gradually diminishes toward the edges. Try placing a point light directly above a plane in your 3D application and do a quick rendering to see what I mean.

FIGURE **9.10** *Rendering of a scene lit by a point light source, notice the large shadow flare and how the light is concentrated in the center of the image and then falls off gradually.*

AMBIENT LIGHT

Just about every 3D program allows the user to configure the ambient light settings in the 3D environment. The majority of programs have a global ambient value setting that affects the entire scene. For most applications this setting should be used.

Important. When adjusting the level of ambient light in a scene, remember that ambient light is distributed in a uniform manner throughout. In other words all shaded areas throughout the scene will be lit by the same amount of ambient light, regardless of the distance from the primary light source. This is why most programs do not allow the user to place or move an ambient light source since it really does not make a difference where it is located.

In more sophisticated programs you can create and place an ambient light that works in much the same way a point light does, except instead of casting illumination, it casts ambient light. Since ambient light is distributed evenly you're probably wondering why you would use an ambient light source at all? The benefit is being able to control the direction and falloff of the ambient light source from a specific area. If, for example, you were trying to create a scene where only certain areas are lit by ambient light you would need to be able to place and then set the falloff of an ambient light source.

FIGURE *An ambient light source casts ambient light in a uniform*
9.11 *manner from a specific point in space.*

TUBE LIGHTS

A tube light is most like a fluorescent bulb, which is long and cylindrical. These lights are useful for things such as neon, laser beams, or fluorescent lightbulbs. Light is cast from a tube light much in the same fashion as a point light, except that light is cast along the entire length of the light source.

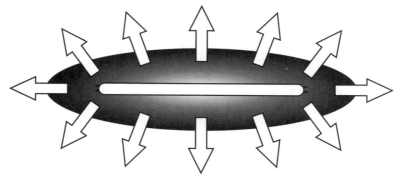

FIGURE
9.12 *A tube light source is most like a real-world florescent lightbulb. Light is cast along the entire length of the bulb.*

BLACK LIGHTS

Black lights are your own personal black hole. Not many programs support this feature but it does come in handy on special occasions. By entering a negative value in the intensity field of a light source, a light can be made to absorb rather than cast light. In a scene where there are multiple light sources and the image appears either overexposed or plagued with hot spots, a black light can be configured to absorb the excess.

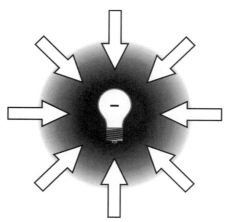

FIGURE
9.13 *Black light sources absorb rather than cast light. This feature is useful for overexposed scenes with multiple light sources.*

SECTION THREE: ANGLE OF INCIDENCE, LIGHT ATTENUATION, AND SHADOWS

Angle of Incidence

It's time to rethink some of the misconceptions you might have about lighting. To illuminate the surface of an object evenly, you have to move a light source further away from rather than closer to an object. As a light source moves further away from the surface being illuminated, the surface becomes more evenly illuminated.

The angle of the light source in relation to the surface of the object is referred to as the *angle of incidence*. As the angle of incidence approaches 90° the illumination of a surface becomes more even. The angle of incidence applies to both point and spotlights but not to parallel lights. It really doesn't matter how far or close a parallel light source is located to an object since the rays of light are parallel.

T
U
T
O
R
I
A
L

ANGLE OF INCIDENCE TUTORIAL

Try this exercise yourself. Create a square-shaped plane in your 3D application. Turn off any default lighting. Place a point light source directly above the plane. Move the light source various distances away from the plane and observe the change in illumination.

POINT LIGHT

FIGURE
9.14 *The point light is placed directly over a plane and has an angle of incidence of 3° (left), and only illuminates a small portion of the plane (right).*

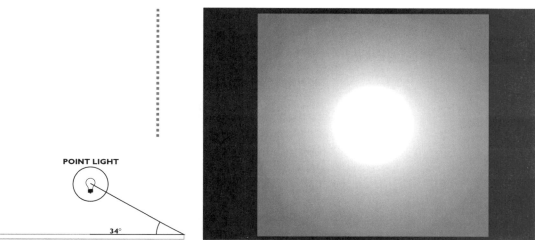

FIGURE 9.15 *The point light is moved further away from the surface and has an angle of incidence of 34° (left), and illuminates the plane more evenly (right).*

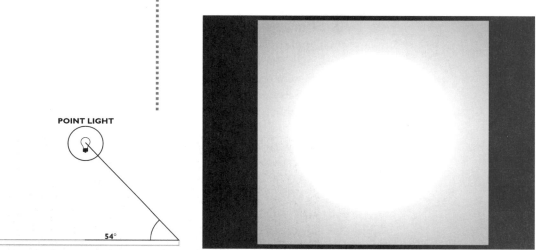

FIGURE 9.16 *As the point light is moved even further away and angle of incidence approaches 54° (left), the surface of the plane becomes more evenly illuminated (right).*

As a light source's angle of incidence approaches 90° the surface being illuminated becomes more evenly lit since more of the object is exposed to the light rays. If your program does not support parallel light sources, you can move a spotlight an extreme distance away from your scene to mimic the effects of a parallel light.

Tip. Take a flashlight into a darkened room and shine it on the wall. As you bring the light closer to the wall, the spot being illuminated becomes brighter yet the overall illumination on the wall is reduced. As you move the flashlight further away from the wall, more surface area becomes more evenly illuminated yet with a slight reduction in intensity.

Light Attenuation

Even though we don't live in a perfect world, our 3D one is almost flawless in most respects. In reality, light experiences *attenuation,* which is the gradual falloff in intensity of light over distance. The atmosphere around us is full of particles that refract beams of light. After a certain distance, a light source becomes so refracted the light is no longer transmitted or visible. Since our 3D world is generated by computers, it tends to be a little too perfect. Most 3D applications have the falloff for a light source set to an infinite value as a default. Light will keep on traveling until it intersects an object regardless of the distance that it has to travel. In reality light rarely works this way unless in a complete vacuum.

In some cases the falloff factor really isn't important, but when trying to create a realistic scene, light attenuation is absolutely imperative. For example, if you create an animated car with spotlights for headlights, you have to set the attenuation of the lights for a number of reasons. If you keep the light sources at the default settings of infinity, you will end up with strange or unrealistic results. Any object at a distance that falls into the beam of the headlights will be completely illuminated regardless of the distance of the object from the lights.

This scenario sounds right but the physics of the situation are slightly off. In reality if a distant object falls into the beam of a headlight it would be dimly lit rather than completely lit. Since the light has to travel over a distance from the headlight to the object, the intensity should decrease rather than remain constant.

If you're having problems visualizing this, imagine driving a car at night up a long straight driveway. The house at the end of the drive would only be dimly lit by your headlights, but as you come closer it becomes more illuminated. In a 3D application with the falloff set to infinity, the house would appear completely lit even when the car is at the far end of the drive.

To correct this imperfect perfection, 3D applications allow the user to set the attenuation or falloff of a light source. In many cases, it does not make sense to set the falloff of a parallel light source because the intensity of sunlight is constant. Since the sun is such a powerful illuminator, the light cast is both steady and even. On the other hand, it makes perfect sense to set the falloff of both point lights and spotlights. Most 3D programs allow the user to set the falloff of point and spotlights by entering a value for the radius of an inner and outer sphere. The area defined by the inner sphere is referred to as the *hotspot,* while the area defined by the outer sphere is regarded as the *falloff* or *dropoff.*

ATTENUATION OF POINT LIGHTS

The shape of the light rays cast by a point light are spherical. The attenuation for light rays cast by a point light is controlled by two imaginary concentric spheres in just about every 3D application. The user can define the radius of both the inner and outer sphere. The inside sphere represents the hotspot and the outside sphere represents the falloff or level of attenuation. Any object that falls within the area of the inside sphere will be illuminated in a completely even manner and the level of illumination will be 100% of the point light's intensity.

In the area defined from the surface of the inner sphere to the surface of the outer sphere, the level of illumination is reduced according to a variety of formulas. Some programs allow the user to configure the rate of falloff. Falloff can either be set to a linear falloff or the square of the distance, which is more accurate. If the falloff is set to be linear, the light's intensity decreases on a linear basis. For example, if an object is twice as far from the light source, it will receive one-half the illumination. In reality, the falloff of light decreases exponentially so if an object is twice as far from a light source, it will receive only one-quarter of the illumination. Any object that falls outside of the volume of the outer sphere receives no light at all from the point light source.

Tip. Why set the falloff for a point light source? If you were modeling a table lamp for example, you would have to define how far the light would travel in a dark room. If you left the falloff at infinity, the lamp would illuminate the entire scene. Have you ever seen a table lamp do this in reality?

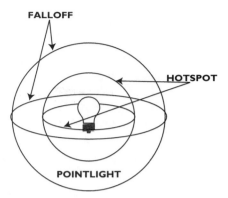

FIGURE **9.17** *Any object that falls within the inner sphere will be illuminated at 100% of the light's intensity. Any object that falls between the inner and outer sphere will receive only a percentage of the light's intensity depending on the rate of falloff.*

ATTENUATION OF SPOTLIGHTS

The shape of the light rays cast by a spotlight resembles two concentric cones with both of the tips of the cones located at the coordinates of the spotlight. Unlike a point light, a spotlight's attenuation is slightly more involved.

If you look at a spotlight from above as in Figure 9.18 you can see that the falloff has to be configured both for the width of the cone as well as for the length of the beam. The inner cone defines the hotspot where the level of illumination is both constant and at 100% intensity. The outer cone defines the falloff. Anything outside of the outer cone receives no illumination from the spotlight at all. The rate of falloff in the area between the two cones can be either linear or cubic depending of course on your application.

To set the falloff for the length of the spotlight beam, most programs allow the user to set the radius of two imaginary spheres that are centered on the light source's coordinates. By entering the radii of both the inner and outer sphere, the user can define the hotspot and falloff, respectively. Any object that falls within the inner sphere as well as the inner cone will be illuminated at 100% of the spotlight's intensity. Any object that falls between the inner and outer sphere, as well as the inner and outer cone, will receive a percentage of light according to the rate of falloff established by the user.

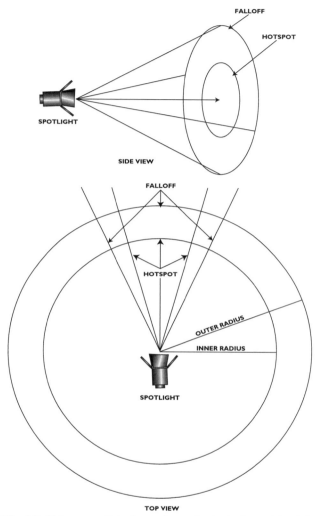

FIGURE
9.18
The falloff for a spotlight has to be set for both the width of the beam and for the length of the cone.

Shadows

First of all, if you can get away without using shadows in an animation or a still image then don't use them. Shadows can add unwanted rendering time to a project and if the viewer doesn't notice their absence then don't bother to render them at all. For example, not many flying logos use shadows. Just watch the flying logos used by many of the networks as well as local television stations and you'll notice that very few of them incorporate shadows into their animations. On the other hand, if the scene looks unnatural without shadows then by all means use them. For example, if an object is placed directly on a planar surface, and there are no shadows in the rendering, then the object will tend to look as if it is floating above the surface of the plane.

Shadows add a dimension of depth and location and can even set the mood in a rendering. A room full of dark shadows can evoke feelings of mystery while a brightly lit room can appear antiseptic. One of the major problems faced by amateur 3D enthusiasts is that their renderings always appear overexposed. By carefully balancing both the lightness and the darkness in an image, a scene can be made to seem more realistic. Shadows are the key to controlling the darkness.

Perhaps the first issue to be covered is which light should cast shadows in a scene. Even though every situation is different there are a few tips that apply to most scenes.

- Try to set only one light as a shadow caster. Most of the time this light should be the main light, which provides the majority of the illumination in a scene. The viewer can become confused by multiple shadows coming from one object. This occurs when more than one light source is casting a shadow. Most applications let the user set whether or not a light can cast a shadow. By enabling only the main light as the shadow caster, you reduce rendering time. On the other hand if the scene has several obvious light sources, then you will need to enable multiple shadow casting lights.

- Even though the user has a variety of light sources from which to choose, each type of light source casts a different type of shadow. For example, a parallel light source casts shadows that are drawn toward the vanishing point in a scene. On the other hand, a point or spot light source flares the shadow outward away from the vanishing point. This phenomenon is known as *shadow flare*. Since the light beams of a parallel light source are all parallel, the shadows created tend to converge on the vanishing point. On the other hand, since the beams of light from a point or spotlight emanate outward from a fixed point, the resulting shadows tend to flare outward as well.

The amount of shadow flare from a model is usually a good cue about the scale of the scene. For example, a group of skyscrapers would look unnatural with a large amount of shadow flare since they are usually illuminated by a parallel light source such as the sun. The amount of shadow flare that a point or spotlight creates depends entirely on how close to the object the light source is located. The amount of shadow flare increases when a light source is closer to an object and decreases as the light source is moved further from an object.

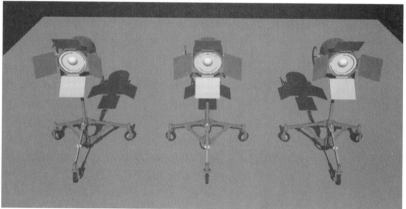

FIGURE **9.19** *Rendering of a scene illuminated by a parallel light source. Notice how the shadows tend to converge toward the vanishing point.*

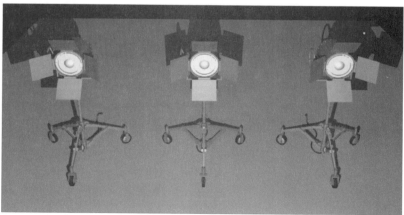

FIGURE **9.20** *Rendering of a scene illuminated by a point light source located close to the lamps. Notice that the shadows flare outward toward the edges of the scene.*

Tip. If your 3D application does not support parallel light sources, you can use either a point or spotlight source instead. But it is important to place the substitute light source at a far distance away from the object being illuminated in order to reduce shadow flare. As a light source is distanced from the object that it is illuminating, the amount of shadow flare is reduced!

- Shadows can never be any darker than the ambient light value, which is something to keep in mind when you are compositing a background image in postproduction. Also keep in mind where the light sources are coming from in both the animation and background.

Tip. Several programs allow the user to set which objects cast shadows and which objects do not. In general most objects when they are created default with this option activated. To conserve on resources, turn off the shadow casting capabilities for the ground plane. Since everything is located on top of the plane, it does not usually cast a shadow.

- Here's a trick that I learned from a company creating extremely complex images. They had limited rendering resources so they couldn't create a parallel light source that cast shadows since there was too much geometry in the scene for the computer to handle. What they did was link a shadow casting spotlight to the camera so as the camera moved forward in the animation, it carried along a shadow casting light source. Only the area directly in front of the camera would have a shadow-saving valuable rendering resources.

SECTION FOUR: LIGHTING A SCENE

In this section we're going to cover the basics of how to place and set the color and intensity of the lights in your scene. This will probably be the most time consuming step in the entire animation process because you have to render the scene each time you adjust a light just to see the effects it has on the rendering. Once QuickDraw 3D becomes more integrated with existing software packages, we hope that will all change. But for now, when doing a preview rendering, make sure to use a fast rendering algorithm and turn off features such as reflection, transparency, and bump mapping until you go to render the final image. You will save a lot of time by disabling these features.

While there is no hard and fast rule for lighting a scene, there are a few good rules of thumb to follow. In this section were going to cover the basics of a studio setup. In Chapter 11 we'll cover the finer points of simulating a specific type of environmental setting. The goal in this section is to get you a little more familiar with how your lights work and how they work with each other.

Three-Light Studio Setup

Depending on who is lighting the scene and what is being lit, several different types of lighting models are available from which to choose. The most basic lighting model involves three lights:

- Key or primary light
- Fill light
- Back or rim light

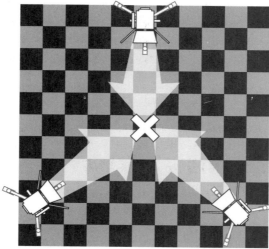

TOP VIEW OF STUDIO LIGHTING SETUP
BACK LIGHT
25% INTENSITY

KEY LIGHT
75% INTENSITY

FILL LIGHT
25% INTENSITY

FIGURE 9.21 *A typical studio lighting setup uses three lights placed in key positions around the central object.*

KEY LIGHT

The key light provides the most illumination and should be the brightest light in the scene. The key light should also be the light that casts the shadows. When configuring the intensity of this light, it's important to try various settings. While most programs set the default value of a new light at 100%, it's a better idea to set the light to around 75% intensity and then gradually increase the value if needed. At 100% intensity, there might be too much contrast between the shadows and the illuminated areas on the surface of the model.

The key light should be located at a 45° angle to the front face of the model either to the left or the right of the camera. The height of the light should be a little bit over head-high or a few units higher than the top of the model. Try using a spotlight with a wide cone as your key light.

FILL LIGHT

The fill light gets it name from the fact that it is used to fill the shadowed areas on a model. It's used to soften the contours of a model, making the transition from bright to dark areas more gradual. The fill light should be set to approximately 25% intensity and gradually increased if needed. If the intensity of the fill light is too high, then the model will appear flat because of the lack of contrast between the lighted areas and the shadows.

The fill light should be located on the opposite side of the key light at a 45° angle to the model. Try setting the height of the fill light a little lower than that of the key light, or even try angling the light upward from the floor for a more interesting effect. You can use either a spotlight or point light as a fill light. To save on rendering resources, consider disabling the shadow casting feature of the light source. Any shadows cast by the fill light are usually overpowered by the key light anyway.

 Tip. Here's a useful tip to create the illusion of scale using only lighting. Try placing the light sources at the base of the model and have the lights point upward. Most buildings, statues, and monuments are lit in this fashion.

BACK LIGHT

Placed behind the model, back lights serve to cast a halo or rim of light around the object. A back light defines the edges of a model from the background. The back light should be first set at 25% intensity and then increased if needed. If the model seems to blend into the background, try increasing the intensity of the back light. The back light should be placed directly behind or below the model for the best results. You can use either a point or a spotlight for the job.

FIGURE 9.22 *The three-light studio setup uses key, fill, and back lights.*

FIGURE 9.23 *The figure is illuminated with three lights from a variety of angles using the three-light studio model.*

Four-Light Studio Setup

The four-light studio setup is based on the same model as the three-light setup. But instead of placing the back or rim light directly behind the model, it can also be placed directly opposite the key light. In addition, a grazed background light can be used to illuminated a backdrop screen or cyclorama.

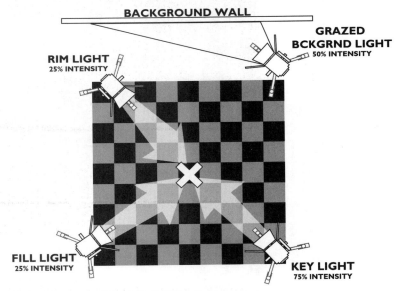

TOP VIEW OF STUDIO LIGHTING SETUP II

BACKGROUND WALL

GRAZED BCKGRND LIGHT
50% INTENSITY

RIM LIGHT
25% INTENSITY

FILL LIGHT
25% INTENSITY

KEY LIGHT
75% INTENSITY

FIGURE *Diagram of the four-light studio setup.*
9.24

GRAZED LIGHT

The settings for the key, fill, and back lights are virtually identical to the three-light studio setup. The major difference in this case is the addition of a grazed background light. A grazed light that illuminates a background screen or cyclorama should be placed close to the base of the screen, near the ground plane. The beam or focus of the grazed light should be set to point upward at a 45° angle.

ACCENT LIGHT

Another type of light that can be added to either the three- or four-light setup is an *accent* light. An accent light serves to highlight specific objects or features on a model or within a scene. Try using a spotlight set to 75% intensity with a narrow falloff. Make sure that the shadow cone around the pool of light that is cast from the spot light is soft or fuzzy. A sharp-edged shadow will draw too much attention to the highlighted area.

FIGURE *Rendering of four-light studio setup.*
9.25

FIGURE *This model was lit using the four-light studio setup. Notice that*
9.26 *the background is lit by a grazed light.*

Tip. In a photography studio, most backgrounds used in a photo shoot are large curved sheets of flexible material with a matte finish. These backgrounds are usually referred to as a *cyclorama*. A cyclorama provides a seamless as well as shadowless gradient fill background. A cyclorama can be either vertically or horizontally oriented.

Basic Lighting Considerations

Now that you've gotten the concept of a studio lighting setup down pat, and you want to branch out and try different lighting models, here are a few pointers to keep in mind.

- As you add more lights to a scene, the general level of illumination increases. To keep the scene from being overexposed, reduced the overall intensity of all of the lights. This rule is extremely important when dealing with multiple point or parallel light sources. Since the light from these sources tends to travel in an all-encompassing manner, the entire scene can easily become washed out. Add up the intensity values of all of the point and parallel light sources in your scene. Make sure that this value does not exceed 100%. For example, if you have one parallel light set to 40%, and two point lights set to 60% and 75% the total is 175% intensity. Chances are the scene will be overexposed. If you want to keep the lights at their highest intensity, try scaling the falloff of the light sources so that they do not overlap and create hotspots.

- The term hotspot can also be used to describe the area where the beams of several light sources converge. This area tends to become overexposed and washed out. For obvious reasons this phenomenon should be avoided. In reality, when lighting an indoor scene that is illuminated by several light sources such as track lighting, table lights, and so on, the professional lighting designer tries to avoid creating sharp shadow lines or bright pools of light. Most amateur 3D designers try to show the result of every light that is added to a scene. This is both unnecessary as well as counterproductive. The subtle approach is much more attractive. A good example of lighting misuse is the use of sharp-edged spotlights in an interior scene.

• When initially setting up the intensity of your lights in a scene, set the ambient light value to around 7% intensity and then gradually increase it if need be. The primary role of ambient light is to provide contrast in a scene. As the amount or value of the ambient light is increased, the amount of contrast in a scene is decreased, thereby flattening the image. Another useful tip is to set the color of the ambient light to the complementary color of the main or key light.

• When working with the studio lighting setup, try using a variety of lighting intensities in different combinations. The chart in Figure 9.27 offers several different lighting models for you to try.

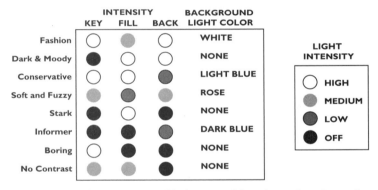

FIGURE *Chart of various types of lighting models to be used in the studio*
9.27 *lighting model.*

CHAPTER
10
Simulating Environments with Lighting

Lighting a Real-World Environment

While the studio lighting setup in the previous chapter was a good start to lighting a scene, the rendered results often look too polished or perfect. To make our renderings look more realistic, we have to gain a better understanding of the world around us and how light reacts under certain circumstances. The aim of this chapter is to explain and describe how to light a scene relative to its location and seasonal changes.

An infinite number of variables make one day look different from the rest. These variables range from the relative humidity in the air to the pollen count. But when it comes down to it, there are four major elements that play a vital role in lighting a scene:

- Atmosphere
- Light color
- Light intensity
- Light angle

ATMOSPHERE

What do I mean by atmosphere? In any scene that you create in 3D you need to take into consideration the atmosphere that surrounds the model. For example if you're creating a futuristic city scape reminiscent of Ridley Scott's *Blade Runner* you need to consider the high pollution content and how it affects the intensity, color, and attenuation of the light. On the other hand if you're interested in creating an underwater scene, you need to consider how the density of the water will affect the various lighting factors. Be it air, water, pollution, or a complete vacuum, the atmosphere in a 3D scene plays a vital role.

LIGHT COLOR, INTENSITY, AND ANGLE

The color, intensity, and angle of a light source varies dramatically from situation to situation, relative to the time of day, season of year, and location on the planet. For example, a winter scene uses different lighting parameters than that of a summer's day. The color, intensity, and angle of a light source are all fairly self-explanatory; the problem lies in achieving the correct combination relative to the scene that you're trying to light.

This chapter is broken down into various lighting scenarios that you're likely to encounter. As with the rest of the chapters, all of the models and textures in each section are included on the CD-ROM. Before you start this chapter you should have a good grounding of how to create a light source in your 3D application and how to configure it accordingly.

SECTION ONE: SUNLIGHT

The most basic of all of the lighting models, yet still fairly complicated is the creation of sunlight. Learn how to set the color and placement of your light sources relative to the time of day and the season of the year and location on the planet.

SECTION TWO: MOONLIGHT

Use your lights to create a creepy haunting feeling or a romantic evening. Learn how to set the color of your light sources and the level of ambient light in your nighttime scene

SECTION THREE: FOG AND ATMOSPHERIC CONDITIONS

Snow, sleet, hail, rain, smog, everything that you could possibly throw at the U.S. Postal Service and more are discussed in this section. Use fog to create the illusion of depth of field or add a little bit of imperfection to our perfect 3D world.

SECTION FOUR: OUTER SPACE

This choice is perfect for your science fiction epic animations. Learn how to become the next George Lucas or James Cameron.

SECTION FIVE: UNDERWATER

Sea Quest, The Abyss — you can create an underwater scene without getting your feet wet. Use fog and visible light sources to create an underwater scene that Nemo would be proud of.

SECTION SIX: ARTIFICIAL LIGHTING

We'll study everything from street lamps to fluorescent lights. Learn how to light your city streets, high-rise buildings, and industrial plants.

SECTION ONE: SUNLIGHT

Sunlight is the most basic lighting model that you can use in 3D. It's fairly easy to use since most of the time all it involves is adding a parallel light source to a scene. But if you're striving for accuracy, creating an artificial sun is slightly more involved.

CAD Lighting

One of the hardest types of lights to judge accurately is sunlight. It might appear deceptively easy, for example, it's a simple matter to place a parallel light source in a scene and then leave it at that. And in most cases this would work, but for more precise applications such as architecture it's extremely difficult to guesstimate sun angle and position.

Why is this so important? For the architect trying to place windows on a wall or trying to calculate which direction to point the house so that it receives the most amount of sunlight throughout the entire year, knowing the angle of the sun is imperative. Depending on where in the world you live, this angle of the sun varies. Countries closer to the equator receive more direct sunlight since the effects of the axial tilt of the planet are less noticeable.

The best application for an accurate seasonal light source is a CAD-based program that is specifically designed to replicate the seasons as well as the country where the model is supposed to exist. If CAD is not your cup of tea, there is an alternative. auto•des•sys's form•Z RenderZone has accurate sun light sources that can handle real-world sunlight placement.

Quick and Easy Sunlight

Like I said, in most cases it won't be necessary to ensure that you have the sun light source placed accurately for Bombay, India, on March 23. So if all you want to do is create a sun, and you're not too concerned with absolute accuracy, you can try the following. First of all, use a parallel light source. A parallel light behaves most like the sun by providing both even and constant illumination. The parallel light should be the only light source in the scene to start with. Once the light has been added to the scene, you need to consider the following factors:

- Time of day
- Season of the year
- Location on the globe

All of these factors influence the following parallel light settings:

- Solar angle
- Light intensity
- Light color

TIME OF DAY

The first factor that you should be considering when setting the light source for sunlight is the time of day. Try to get a general idea of when your scene is set: dawn, sunrise, midmorning, noon, afternoon, sunset, or twilight.

Setting the Solar Angle

Once you've decided on the time of day, you can then set the solar angle or angle of the rays of the light source relative to the X/Z or ground plane of the model. If the entire model and ground plane is centered on the origin (where the X, Y, Z coordinates all equal zero) then set the focal point or the center of interest of the light source to the origin as well. The location of the light source itself can be set to any X, Y coordinates you wish, but do not move the light source along the Z axis! We will do that a little later.

Tip. By drawing a line between the location of a parallel light source and its center of interest, you can define a ray of light. The angle at which the ray of light intersects the ground plane is the solar angle. The solar angle is low in both the morning and evening, and close to 90° at noontime.

Figure 10.1 illustrates the solar angle relative to the time of day. In this step we're just trying to establish the length of the shadows cast by the parallel light source. You've probably noticed that in reality, the shadows at sunrise and sunset are the longest in the entire day. As the time of day approaches noon, the rays of light cast by the sun come close to perpendicular to the ground. At noon, the shadows are the shortest and tend to pool at the base of objects since the sun is directly overhead. Your 3D program automatically calculates the length of the shadows; all you have to do is locate the light source.

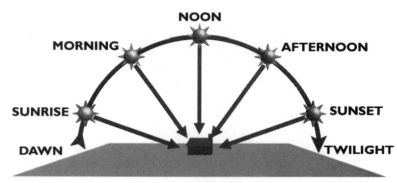

FIGURE **10.1** *The solar angle is relative to the time of day and controls the length of the shadows in your 3D scene. Shadows tend to be longer in both the morning and at sunset since the solar angle is low.*

Setting the Intensity of the Light

Once again, depending on the time of day, the amount of light in a scene varies. In the early morning before sunrise or dawn, and in the late evening after sunset or twilight, there is not much direct illumination from the sun itself. The light tends to be weak but you can usually see things fairly clearly because of the reflected light from the sky. When recreating this scenario in your 3D world try using a radial light source set from 10% to 20% near the center of your scene, and set the ambient light to a medium intensity.

Once the sun crests the horizon, it becomes a little easier to configure your light source. In this case use a parallel light source with a low solar angle for sunrise or sunset scenes. The intensity of the light should be anywhere from 25% to 50%. Think of the dark purple shadows that you see during a sunset. That's what you're trying to achieve, so keep the ambient light value low and set to a dark violet color.

At noon feel free to set the light source close to 100%, but be careful not to overexpose your image. Try setting the ambient light values to a medium to high level if your shadows become too dark. There is usually a high level of ambient light at noon because sunlight is very strong and tends to be reflected off of the surroundings. If your shadows are too dark try adding a radial light source set to 10% to 15% intensity to fill the darker areas.

Tip. When creating a scene set at noon, don't automatically place your light source at a 90° angle to the ground plane. The shadows will obscure the base of your objects and it will tend to look a little unusual. Offset the solar angle a couple of degrees so that your shadows gain a little length.

Setting the Color of the Light

This is perhaps the most important step of all. Color always sets the mood of a scene. But before you set the color of the parallel light to just any shade, you should first consider how the sunlight becomes colored in the first place.

The key to understanding this concept is to understand the atmosphere around us. As light travels through the atmosphere, it gains more color. Why does it do that? The atmosphere is composed of an immeasurable number of water, dust, oxygen, nitrogen, and pollution particles, all of which refract the light that passes through. Remember that sunlight or white light consists of all of the colors of the spectrum. As sunlight passes through the atmosphere, it becomes refracted, splitting up into its component colors. Since sunlight has to pass through more of the atmosphere at both sunrise and sunset, the light becomes more refracted or more colorful. At noontime, since sunlight does not have to pass through as much atmosphere to reach the viewer as in the morning or evening, the light tends to be closer to white.

When it comes to actually setting the color of your light source, take into consideration the time of day. For sunrise and sunset try using a lot of purple, magenta, and oranges. Since the sunlight has to pass through more of the atmosphere to reach the viewer, it becomes more refracted and thus more colorful. At noontime set the light color to a near white color. Since the sunlight has the most direct route to the viewer and it passes through a minimum of the atmosphere, the light is less refracted and thus closer to white.

In the midmorning and afternoon, use a warm yellow light since the sunlight is only partially refracted. Practically speaking, the best method for setting the color of sunlight is to simply stick your head out the window and look around. Once you know what to look for, the rest is easy.

Tip. In some cases you can actually create the illusion of a sun or bright star in the sky. A lens flare can be added in postproduction in a program such as Photoshop for a still image, or in After Effects or Premiere for an animation. The only 3D program that currently offers lens flares built into the application is Electric Image.

Important. Do not set your light source to be absolutely white. Most programs set the light sources at white as a default. Add a touch of blue or yellow to the light to make the scene appear more realistic! Even when lighting in a studio or natural setting, add a little bit of color to the lights.

Seasons

The last step in the procedure is compensating for the seasons. Sunlight looks much different in the summer months than it does in the winter months.

If you want to make the scene look as if it is set in the summer, keep the Z coordinates of the location of the parallel light close to zero. The path that the sun takes across the sky defines the solar plane. As the solar plane comes close to being perpendicular to the ground plane, the season is closer to the summer months. As the plane becomes close to being parallel to the ground plane, the season is closer to the winter months. The Z coordinates of the parallel light source control the angle of the solar plane.

When it comes to compensating for the winter season, lower the Y-coordinate value of the parallel light source while increasing or decreasing the Z-coordinate value. The idea is to offset the location of the parallel light source from the Y and X axis in either direction.

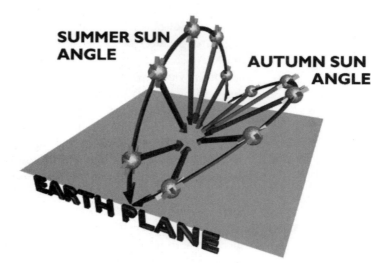

FIGURE *The summer solar angle is close to being perpendicular to the ground plane*
10.2 *and the winter solar angle is close to being parallel to the ground plane.*

As the solar plane becomes close to being parallel to the ground plane, the shadows cast by the sun become longer. Shadows tend to be longer in the winter than in the summer since the sun is lower in the sky during the winter months.

Global Location

The angle of the solar plane relative to the season depends on where you're located on the planet. Equatorial countries are affected less by the seasons than are countries located in the upper and lower hemispheres.

Also remember, since the solar angle is decreased in the winter months, the color of the light will change as well since the light has to pass through more layers of the atmosphere. That's why the color of the light seems cleaner in the summer, and more rich and varied in the autumn months.

T U T O R I A L

CHAIRS TUTORIAL

In this tutorial you can experiment with lighting this model. Try the various light positions, intensities, and colors to achieve different results.

FIGURE **10.3** *Sample rendering of a scene at midafternoon in Strata StudioPro.*

SECTION TWO: MOONLIGHT

Although the moon does not emit any light of its own, it does provide illumination since it reflects sunlight from its surface. The amount of illumination is far less than that provided by the sun. Like the sun, the color cast by the moon is relative to its position in the sky. Since the light has to travel through more layers of atmosphere when it is low in the sky, relative to the position of the viewer of course, the light becomes refracted. A young moon is usually a yellowish orange and it grows whiter as it climbs in the sky. The atmosphere also creates another unusual optical illusion. The moon appears much larger when it is low in the night sky, and then shrinks as it climbs higher. The refraction caused by the atmosphere not only serves to split the light into its component colors, but it also magnifies the size of the moon.

When you're trying to light a scene by moonlight in your 3D application you should use the following guidelines:

- Create one parallel light source as your primary light. Set its intensity to around 25% to 30% and the light color relative to the moon's position in the sky.
- Set the ambient light's intensity level very low and to the complementary color the primary light source.
- The key to a convincing moonlight rendering is soft-edged shadows. Some programs let you set how defined a shadow edge appears when it is rendered. The fuzzier the better.

SECTION THREE: FOG AND ATMOSPHERIC CONDITIONS

The weather, amount of pollution, or humidity can affect the color and density of the surrounding environment or atmosphere. The atmosphere in turn influences the color of the light passing through it. In this section we're going to use a new tool in our arsenal: *fog*. In later sections we'll use fog to create a variety of atmospheric conditions such an underwater scene.

Fog

The reason fog is so important in a rendering is that the user can use it to create the illusion of depth. Once again the problem lies with the computer being a little too perfect in the way that it does things. In reality, as an object recedes into the distance, it becomes out of focus and then eventually blends into the background. On a particularly hazy day, the horizon, ground, and sky often are one unintelligible blend of color. This occurs because of the atmosphere. As an object moves further away from the viewer, the light being reflected off of the surface of the object becomes more obscured by particles of dust, smoke, water, and so on floating around in the atmosphere. Your computer however is not affected by this phenomenon.

When you render a scene in your 3D application such as the image in Figure 10.4, the objects in the both the foreground as well as the background are in perfect focus. While it would be nice if we could look at everything this way, it isn't very realistic.

FIGURE *Notice how both the foreground as well as background objects are in*
10.4 *perfect focus.*

The rendering appears to be flat since we don't have any visual depth cues. There are two major types of depth cues: *depth of field* and *atmospheric conditions.* Depth of field is the phenomenon that as objects recede into the distance they become more out of focus. Atmospheric conditions such as fog, haze, or pollution affect the visibility of objects in the distance.

While most beginning 3D designers use fog to create depth of field, it is not the most accurate method. Fog obscures objects in the distance, and in reality depth of field only blurs object in the distance. We cover depth of field in more detail in Chapter 12, Perspective and the Virtual Camera, and offer a better method for creating this illusion. For now, we're going to concentrate primarily on fog.

How Fog Works

The most common application for fog is for creating the illusion of haze or atmosphere. Using fog in this manner is particularly useful since one of the more difficult problems with 3D rendering is creating a realistic background for a scene. A tremendous amount of 3D work looks unnatural since everything is in perfect focus, and the horizon line is perfectly sharp. When using fog you can also create a gradual transition from foreground to background. In Figure 10.5 we've used a

FIGURE 10.5 *Black fog applied to the image to create the illusion of the attenuation of a light source.*

little fog applied to the scene to mimic the attenuation of a light source. The color of the fog is black, which also matches the color of the background.

Fog works in much the same way as the dropoff of light sources. Two imaginary concentric circles define the boundaries of the fog and the user sets the radius for both circles. The inner circle defines where the fog is to start. Any object that falls within the inner circle will be rendered as completely clear. Any object that falls between the inner and outer circle will be rendered as slightly obscured depending on the distance from the center of the fog. Anything outside the outer circle which defines the outer boundary of the fog will be completely obscured.

The amount by which an object becomes obscured by the fog when it is located between the two circles depends on the type of falloff used to define the fog, which is either linear or cubic. For the linear method, as an object moves twice as far away from the center of the fog, it will become twice as obscured. The cubic method works on the principle that as an object moves twice as far away, it will become four times as obscured.

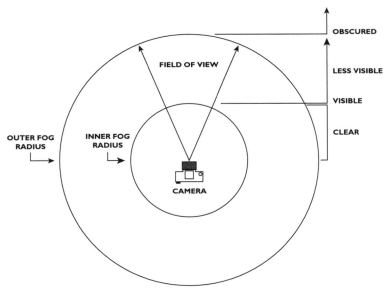

FIGURE **10.6** *The inner circle defines where the fog starts, and the outer circle defines the limit of visibility. Any object that falls outside the outer circle will be completely obscured by the fog color.*

USING FOG

The user can also choose the color of the fog to create a variety of effects. In Figure 10.5 we used a black fog to create the illusion of the falloff of a light sources. But if we used a white color we could have created the illusion of haze or mist. A brown fog can easily be seen as pollution. Purple fog could be a poisonous gas.

FIGURE *By using white as our fog color, we can create the illusion of mist*
10.7 *or haze.*

When it comes to configuring the inner and outer radii of fog try setting the inner circle radius to 0 or centered on the camera. By using this method, the fog starts directly at the "lens" of the camera creating the illusion that the camera is immersed in the fog.

The density of the fog in a scene can be altered by manipulating the inner and outer circles for the dropoff. If you want to create a denser fog, keep the circles closer together with the inner circle located near to the camera. For a lighter haze try spacing the circles further apart with the inner circle further away from the camera. Also the falloff of the fog depends on your 3D application. Some programs let the user define a cubic or linear falloff for fog, which controls the amount of visibility over distance.

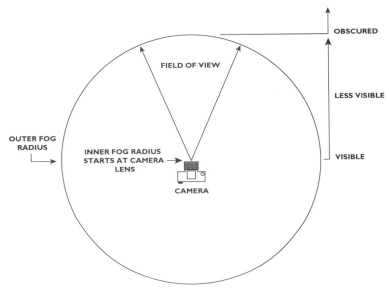

FIELD OF VIEW

OBSCURED

LESS VISIBLE

VISIBLE

OUTER FOG RADIUS

INNER FOG RADIUS STARTS AT CAMERA LENS →

CAMERA

FIGURE **10.8** *The fog starts directly at the camera lens...*

FIGURE **10.9** *...and creates the illusion that the camera is immersed in the fog.*

DEPTH OF FIELD WITH FOG

If you're intent on using fog to create the illusion of depth of field then read this section. If you want to use a better method, flip ahead to Chapter 12.

When trying to create the illusion of depth of field, try to set the color of the fog as close to the color of the background as possible. By using this method, the transition from foreground to background will appear more gradual. For example, if you were creating a scene with mountains in the distant background, you would set the color of the fog to a light sky blue color and have the mountains located just inside the outer circle, which defines the dropoff of the fog. In this way the mountains would be still visible, but on the threshold of becoming obscured. As a rule of thumb, try keeping the objects that are furthest away from the center of the fog just within the outside dropoff circle. Set the inner circle, which defines where the fog starts, at around 50% to 75% of the size of the outside circle.

Atmospheric Conditions

Now that you've gotten the basics down about fog you can use it for other weather or atmospheric conditions as well.

POLLUTION

For an atmosphere full of pollution such as that seen in Ridley Scott's *Blade Runner*, you can use fog. The idea is to make a light haze with the dropoff close to the outer boundary of your scene. Try using a light brownish orange for the color of the fog, and keep the fog density low. Remember to set the inside and outside circles a fair distance apart. Set the inside radius of the fog close to the camera so that the entire scene appears to be slightly fuzzy.

The lighting in the scene should be muted yellows and oranges, very deep in tone. Use multiple point lights with the intensity set to around 60% to 75%. Make sure to set the falloff of these light sources so that you don't overexpose the scene. The color of the ambient light should be a very dark bluish black. The level of ambient light should also be reduced so that there's a lot of contrast between the illuminated areas and the areas in shadow.

RAIN AND SNOW

When it's raining or snowing, there's usually a very high water content in the atmosphere. Use a little bit of fog to create a slight haze in the scene.

On rainy or snowy days it's usually overcast with many low lying clouds. The amount of illumination coming from the primary light source should be lowered to around 60% with the colors set to cool blues and grays. The level of the ambient light should be increased since there is a fair amount of light reflected from the low ceiling of clouds.

Tip. When you're creating a rainy or wet scene, remember to increase the reflectivity and specularity of your texture maps. Since the objects would be wet, they should appear slightly shiny or glossy.

SPECIAL LIGHTING CONSIDERATIONS

In reality any light source located in a setting with high atmospheric density tends to glow. For example, on a foggy day you can see the beams of light cast by street lamps or headlights. If you are creating a scene in your 3D application and using a high degree of fog to mimic an atmospheric effect, you should consider creating visible light sources. Unfortunately, this feature is not available in all programs. At the time of this writing, only three applications have visible light source features: Electric Image Animation System, form•Z, and Extreme 3D.

But don't despair, there are several ways to get around this limitation and is discussed in Chapter 11, Lighting Special Effects.

Tip. As a general rule of thumb, as the atmosphere becomes more dense, the amount of glow of a light source increases.

SECTION FOUR: OUTER SPACE

After watching so many different science fiction epics set in the deep recesses of outer space, or the thousands of news bites downloaded from the space shuttle, you can see that light from outer space behaves much differently than from on earth. The main reason that a scene looks so unique is that there is no atmosphere out there among the stars.

Vacuum

In a vacuum there is no dust or pollution to distort the transmission of light. That fact, in combination with the total absence of any gaseous atmosphere makes light react differently in outer space. Light does not attenuate noticeably in a vacuum. Since there is nothing in a vacuum to defract light beams, they tend to travel over a greater distance without dispersing. As a result, shadows tend to be very sharp and clearly defined.

Another consideration is that you should use a minimum number of light sources in an outer space scene. Use only one parallel light to achieve the most realistic results. Set the intensity of the light fairly high, close to 90% to 95%. The idea is to mimic the light cast by the sun or a distant star. The color of the light should be fairly close to white, and once again since there is no atmospheric distortion in outer space, the light does not become colored through refraction.

If you're using a spotlight in a scene for example, make sure that the edges of the light are sharp instead of soft, and the falloff set close to infinite. Another consideration is that you shouldn't use too much fog to create depth of field, if any at all. Without atmosphere objects in the far distance tend to be in sharp focus just like the objects in the foreground.

Ambient Light

One of the most important settings to consider when creating a scene set in outer space is ambient lighting. The ambient light level should be set to zero or turned off entirely. There is very little matter in space to reflect ambient light, so the areas in shadow should be completely black. The key to a realistic outer space scene is contrast between the areas that are lit and those in shadow.

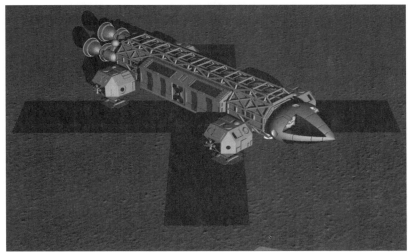

FIGURE *In this outer space scene rendered in StudioPro, there is a single parallel*
10.10 *light source, sharp-edged shadows, and zero ambient light.*

SECTION FIVE: UNDERWATER

The entertainment industry always seems to be setting movies and television shows in the deep briny blue. Everything from *Flipper* to Sea Quest have scenes set in the shallow tide pools and the deepest submarine trenches beneath the waves. The trick is knowing how to replicate these environments in your 3D application.

Depth

Before you even start to set up your lights and models, the first consideration is how deep is the water in which the action is occurring. Light reacts differently at various depths. Since water is a thousand times denser than air, the attenuation of light occurs over a much shorter distance. The intensity of your primary light source or sun should be configured to a higher intensity if the scene is to be set in shallow water. As the depth increases, the intensity of the primary light source should decrease. Since the light has to travel through much more water to reach the deeper regions of the ocean, the overall intensity of the light will be diminished. To recreate sunlight coming from above, use a parallel light source set close to perpendicular to the viewing plane.

The color of the light source should also be set according to depth. A scene set in shallow water would have a light blue green light while a scene set in a deep abyss would have a dark bluish black light if any at all. The amount of ambient light should also decrease according to the depth of the scene.

Tip. Try using an animated gel to reproduce the effect of sunlight passing through the waves on the surface of the water.

Fog

The most important factor in creating an underwater scene is fog. The fog setting can create the illusion of the density of the water as well as the amount of sediment or particulate in the surrounding environment.

Set the color of the fog to the color of the background. In many cases this color should be fairly dark. The minimum radius of the fog should be set directly on top of the camera or to a negative value if possible. The scene will tend to look more realistic since the camera appears to be immersed underwater or directly within the scene. Set the maximum radius of the fog close to the camera as well. Light does not travel far underwater and tends to fall off quickly.

Background

The color of the background depends entirely on the depth of the scene. For a scene set closer to the surface of the ocean, try using a gradient background with a lighter color near the top of the image and a darker color along the bottom. For a deep water scene use a solid colored background with deep blues, blacks, or greens.

Lighting

In deep water scenes there is a complete absence of natural illumination from above. Your scene should be lit by man-made light sources. Be sure to create models of objects that cast illumination, for example, spotlights on an underwater vehicle or strobe lights on a mining platform.

When it comes to setting the characteristics of underwater lights you should use both visible light sources or glowing lights in combination with lens flares. The base or origin of a light should have a lens flare, while the beam of light itself should also be glowing. You will need two types of lights to represent one light in a scene. A spotlight, for example, should have a lens flare at the point of the cone and the cone itself should be visible. Set the attenuation of all of the lights in the scene to be relatively small. Remember that light does not travel well underwater.

Tip. Don't have visible light sources? Read Chapter 11: Lighting Special Effects, for a work-around.

FIGURE *By using fog in this scene, the rear of the submarine blends into the*
10.11 *color of the background.*

SECTION SIX: ARTIFICIAL LIGHTING

You've spent days creating the perfect model, even longer creating your texture maps. Don't blow it all by just dropping one parallel light set at 100% intensity in the middle of your scene. Take the time to configure your lights carefully before committing to the final rendering.

Types of Artificial Lighting	Whether you're trying to light a boardroom or create a parking lot at night, you have to configure your artificial lights accordingly. Different types of light sources cast different types of light. For example, the professional lighting designer usually tries to work with halogen lights since they provide a light color that is closest to sunlight. But for other industrial applications such as street lamps, fluorescent lighting fixtures, or track lighting, a more industrial incandescent bulb is used.

HALOGEN

The closest of all of the artificial lights to natural sunlight is the halogen light. Halogen lights have bright whites that tend to be very warm. When recreating a halogen light in 3D, try to use a very focused light source such as a spotlight. If you use a point light, it might overexpose the scene and ruin the illusion. The falloff of a halogen light is fairly long, which is why they make excellent headlights or flashlights in reality.

LIGHTBULBS

This type of light source is perhaps the warmest of the lot. Use a point light to recreate a lightbulb, but be sure to set a very limited falloff for this light source. The color should be a warm yellow, and if your program has the visual light source capabilities, try adding a little bit of glow to the light.

FLUORESCENT

Perhaps the ugliest or the most unflattering of all light sources are the fluorescent lights. Fluorescent light tends to be a whitish blue green, which washes out its complementary colors of red and orange, which also happen to be very close to skin tones. Most people tend to look terrible under fluorescent lighting for this reason. Try using a tube light source for a fluorescent. Set the ambient color of the scene to a medium-grade gray that is close in color to the primary light source.

Sodium Vapor

These lights give you that weirdish orange yellow color. You see sodium vapor lamps used in industrial settings and in street lamps. Try using point lights that have a medium falloff and are set to a very saturated orange or yellow color. You'll notice that the color blue will become flattened and render out as more of a dark black.

Neon

Neon light sources are fairly easy to produce in a 3D program and it's usually a good idea to use a model to represent the neon. Make sure you increase the glow of the model's material and use a glow map in conjunction to create a convincing illusion. Neon tends to be very saturated in color.

CHAPTER

11

Lighting Special Effects

CHAPTER REQUIREMENTS
Basic understanding of
either Illustrator or
FreeHand, and
Photoshop.

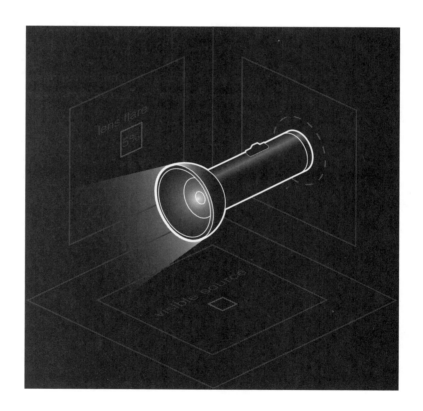

The Lighting Toolbox

Once you've configured all of the lights in your scene, established their spatial positions and set the color and intensity, the next step is to add a little bit more realism to the rendering. In the previous sections we dealt with the attenuation or the falloff of light and the density of the atmosphere. In this chapter we're going to cover lighting special effects that are available in some of the higher level programs, and work-arounds that will mimic them in lower level applications. The following sections cover lighting special effects that can make your work more realistic.

SECTION ONE: GELS, PROJECTORS, AND GOBOS

Just about any lighting professional involved in either Hollywood or Broadway is familiar with either gels or gobos. A good gel or gobo can change the mundane mood of a scene to the dramatic. Closely related to gels are projectors which are like slide or movie projectors. Projectors can be used for more common applications such as projecting a movie onto a surface or for more subtle effects such as mimicking light shining through water or the flickering flames of a fire.

SECTION TWO: VISIBLE LIGHT SOURCES

In the previous chapter we covered the use of fog to create a tangible atmosphere in a scene. In this chapter we'll take this a step further and create visible light sources. In reality, visible light sources occur when rays of light illuminate particles in the atmosphere. One example of this phenomenon is the visible beam of light cast from a lighthouse on a foggy night or from the headlights of a car. Even if your application doesn't support this feature, there are several work-arounds that can provide comparable if not superior results.

SECTION THREE: LENS FLARES

The irony of lens flares is that most videographers and cinematographers try to avoid this optical aberration. A lens flare occurs when light is refracted from the lens of the camera and creates a star burst effect. This usually occurs when either the camera is pointed directly at a light source or if a light source is particularly intense. For the 3D designer, this optical imperfection can be used to create effects ranging from duplicating the effects of a bright light to mimicking a star in the sky or the flash of an explosion.

SECTION ONE: GELS, PROJECTORS, AND GOBOS

In the most traditional definition, gels are translucent films of plastic that cover the opening of a spotlight. They are used solely to change the color cast by the light. In the theater and in film, a gel is usually a solid color, but in 3D the definition becomes slightly blurred. With most 3D applications you don't have to apply a gel to change the color of a light source since programs have a specific parameter for that function. A gel in 3D implies the ability to apply an opaque or colored pattern to a light source. Check your user's manual to see if your application supports this feature and read up on how to apply a gel to a light source.

Simple Gels

The simplest type of gel you can use in a 3D rendering is a black and white image. This image can be created in Photoshop and then imported into your 3D application. The areas that are white will let light shine through while the black areas will be completely opaque. Any area that is gray lets only a specific amount of light through relative to the brightness or darkness of the shade.

**T
U
T
O
R
I
A
L**

SIMPLE GEL TUTORIAL

For the following tutorials we're going to use Strata StudioPro as our primary application. The Strata model of the scene is included on the CD-ROM with all of the lighting, textures, and gels already preconfigured. If you don't have a copy of StudioPro, a save-disabled version is included on the CD-ROM. Since both the DXF models as well as the appropriate color maps are included on the CD-ROM, you can also modify the following tutorials to suit your own 3D application.

STEP ONE

We can start by either creating our own gel in Photoshop or using one of the presets in StudioPro. When creating your

CHAPTER ELEVEN

own simple black and white gel remember to set the bit depth to 8 bits per pixel to conserve on rendering resources. Since a grayscale gel uses only 256 shades of gray, you do not need to use a 24-bit image.

When you create your own gel such as the image in Figure 11.1, make sure you apply a little bit of Gaussian blur to the image. The idea is to make the edges of the shadows softer by creating less of a sharp edge. The gel, once it is applied to a light source, will mimic sunlight streaming through the panes of glass in a window.

FIGURE
11.1 *The white area in this gel will let light pass through and the black area will restrict the passage of light.*

STEP TWO

The next step in the process is to import the gel into your application and then apply it to the light source. In this case a parallel light should be used. The light should be set at approximately 80% intensity. Depending on your 3D application, you have the option to map an infinite number of repetitions of the gel onto the light source. In this case we're going to apply the gel infinitely on both the X and Y axes.

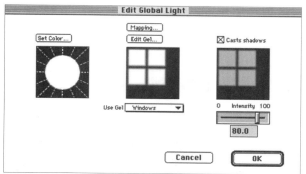

FIGURE **11.2** *Strata StudioPro allows the user to apply a grayscale image onto a light source as a gel.*

STEP THREE

Once the gel is applied to the parallel light source do one or two test renderings to make sure that the light is aligned properly before committing to the final rendering.

FIGURE **11.3** *The windows gel has been tiled onto a parallel light source and then rendered.*

ANOTHER SIMPLE GEL

You can use a simple grayscale gel to create different moods or atmospheres in your renderings. Try using a variety of different gels to achieve various results. It's easy to create the illusion of jungle sunlight streaming through a rain forest canopy or late afternoon light coming through venetian blinds.

FIGURE *This grayscale image can be used as a gel to* **11.4** *create the illusion of venetian blinds.*

FIGURE *Rendering of scene with venetian blinds gel.* **11.5**

T
U
T
O
R
I
A
L

CREATING CUSTOM GELS TUTORIAL

The previous two examples were fairly simple applications of a gel. In this section we're going to create a more complex gel to show how it can alter the entire mood of a scene. In this tutorial, we've used Onyx's TreePro to create the gel. Try following along with the save-disabled version of TreePro included on the CD-ROM.

STEP ONE

Launch the TreePro application. Set the color of the leaves and branches to black. Try using various types of leaves and branch sizes to create an interesting image. Manipulate the viewing angle of the tree until you're satisfied with the results. In the working version of the program you can save the image on screen as a PICT file. Since this is a save-disabled version, we've already included a gel created with TreePro.

FIGURE 11.6 *The TreePro application can also be used to create a custom gel for our 3D application.*

STEP TWO

Import the PICT of the tree into Photoshop. Apply a little Gaussian blur to the image and then save the file.

FIGURE
11.7
The grayscale gel of tree branches and leaves was created in TreePro.

STEP THREE

Open the model of the scene in StudioPro. Do a quick rendering of the scene without the gel applied. The image looks pretty good, but by applying a gel to the global light source we can make it better.

FIGURE
11.8
Rendering of the scene using a global light source with no gel applied.

STEP FOUR

Import the gel of the leaves into StudioPro and then apply it to the global light source using zero repetitions in the mapping dialog box.

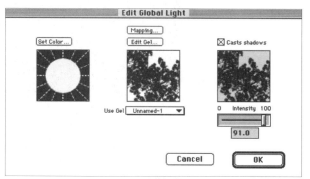

FIGURE
11.9 *Strata StudioPro lets the user apply a grayscale image as a gel to a light source.*

STEP FIVE

Configure the light color, intensity, and placement to your liking. Render the scene. Notice how the gel changes the entire look and mood of the image.

FIGURE
11.10 *Final rendering of the scene with a grayscale gel of leaves applied to the global light source.*

Tip. In a scene such as shown in Figure 11.10, with a large amount of shadows, try adding a low-intensity point light to fill some of the darker areas.

Complex Colored Gels

In the previous sections we used simple grayscale gels to create the illusion of light passing through trees, blinds, and windows. In this section we're going to use a multicolored gel to create more complex and interesting effects. Don't limit yourself to thinking only in terms of black and white; a gel is more than just an interesting way to create shadows.

T
U
T
O
R
I
A
L

STAINED GLASS TUTORIAL

In this tutorial we're going to create the illusion of sunlight streaming through a stained glass window to create a pattern of colored light on the ground. Once again the preconfigured StudioPro project file is included on the CD-ROM for your convenience.

STEP ONE

Import the model into your 3D application. Do a quick rendering of the scene so that you can get an idea of what the model looks like and where you would like to place your camera. Apply textures to the walls, floor, and wooden beams.

STEP TWO

Set up the lighting in the scene. Create a point or radial light source set to around 35% to 45% intensity in the middle of the model. Create a spotlight and place it close to the center of the round stained glass window. The spotlight will serve to recreate the light coming through the stained glass.

Tip. Notice the small target object out of view of the camera, below the floor of the chapel. By placing the target object where you want the center of the spotlight to fall and using the **Point At** function that is available in most 3D applications, you can save a tremendous amount of time aligning your light sources.

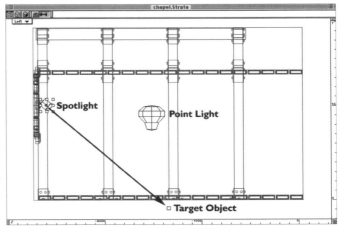

FIGURE *Side view of the chapel in Strata StudioPro.*
11.11

STEP THREE

Import the image of the stained glass window image into your 3D application. Apply the stained glass image to both the window as a texture and to the spotlight as a gel. Set the mapping of the gel to occur only once. When it comes to setting the physical attributes of the glass of the window, make the material 99% transparent and try using 1% glow (Figure 11.12).

Tip. The image of the stained glass window was first created in Illustrator and then rasterized in Photoshop. Another technique to try is scanning a photograph into the computer and then using Adobe's **Stained Glass** filter included in Gallery Effect 3.

STEP FOUR

Do a quick test rendering. Make sure that the angle of the cone of the spotlight is not larger than the colored area of the gel. Render away (Figure 11.13)!

Tip. If your program does not support gels, an easy work-around is to create a 2D rectangle in your scene and then apply a color map of the gel image to the rectangle. Set the material property of the rectangle or the color map to 99% transparency and then place a spotlight directly behind the rectangle. Make sure you use Raytracing as your rendering algorithm and then you're set.

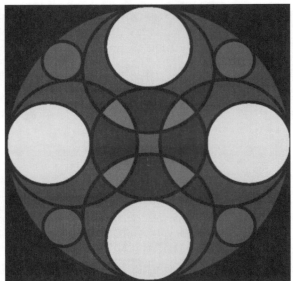

FIGURE 11.12 *The stained glass image should be used as both a gel for the spotlight and as a color map for the window in our 3D scene.*

FIGURE 11.13 *Final rendering of the scene using a colored gel to cast the image on the floor.*

Projectors

Projectors are closely related to gels, with the difference between the two being very slight. The primary distinction between a projector and a gel is that a projector can support moving pictures and is most like a real-world movie projector like that you would find at a theater. A gel on the other hand is only able to cast a static image. Another more subtle difference between the two is that the beam of light cast by a projector is rectangular and has sharp edges, while the beam of light cast by a spotlight with a gel is round and has softened edges. Simply put a projector is a rectangular spotlight with an animated gel attached.

In programs such as Strata StudioPro, you can apply a texture to a light source to create a multicolored gel. In the same vein, an animated texture can also be mapped to a spotlight to create a passable projector. The major problem with using this method is that the light cast will have a round shape.

FIGURE *This color map can be used as a gel for a spotlight.*
11.14

You'll notice that the image in Figure 11.15 is not cast from a true projector since the shape of the light is round rather than rectangular. The only program at the time of this writing that supports true projectors is VIDI's PresenterPro 3.0. But don't despair, if you desperately need a projector light there's an easy work-around that can mimic the effects of a projector.

FIGURE *The gel applied to a spotlight casts a round beam of light.*
11.15

T
U
T
O
R
I
A
L

PROJECTOR BOX TUTORIAL

There are a few software requirements that need to be considered before you start this tutorial. To create a work-around for projector lights you need a program that can handle animated color maps and also has a Raytracing engine.

STEP ONE

The key to creating a work-around for a projector is to first build a 3D model of a projector box. Start in your modeling application by building a box. Cut a space out of the front of the box where you want the light to shine through. Create a rectangle that fits into the window that you recently cut out of the front face of the box. Make sure that the dimensions of the rectangle match the proportions of your animated color map.

STEP TWO

Place a spotlight in the center of the box. Set the angle of the cone to 90°. Make sure that the beam of light cast by the spotlight shines through the window in the front of the box.

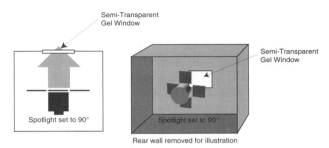

FIGURE 11.16 *By creating a 3D model of a projector you have a partial work-around for projector lights.*

STEP THREE

Create an animated color map and then map it onto the rectangle that you placed in the window in the front of the box. Set the transparency of the animated color map to 99% with the specular levels set to 0% and the ambient and diffuse levels around 30% to 50%.

STEP FOUR

Group the box, light, and rectangle together. Point the front of the box at where you want the light to fall. Make sure you use Raytracing as your algorithm when you render the image.

FIGURE 11.17 *Rendering of a scene lit by a projector box.*

Tip. If you have trouble with your projector box, such as the light still appearing round, make sure that your spotlight's cone angle is set to 90°. If that doesn't work, try moving the spotlight closer to the front window.

T
U
T
O
R
I
A
L

SUBMARINE TUTORIAL

In this tutorial, we're going to use the same animated texture map that we used in the Rippling Reflection Tutorial in Chapter 8. But instead of using the animated map as a reflectivity map, we're going to use it as a projector gel. If you don't have an application that supports projectors, go ahead and create a projector box as in the previous tutorial. Remember to use Raytracing as your rendering algorithm.

The goal of this section is to recreate the effects of sunlight shining through the surface of rippling water. By using a projector, we can create patterns of light on the body of a submarine.

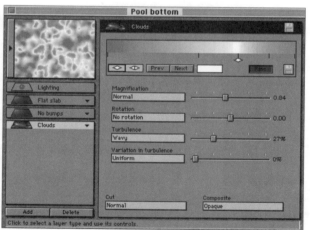

FIGURE *Adobe's TextureMaker was used to create the animated color*
11.18 *map for our animation.*

STEP ONE

The first step in the process is to create an animated color map. In this tutorial, Adobe's TextureMaker was used to create the color map (Figure 11.18).

Tip. When it comes to creating an animated map to be used in an animation, make sure that you know the length of the animation ahead of time. For example if your animation is 3 seconds long, make sure that all of your animated maps have a duration of 3 seconds. Another alternative is to loop your animated maps for the duration of the animation.

STEP TWO

Import the submarine model into your 3D application (Figure 11.19). When it comes to setting up the lighting, be sure to use a blue fog to simulate an underwater environment (see Chapter 10 for more information on this topic).

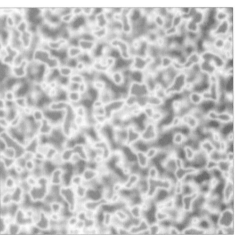

FIGURE **11.19** *Still image from the rippling water animated gel.*

STEP THREE

Map the animated color map onto the rectangle in your projector box or onto a light source. Render the scene using a Raytracing algorithm if necessary (Figure 11.20).

FIGURE   *Notice the rippling effects of the light on the surface of the*
11.20   *submarine created by using an animated gel.*

Gobos

If your 3D application doesn't support either gels or projectors, and all of the work-arounds have failed, you can always resort to gobos. In reality, gobos are simply 2D cutouts of shapes that are placed in front of a light source to create shadows. It's a lot like shadow puppets or making animals on the wall with your hands and a flashlight.

In 3D the process is very close to the tried and true flashlight and hand trick. When it comes to making your own gobos, a program such as Illustrator or FreeHand comes in very handy. Since gobos are usually extruded 2D shapes, using an illustration program can speed up modeling time tremendously. Also if your modeling program does not support Boolean functions, which is absolutely necessary when it comes to creating custom gobos, you will need to use one of the afore-mentioned programs in the modeling process. Refer back to Chapter 6 to the section on modeling with EPS files for more information.

A gobo in a 3D program is a 2D plane or an extruded object. It's just like a cardboard cutout placed over a light source. Gobos perform just about the same function as black and white gels, and if you have the choice of using either in your 3D application I would recommend using gels. Adding any unnecessary geometry to a rendering will only increase rendering time. The main problem with gobos is trying to configure the other lights in the scene around the gobo itself. If you're using a parallel light source in a scene with a gobo you have to be careful not to let the edges of the gobo cast a shadow. Another considera-tion is that the gobo itself should be out of the field of view of the camera so that it does not end up in the rendering.

T
U
T
O
R
I
A
L

GOBO OF STARS TUTORIAL

In this tutorial we're going to create a gobo in Illustrator and then import it into a 3D application.

STEP ONE

Create a series of stars in Illustrator using the **Create Stars** filter. Create a square and then subtract the stars from the square using the **Pathfinder** filter. Save the document as an EPS file and then import it into your 3D application.

FIGURE *Start by creating your gobo in Adobe Illustrator 5.0...*
11.21

FIGURE *...and then save the document*
11.22 *as an EPS file.*

STEP TWO

Place the gobo in front of a spotlight. Make sure that the cone of the spotlight does not cross the edges of the gobo. Group the gobo and spotlight together. Align the group accordingly and then render away.

FIGURE *Make sure that the cone of the spotlight does not cross the*
11.23 *edges of the gobo when aligning the objects in your 3D scene.*

SECTION TWO: VISIBLE LIGHT SOURCES

If you want to create an animation of a lighthouse on a foggy night or of a nuclear submarine cruising along in the depths of the ocean, the key to realistic results for either of these animations is visible light sources. The problem is that only three programs currently support this feature: Electric Image Animation System, Extreme 3D, and form•Z. Adding to this dilemma is the fact that form•Z does not have any animation features. Don't fret, there's a work-around that can replicate visible light sources with a minimum of fuss and hassle, and sometimes the results look even better than what's included in any of these programs.

Creating Visible Lights

Light sources become visible or glow when there is a high quantity of particles of matter in the surrounding atmosphere. That's why, on a foggy night, you can see the headlights of your car much easier than on a clear evening. In the case of underwater scenes, keep in mind that the atmosphere underwater is several thousand times denser than air, lending itself to visible lights much easier than on dry land.

Glowing Radial and Spotlights

Configuring a glowing light source in a 3D application is almost the same as setting the dropoff or attenuation of a normal light. A glowing light is usually composed of two separate parts, an inner and an outer halo. The inner halo should correspond to the hotspot of the light while the outer halo should be equal to the falloff. The glow of a visible light source is strongest in the inner circle of the light source and it falls off to a preconfigured level at the outer circle.

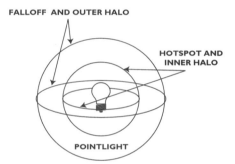

FALLOFF AND OUTER HALO

HOTSPOT AND INNER HALO

POINTLIGHT

FIGURE 11.24 *The glow of a visible radial light source is configured in the same manner as the falloff.*

FIGURE 11.25 *Rendering of a glowing radial light source from Electric Image.*

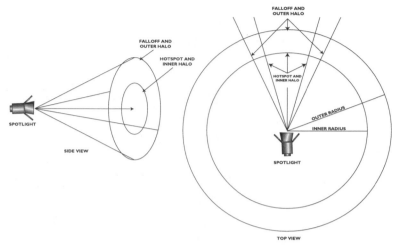

FIGURE
11.26

The falloff and glow of a visible spotlight source are configured in the same manner as the falloff.

FIGURE
11.27

Rendering of a glowing spotlight source from Electric Image.

The radius of the circle defining the glow should not exceed the falloff for obvious reasons. Resist the temptation to keep the setting for the falloff of either type of light source set to infinity. If a light source is glowing, the edge of the glow should be the terminating line for illumination. Remember that if the atmosphere is dense enough to support a visible light source, the light will not be able to travel far because of all of the particles obscuring the rays of light.

Visible light sources are great for recreating the effects of light in a dense atmosphere. Glowing radial light sources make wonderful red beacons or strobe lights on ships and airplanes. Also with a little bit of fiddling around you can create the illusion of a sun or a moon in the sky. Glowing spotlights can be used for just about any model that casts light such as a lighthouse or street lamp.

Tip. Whenever you use a visible light source in a rendering, make sure to use some degree of fog. If the atmosphere is dense enough for lights to glow, then the visibility level in the scene should be low.

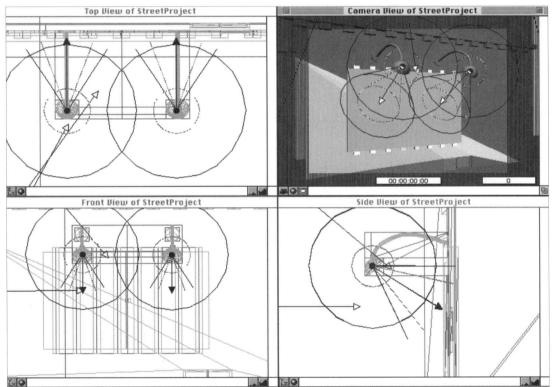

FIGURE *Wireframe of a scene with visible light sources in Electric Image 2.5.*
11.28

FIGURE
11.29
Rendering of the scene with visible light sources done in Electric Image.

MAKING YOUR OWN VISIBLE LIGHT SOURCES

Now that you've been tempted by what you can't have, you can either resign yourself to the fact that there won't be any visible light sources in your renderings or you can learn how to make your own. Making your own visible light sources is a three-step process, involving modeling, texture mapping, and material creation.

T
U
T
O
R
I
A
L

DESK LAMP TUTORIAL

In this tutorial we're going to create our own visible light source for a desk lamp. The goal of this section is to construct a convincing illusion of a beam of light in the scene. Instead of relying on the software to create a beam of light we will construct a beam in our 3D modeling program. After that we'll create a material that will look like a ray of light complete with a transparency map.

STEP ONE

The first step in the process is to make the beam of light in your 3D modeling program. You should use a certain degree of precision when it comes to aligning the beam to the head of the lamp. In this case since the lamp is like a spotlight, we're going to use a cone-shaped object for the beam. If we were making a glowing radial light source we would use a sphere.

When making the cone for the beam be sure to construct only the sides of the cone and not the base and top. In this case a good method would be to draw a line from to bottom of the head of the lamp to the surface of the desk. The next step would be rotate or lathe that line around a central axis to create the beam.

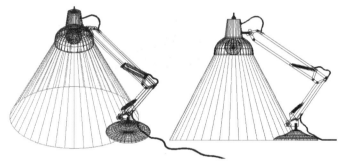

FIGURE **11.30** *The first step is to create a 3D model of the beam of light cast by the table lamp.*

STEP TWO

Once the model has been completed and imported into your rendering application, you need to create a material or set the physical properties of the light beam. Try using the following settings:

Ambient:	50%
Diffuse:	50%
Specular:	0%
Transparency:	99%
Glow:	1% to 99%

The idea is to set the physical properties so that the beam of light appears to glow, is evenly shaded, and is transparent all at the same time. For the rest of the lamp, apply a metallic substance to the model.

Edge Density

One of the physical properties not mentioned in the previous chapters is edge density. If your program supports this feature it is very useful when creating glowing objects. By altering the edge density or the level of transparency of the edges of a material, the user can make the object appear to glow or radiate light. Edge density simply controls the level of transparency of an object's edges independent of the rest of the object. Edge density works best on curved or rounded shapes rather than straight-edged objects. In form•Z, for example, the user can set the density of both the inner and outer area of an object.

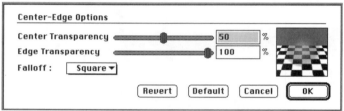

FIGURE 11.31 *form•Z RenderZone 2.75 lets the user set the inner and outer edge density of a material.*

In the case of this model, we would want the density of the edge of the beam of light to be more transparent than the center of the beam. By setting the edge density or amount of transparency of the center of the beam to 50% and the density of the outer edge to 100% you can create a convincing illusion of a glowing light (Figure 11.32).

STEP THREE

The next step is to apply a grayscale image as a transparency map to the beam of light. The transparency map was created in Photoshop using the gradient fill tool. By using a transparency map that has a gradual vertical transition from black to white, the beam of light can be made to look as if it is semitransparent near the head of the beam, and then completely transparent near the base (Figure 11.33).

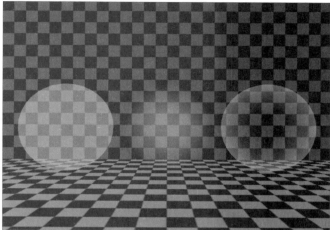

FIGURE **11.32** *This figure uses 50% center transparency/50% edge transparency (left), 50% center transparency/100% edge transparency (center), 100% center transparency/50% edge transparency (right).*

FIGURE **11.33** *The transparency map for the beam of light is a gradient fill created in Photoshop. The map will make the beam opaque at the top and transparent at the bottom.*

STEP FOUR

Create a spotlight and then center it within the head of the table light. Point the light downward toward the table top. Make sure that the circle cast by the spotlight matches the exact diameter of the model of the light cone. Set the intensity of the spotlight to around 90%. Add an additional parallel light source to the scene set to around 30% intensity.

Step Five

For an added touch of realism we're going to create a smoke effect for the cigarette in the scene with a transparency map. Figure 11.34 shows what the model of the cigarette looks like in wireframe mode. Notice that above the cigarette where the smoke would appear is a 2D rectangular shape. By mapping a color map to this shape, in addition to a transparency map, we can create the illusion of smoke.

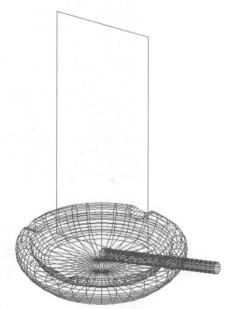

Figure **11.34** *A color map of smoke is applied to the 2D shape to create the illusion that the cigarette is smoking.*

The color map was created in Photoshop with the airbrush tool, and then distorted with the smudge tool. The color map can then be inverted if necessary and used as a transparency map.

FIGURE
11.35
Color and transparency map for the smoke

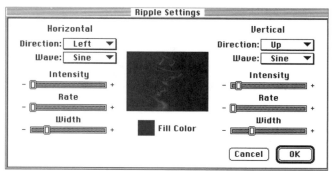

FIGURE
11.36
*By using the **Ripple** filter in Adobe Premiere 4.0 we can transform the smoke image into an animated map.*

Tip. If you want to animate the smoke, import the still image into Premiere or After Effects and change the duration or length of the still to 3 seconds. Apply the **Ripple** filter to the clip (Figure 11.36) and then render the movie (Figure 11.37). Import the clip into your 3D program and then apply it to the rectangle as both a color and transparency map. See Chapter 14, Animation Special Effects, for more on this subject.

FIGURE **11.37** *The animated map can be applied to the 2D rectangle and then rendered to create the illusion of smoke.*

FIGURE **11.38** *Final rendering of the scene using a 3D model for the visible light source coming from the table lamp.*

STEP SIX

Apply textures to the rest of the objects in the scene and then do a test rendering to make sure that your lights and textures are configured correctly. Render the scene (Figure 11.38).

Tip. For a more realistic effect, try modeling two cones for your spotlight. The inner cone should be brighter and slightly less transparent than the outside cone. Make sure that the inner cone corresponds to the diameter of the hotspot of the light source and that the outer cone matches the diameter of the falloff.

SECTION THREE: LENS FLARES

It's ironic that one of the most sought-after special effects on the Mac platform is usually a sign of poor cinematography. Lens flares occur when a camera is pointed directly at a light source, causing light to refract off of the surface of the lens. This refraction creates a star burst or glowing halo around the light source within the field of view of the camera. Of course, in the virtual world of 3D, the camera has to be configured for the optical distortions created by a nonexistent lens. In order for an animation to appear more realistic, imperfections have to added to our perfect world.

A lens flare is particularly useful to the 3D designer for a number of reasons. A lens flare can be used to create the illusion of a distant sun in the sky, it can be animated to look like an explosion, or it can simply be applied to a light source so that it looks more realistic to the viewer.

There are two major drawbacks to using lens flares in 3D. The first problem is the fact that it is one of the most overused and misapplied special effects. Just about every low-budget television commercial using CGI (computer-generated imagery) tends to use lens flares.

The key to using a lens flare is subtlety. It's easy to get caught up in the flashy look, but a more subtle effect is more realistic. Since bright lights are the most common source of lens flares, there are a few rules of thumb when it comes to using a lens flare in conjunction with a light source:

- When using multiple lens flares in a scene, keep the brightness level low. Don't overpower the scene and obscure the action. Remember cinematographers try to avoid this effect!
- When applying a lens flare, start at a low value and then gradually increase the brightness level of the flare.

- Use different brightness levels for each light source in a scene. Don't set every flare to the same level.
- Use your common sense when applying a lens flare to a scene. Make sure that the light source will first of all be visible to the camera, and that it is strong enough to cast a flare. Lens flares are most evident with strong, intense light sources. The flame from a blowtorch for example casts a very bright lens flare.

The second problem associated with lens flares is the fact that only one 3D rendering program supports this feature. Electric Image lets the user attach a lens flare to any light source in a scene. If you're not using Electric Image, your only alternative is to add a lens flare in postproduction in a program such as Adobe's After Effects or Premiere. In this chapter we're only going to cover the basics of the different types of lens flares, and when to use one. In Chapter 16 we'll cover how to add a lens flare in postproduction.

Types of Lens Flares

In reality you get a different type of lens flare with a different type of camera lens. In 3D you don't even have a lens much less a real camera. All of the optical aberrations and imperfections caused by a camera lens such as focal distance, distortion, and lens flares have to be calculated via the software.

Programs such as Electric Image, Photoshop, Premiere, and After Effects let the user choose from three different types of camera lens, which produce three different types of flares. Figure 11.39 shows the lens flare interface from Adobe Photoshop. While Electric Image lets the user configure just about every aspect of the lens flare ranging from ring size to halo color, most users will only be concerned with the brightness of the flare.

Tip. One problem with adding a lens flare to an animation in postproduction is that the light source creating the lens flare can become obscured by an object in the foreground. One work-around is to render the foreground model first with the background as an alpha channel. The next step is to render the background without the foreground model. Then add the animated lens flare to the background in your postproduction application. Finally add the foreground model to the lens flare and background composition.

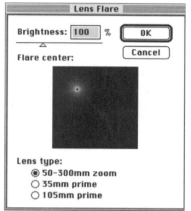

FIGURE **11.39** *The Adobe Photoshop lens flare plug-in filter can be accessed in just about any program that supports the plug-in architecture.*

FIGURE **11.40** *Lens flare created with a 50–300mm zoom lens.*

FIGURE *Lens flare created with a 35mm prime lens.*
11.41

FIGURE *Lens flare created with a 105mm prime lens.*
11.42

Uses for Lens Flares

Now that you've gotten a basic grounding on what lens flares are, you can start using them in your animations. Some of the more basic uses of a lens flare range from distant stars, to explosions, to bright light sources in a scene.

LENS FLARES AND LIGHT SOURCES

When creating a lens flare for a light source in postproduction, it's a good idea to center the flare on the light source itself. Remember that a lens flare is only visible if the object that is casting the light is visible. For example, if you wanted to add a lens flare to a model of a table lamp, there would only be a flare if the bulb is visible to the viewer.

 Tip. Try using a lens flare in conjunction with a glowing radial light source when creating the engine exhaust of an airplane or rocket ship.

FIGURE *Rendering of a scene with two light sources with lens flares.*
11.43

LENS FLARES AND EXPLOSIONS

By animating the brightness of a lens flare over time, it can be made to seem as if there is an explosion occurring on the screen. In Chapter 14, Animation Special Effects, we'll cover creating an animated color map to be used in conjunction with a lens flare to create a first-class explosion with a shock wave.

Tip. Tired of using tube lights as laser beams? Try using a lens flare instead. In your outer space epic, a lens flare makes a great sci-fi torpedo or missile.

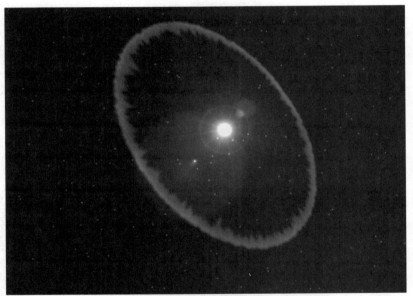

FIGURE *Rendering of a lens flare used in conjunction with an animated color*
11.44 *map to produce an explosion with a shock wave.*

LENS FLARES AS STARS

Using a lens flare as a star is one of the more gratuitous effects that you can create on screen. The easiest method is to add them to your background images and then composite the entire image in postproduction. We'll use the image in Figure 11.45 again in Chapter 16, Postproduction, as a composited background.

Perhaps one of the most visually inspiring applications for a lens flare is to place the flare behind a planet, and then pan the camera slowly around so that the flare peeks out slowly from behind the planet. Many of the larger studios use this technique in their theatrical trailers.

FIGURE
11.45
A lens flare can be used in a background image as a star.

FIGURE
11.46
Rendering of a lens flare placed near the edge of a planet.

12 Perspective and the Virtual Camera

CHAPTER REQUIREMENTS
Basic understanding of
Photoshop.

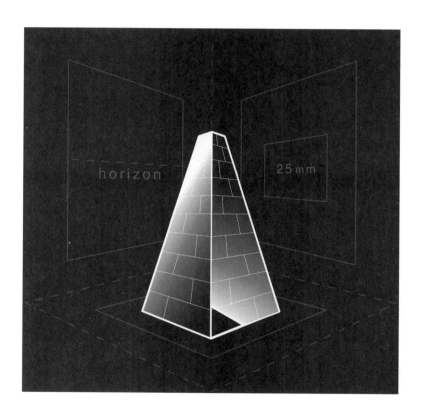

We already know how to light our scene, now we have to figure out how to shoot it. Our most basic tool in animation is the camera. The key to good cinematography in 3D is knowing about two things: perspective and the virtual camera.

SECTION ONE: PERSPECTIVE

The groundwork for this chapter is learning about perspective. You see it every day, but can you explain how it works?

SECTION TWO: THE VIRTUAL CAMERA

How a real world camera corresponds to the virtual camera is of importace to 3D animators. Here we give an explantion of focal length and of field of view and its relation to perspective.

SECTION THREE: DEPTH FIELD

We'll discuss what depth of field is and how to recreate the illusion of depth of field accurately.

SECTION ONE: PERSPECTIVE

There are many things that we take for granted on a daily basis and there are things that we don't even realize exist until they're no longer there. Perspective is one of those funny little things. As objects move off into the distance, they appear smaller. That's a fairly easy concept to grasp. Try moving a pen forward and backward in front of you. The pen grows smaller as you move it further away from your eyes. Now that you've gotten the basic premise down, think about this one. As parallel lines recede into the distance, they appear to converge.

A real-world example of this phenomenon is a long straight road or railroad track heading toward the horizon. As a pair of railroad tracks recedes into the distance, the space between the two rails appears smaller. The two rails which are parallel in reality, seem to coverage at a certain point close to the horizon. These two concepts, parallel lines converging and objects shrinking as they are moved further into the background, are two of the more important traits of perspective.

FIGURE **12.1** *Parallel lines appear to converge and objects appear to shrink when receding into the background.*

Orthographic vs. Perspective Views

While you and I might notice the optical aberrations of perspective, our computers might not. After all they're only a box full of chips and wires and, excluding concepts such as fuzzy logic, they tend to deal only in absolutes. Our computers don't notice things such as perspective unless we tell them to. Humans on the other hand need perspective in order to judge concepts such as depth and distance. Images created without perspective tend to look a little unusual or unbalanced. Take art from the Dark Ages for example, all of the illuminated manuscripts and paintings were devoid of perspective and they tended to look flat. On the other hand, paintings and drawings from the Renaissance had more depth because they managed to convey perspective.

Strangely enough, modern-day 3D artists have to work in an axonometric or orthographic environment when modeling and animating. When creating a model in a 3D application, we have to model in an orthographic or axonometric mode or without perspective. If we tried to model with perspective turned on, the results would be disastrous. Since we're dealing with 3D objects on a 2D monitor, we have no depth cues to determine distance or spatial relationships.

It's far easier to understand 3D when given absolutes. For example, if we were looking at three cubes of the same size head on, they would look like the image in Figure 12.2.

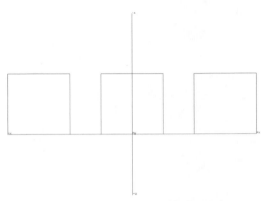

FIGURE
12.2 *Three cubes viewed in an orthographic or axonometric viewpoint in form•Z.*

Since we're looking at these cubes with perspective turned off, we can tell that they are all the same size and rest on the X axis. But if we looked at the same model with perspective turned on, the entire image changes. In Figure 12.3 we can see that the three cubes are at different depths. The problem is since we have no depth cues such as depth of field or atmospheric haze, we cannot judge the relative size of each cube.

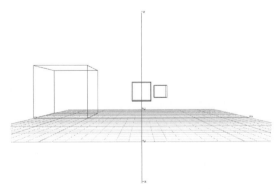

FIGURE
12.3 *The same three cubes viewed with perspective turned on in form•Z.*

When modeling in the orthographic mode, we're able to view the 3D model in absolute terms. By using tiled windows, we can see several perspectives of the model and then judge depth and spatial location. Another alternative to tiled windows is to use multiple monitors for various model perspectives.

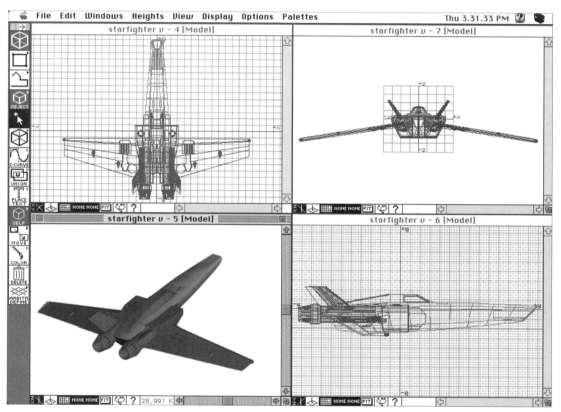

FIGURE *The user can see a model from multiple angles using the tiling option in auto•des•sys form•Z 2.75.*
12.4

While the orthographic mode is fine for creating a model, it does not work well for a rendered animation. For example if we looked at all of our models without perspective, they wouldn't look quite right. They would appear flat or unbalanced. That's where perspective and the virtual camera come into play.

SECTION TWO: THE VIRTUAL CAMERA

Perspective, or the lack thereof, can do a lot to a scene. The absence of perspective can make your image look flat or unnatural; too much perspective and things seem out of kilter or shaky. Is there more than one type of perspective? For the human eye no, but for the camera lens, yes. The camera lens can play all sorts of tricks with light. It can zoom in on far-off objects, or it can pan out and capture an entire panoramic view. And with a little bit of mathematical wizardry on the part of those programming geniuses, all of that can also be done in 3D with the virtual camera.

All About Cameras

First of all we need a brief primer on how a real camera actually works. A camera can be broken down into a couple of major components, the lens and the film. Sure there are many more parts to a camera but these are the ones that are relevant to us.

The lens takes light from the real world and focuses it on a piece of film. The film part is fairly easy to comprehend, it's the lens that can be tricky. A camera lens just isn't a barrel of metal with two pieces of glass stuck in it. There are usually several lenses on the inside of the barrel as well as a few sets of mirrors. To further complicate the issue, there are a multitude of different sizes of lenses available for the consumer ranging from a 10mm to upwards of a 600mm lens.

What exactly do those numbers stand for? Those metric numbers, otherwise known as the focal length of a lens, refer to the distance light travels from the front of the camera lens to the focal plane. The greater the distance light has to travel through a lens, the more magnified the image. Any lens measuring over 50mm is regarded as either a telephoto or zoom lens and magnifies an image. On the other hand any lens in the 15mm to 10mm range is regarded as a fish-eye lense since it can capture a broad, wide-angle panoramic shot.

As lens size or focal length increases two things occur: The field of view grows smaller and the effects of perspective diminish. The opposite occurs when the focal length of a lens decreases: The field of view and the amount of distortion or perspective increases.

Important. The field of view of a camera is inversely proportional to the length of the camera lens. As the length of the lens increases, magnification increases and the field of view and amount of perspective decrease.

FIELD OF VIEW

As the length of a camera lens increases, the field of view decreases. This kind of makes sense if you think that if you zoom in on an object, you will see more of the object in your frame and less of the surroundings. The field of view is basically what you see out of the viewfinder of your camera. The field of view or FOV is measured in degrees and is also referred to as the camera angle.

To better understand how the field of view of a camera works, you should first understand the field of view of the human eye. The field of view of the average human being is 30° to either side of the line of sight. In other words when staring straight ahead, the average person can see objects within a 60° arc. But on an average only objects within 48° arc are in focus. Everything outside of that arc is considered to be peripheral vision and is somewhat fuzzy.

Tip. Try opening and closing one eye to see how much your field of view decreases and increases. Also notice that you lose your depth perception since you no longer have binocular vision. That's what it would feel like to be a pirate.

Even though the field of view of a human is fixed, a camera's field of view can be changed. A camera's FOV is directly related to two factors: the size of the lens and the size of the film. Just when you thought it was getting easy, I've gone and made it more complicated.

By this point you should understand that as the size of the lens increases, the field of view decreases. In reality, depending on the size of the film, the field of view can vary. For example a 35mm camera and a 70mm motion picture camera using the same lens size have vastly different fields of view. But here's the good news. Since our computers have to artificially calculate the FOV for our render-

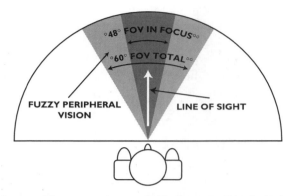

FIGURE *The average human field of view is 60° of which*
12.5 *only 48° is in sharp focus.*

ings, the FOV is based on a set film size regardless of the size of our camera window. Most people understand the FOV associated with their 35mm format cameras so the majority of 3D applications are based on this format. So go ahead and change the dimensions of your rendering window, chances are it won't effect the FOV of the camera dramatically.

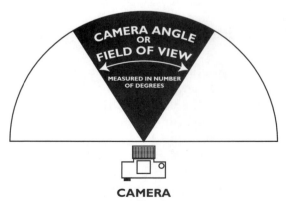

FIGURE *A camera's field of view is much like a human's*
12.6 *except that it can be changed with various lenses*
or film types.

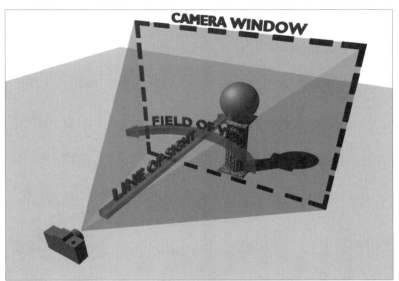

FIGURE *A 3-dimensional representation of a camera's field of view.*
12.7

THE VIRTUAL CAMERA

Finally we get to how a real camera ties in to our virtual camera. Our computer works in absolutes. It has no grasp of depth perception, perspective, or even a sense of humor unless we program it to do so.

Perspective has no real place in the modeling process unless it is to get a preview of what the model might look like when rendered. But perspective is imperative when we finally come to scripting and rendering our animation. Without perspective, a scene looks unnatural and unbalanced. So how do we give the computer a sense of perspective? Since it would be extremely difficult to give our computer a pair of eyes to see the scene with, we instead give it the virtual camera.

Both lens size/focal length and field of view are programmed into the virtual camera. Specially designed algorithms can calculate the amount of magnification and FOV of a scene so that it will appear more natural. But that isn't enough. A real camera experiences distortion of perspective when various types of lenses are used. For example, a 10mm or fish-eye lens can capture a wide-angle panoramic shot but tends to bubble or warp the edges of the image. Conversely a tele-photo or 50mm lens can zoom in on an object far closer than the human eye could, but the image is flattened and the sense of perspective is diminished. The irony of the situation is that while the real-world photographer spends thousands of dollars on lenses that do not distort images, the 3D designer tries to replicate the distortion in order to make the animation appear more real.

As lens size increases, the effects of perspective on the image decrease. Our 3D camera's have been programmed to handle the three major factors of real-world photography: field of view, lens size, and perspective distortion. In the following illustrations, you can see how both the field of view and the effects of perspective change as the lens size increases.

Just about every 3D program available today lets you set either the lens size or focal length and field of view of a camera. Fortunately the computer handles the amount of perspective in the scene. The advantages of being able to use various types of camera lenses are numerous. The entire feeling or mood of an animation can be conveyed through the type of lens used. For example, if you were creating an animation

FIGURE *The camera for this rendering has a 15mm lens with a field of view*
12.8 *of 109°.*

FIGURE 12.9 *The camera for this rendering has a 23mm lens with a field of view of 85°.*

FIGURE 12.10 *The camera for this rendering has a 48mm lens with a field of view of 48°.*

FIGURE **12.11** *The camera for this rendering has a 167mm lens with a field of view of 15°.*

of a fly-through of a city or canyon, you could use a wide-angle lens to get the giddy, unbalanced feeling of high-speed flight. On the other hand, if you were creating an animation of a dancing soup can, a larger telephoto lens should be used to zoom in and focus the center of attention on the product.

SECTION THREE: DEPTH OF FIELD

With a real-world camera, we can adjust the f-stop to blur the foreground, background, or both in a picture. The area in a photograph that is in focus is referred to as the *depth of field*. When I first discovered that I could do this with a camera I had to ask myself why? But once it was explained to me, it made perfect sense. It has to do entirely with composition. If your subject is in the foreground, then you might want the background to be out of focus so it would not detract from the scene and vice versa for a subject in the background. If the subject is in the midground, then you could blur both the foreground and the background.

Tip. Having problems visualizing what depth of field is? Hold out your hand in front of your face. Look at your hand. Notice that as you look at your hand, any object in the background is out of focus as well as any object in the foreground such as your arm or shoulder. The camera lens works in the same way.

The range of the depth of field is controlled by the f-stop or aperture opening in the camera. As the camera's aperture opening increases, the range of the depth of field decreases. In other words more of the picture becomes blurry as the aperture opens wider. The aperture opening on our virtual camera is regarded as a pinhole. What this means is that the image will be completely in focus 100% of the time.

Unfortunately no 3D software application on the Mac lets you change the aperture opening for the 3D camera. But there is a work-around. If you want to create the illusion of depth of field, and have portions of your animation or still image blurry, use the following technique.

T
U
T
O
R
I
A
L

DEPTH OF FIELD TUTORIAL

Many beginning 3D animators just use fog to create the illusion of depth of field. While this method might fool some of the people some of the time, it's just not very accurate. In this tutorial we're going to use fog, but in a completely different manner than what you're probably accustomed to.

STEP ONE

Render your 3D scene or animation normally and then create a copy of your project file (Figure 12.12).

STEP TWO

Open the copy of the project file. Remove all textures from the scene. Turn off any special rendering effects such as bump mapping, glow, shadows, and transparency. Set the ambient light value to 100% or completely white. Turn on the fog in your 3D scene and set the color to

FIGURE *The first step is to render your 3D scene normally.*
12.12

black. You want the fog to start at your camera and the outer perimeter of fog to reach the furthest edge of your 3D model. Choose a fast rendering engine such as Phong and then render the scene. It should take less time than the previous rendering. The resulting image should be completely in grayscale.

FIGURE *The next step is to rerender the scene making sure you turn off*
12.13 *all of the special rendering, set the ambient light to 100%, and use black fog.*

STEP THREE

Import both the color and grayscale image into Photoshop. Take the grayscale image and then invert the colors using the **Convert** > **Invert** command from the **Image** menu. Adjust the **Levels** so that the foreground color is completely black, and that background color is more or less white. Copy the entire image to the clipboard.

FIGURE *The image is then inverted and the levels adjusted.*
12.14

STEP FOUR

Create a new Alpha channel for the color image. Paste the entire grayscale image into the Alpha channel for the color image. Go to the **Select** menu and choose **Load Selection**. Choose **Channel #4**. Go to the **Filter** menu and then choose **Blur** > **Gaussian Blur**. Use anywhere from 1 to 2 pixels for the blur. Click the **OK** button and you're done.

Tip. If you don't invert the color of the image in Step Three the objects in the foreground will be blurry and the background objects in focus.

By using this method you can add a selective blur or depth of field to any part of your image. In Chapter 16, Postproduction, we cover how to add an Alpha channel to a 24-bit movie in DeBabelizer. Once an Alpha channel has been added to a clip, then you can apply the depth of field method to an animation in DeBabelizer.

FIGURE *By using the Alpha channel selection and the Gaussian blur*
12.15 *filter, the illusion of depth of field can be created.*

Layering for Depth of Field

Another method for creating the illusion of depth of field is rendering your animation or still image in layers. Separate the foreground and the background objects into groups or layers and then render them separately with the background as an Alpha channel. In postproduction apply a varying degree of Gaussian blur to each layer before compositing them into one image.

MOTION BLUR

This technique also works for creating the illusion of motion blur. For example, either a foreground or background image could be blurred while the remaining parts of the animation could stay focused. Unfortunately this method is only partially accurate. Motion blur occurs when the shutter and film/video speed of a camera are so slow that a rapidly moving object appears blurred when photographed. Only a few 3D applications offer motion blur, and to this day I still haven't found an adequate work-around for this effect.

CHAPTER

13

Animation: The Magic of Movement

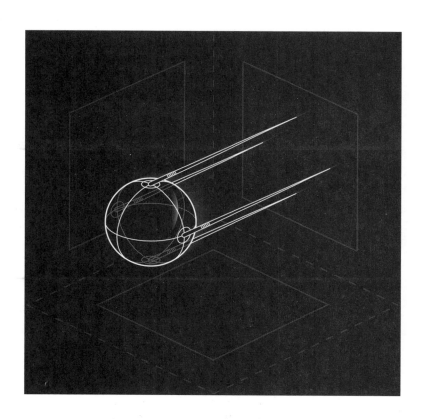

The models have been completed, and the texture maps applied. The long hours that you spent setting up your lights have finally paid off. Now it's time to play movie director and make your models move and dance.

When elaborate cel animation was in its heyday during the reign of Walt Disney, a typical project had a staff of hundreds. Dozens of artists, choreographers, and directors were needed to accomplish the most simple cartoon. Today it's all up to you and your computer.

Even though you don't have the staff of hundreds to back you up you can produce your own feature-length film in probably far less time. It's ironic that even though technology has changed the face of animation tremendously, the technique and theory behind creating an animation remains the same.

SECTION ONE: A BRIEF HISTORY OF ANIMATION

The background of animation and how it relates to 3D is discussed. Learn where the terms *keyframe, cel,* and *tweening* come from.

SECTION TWO: SCRIPTING YOUR ANIMATION

This is the process of putting your ideas to a time line. The concepts of model heirachy, links, and the parent–child relationship are detailed.

SECTION THREE: MOTION THEORY

Velocity, speed, anticipation, and exaggeration make up our study of motion theory.

SECTION FOUR: BASIC CINEMATOGRAPHY

The basic camera movements, pan, zoom, and dolly are explained.

SECTION ONE: A BRIEF HISTORY OF ANIMATION

An animation is simply a series of rapidly changing pictures flashed in front of your eyes. The earliest forms of animation were displayed on rotoscopes or in flip books. A rotoscope is constructed of a pair of cylinders. The outside cylinder is perforated with a series of vertical slits and the inside cylinder is covered in a series of pictures.

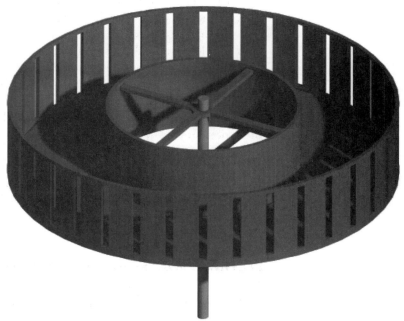

FIGURE
13.1   *The outside cylinder of a rotoscope has a series of slits or windows and the inside cylinder is covered with a series of pictures.*

As both cylinders are spun, the image appears to move when viewed through the slits, which serve as a type of primitive shutter mechanism. Because of an optical phenomenon known as *persistence of vision,* which is when our brain registers an image even after it is gone, the human eye can be fooled into perceiving motion. A flip book works in much the same way. A series of pictures are flipped in rapid succession and through persistence of vision they appear to move. Both television and film work following almost the same principle. A movie projector displays 24 frames per second while a television shoots out 60 fields or 30 frames per second. All that we're looking at is a series of pictures flashed rapidly before our eyes. Animation is simply a series of sequential still frames that, when viewed properly, appear to move.

Cel-Based Animation

Animation is a logical offshoot of the film industry since the technology is so closely related. The problem with creating an animation in the past was the amount of labor required to produce even the shortest piece. The process involved hundreds of skilled artisans and professionals and was a time-consuming process.

Production started with a storyboard, and then went to the top artists who divvied up the workload. Each character in an animation was assigned to individual lead artists to ensure consistency. A lead artist would then sketch out the character on a piece of transparent celluloid film. The celluloid film or cel was transparent so that the background image could be seen through the multiple layers of cels. Using this technique the background would only have to be drawn once. The lead artist gradually became known as the *keyman* since he would only draw the most important parts of the action. Those important segments in an animation then became known as *keyframes*.

The workload would then trickle down to the hundreds of minions who would draw the frames between the keyframes, a process referred to as *tweening*. Once all of the sketches were completed, they were then colored and layered on top of the background to be shot to film.

Computer-Based Animation

Now it's up to you, and your Mac. The process hasn't changed all that much since the days of Disney, but thankfully the technology has. Your role in the animation process is simple: You play the director and the key man or key woman. The computer takes care of all of the grunt work involved in tweening and coloring the frames. The background will be put into the scene in postproduction thanks to the all mighty Alpha channel.

SECTION TWO: SCRIPTING YOUR ANIMATION

Your producer has handed you the storyboard. Your art department has just delivered all of the models. Your job is to make them move. What do you do? Panic, of course; it makes your job look harder than it actually is and someone might actually notice and give you a raise. Another alternative is to script your animation. Your tools? A big piece of graph paper, a pencil, your computer, and your brain.

While just about every Mac animation program is based on a keyframe system, not every one has an easy-to-use interface or offers the same number of features. This is why the scripting process is so important. It's also usually easier to work on a hard copy of a script rather than directly on the computer.

An animation script varies from the storyboard in the fact that it is much more precise in terms of time and spatial location. Also there are no illustrations included with an animation script since the script is usually written by the animator for his or her own personal use.

An animation script is simply a long time line that plots keyframes. It's usually easiest to take a piece of graph paper and write out your time code along the longer edge, and then write the list of the models and the individual parts that you wish to animate along the shorter edge. An EPS template is included on the CD-ROM that you can print out and use for your own projects.

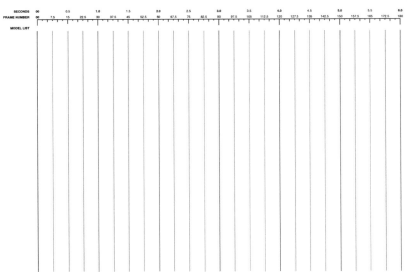

FIGURE
13.2
This is a blank animation template that can be used to script your project.

But before we get to scripting our animation, we need to first cover the concept of a dual coordinate system in animation.

Coordinate Systems

By this point in time you should know the X, Y, Z coordinate system like the back of your hand. When it comes time to animate your models, your grasp of coordinate system geometry will be put to the highest test. You've used it all through the entire modeling process and you should be able to read it as easily as a road map.

WORLD COORDINATES

Whenever you're scripting an animation, it is important to remember that you will be using two coordinate systems. The first coordinate system is fixed and is the absolute coordinate system of the world of the animation. This system is unalterable and remains constant. The map analogy works best in this case. For example, imagine that you're looking at a map of the United States. The direction north will always remain north and south will always be south. Sure you can turn the map upside down, but it still doesn't change the way the country is oriented. This stands true in the world of 3D, your camera angle can show everything completely upside down, but that does not change the way the X, Y, and Z axes are oriented.

OBJECT COORDINATES

The second coordinate system that you will be using is relative to the individual models in your 3D world. When a model is first created or imported into your animation package, it is assigned its own individual coordinate system. You can rotate, roll, or spin your model to your heart's content but the X, Y, Z axes assigned to the model will always remain fixed relative to the model itself. The best way to comprehend this concept is to imagine yourself traveling in a car. Regardless of whether you are traveling north, south, east, or west you will always be facing forward. Now carry this concept over to 3D. Let's say that the length of our model was created along the X axis. If we animate that model in 3D space, the X axis will remain constantly fixed on the length of the model regardless of the direction in which the model is facing.

FIGURE 13.3 *3D animation uses two sets of coordinate systems, one that is fixed on the world of the animation and the other relative to the orientation of the individual models.*

The Keyframe

When it comes time to script your animation, the most important concept that you need to grasp is the keyframe. The keyframe is what makes animation possible. As in traditional cel-based animation, the keyframe is the guide used in the tweening process. You as the designer, create or set the parameters of the keyframe, and the computer will fill in the frames between the keyframes.

Let's say that we want to script an animation of an airplane flying through the air. At this point in time, forget all about the other factors in an animation such as camera angle and lighting and concentrate fully on making the plane move.

Tip. When scripting an animation, it's a good idea to calculate the action occurring in terms of time rather than by frame number. The reasoning is that time is constant, while the frame number might change relative to the frame rate of the playback medium. For example the frame rate of television is 29.97 frames per second (fps) while film has a playback rate of 24 fps, and animation optimized for playback from a CD-ROM drive has a suggested frame rate of anywhere from 15 to 20 fps.

T
U
T
O
R
I
A
L

KEYFRAME TUTORIAL I

This tutorial is designed to show how keyframes work. If you wish to follow along in your 3D animation program, you should have a basic understanding of how your animation sequencer or timeline operates. At the end of the tutorial is an illustration of the animation script that was used to plan the animation.

STEP ONE

Import the model of the airplane into your animation package. Check to see that the aircraft is located on the X/Z or ground plane of the world, and that the X axis runs the length of the aircraft's fuselage (Figure 13.4). If it doesn't, check with your software manual on how to realign the model's axis. Set the frame rate of the sequencer to 30 fps.

FIGURE *The coordinate system for the airplane has*
13.4 *the X axis running the length of the fuselage.*

STEP TWO

The goal of this tutorial is to make the airplane fly across the screen along the X axis. Start by creating a keyframe at time index 0, which is the very beginning of the time line. This keyframe records the current spatial coordinates of your airplane. For our own personal reference, let's call this spot **Point A**.

STEP THREE

Set the time indicator of your animation sequencer to 3 seconds or to frame number 90. Move your airplane along the X axis 1000 units to the right. Depending on the unit of measure in your animation package, 1000 units can be either centimeters, inches, pixels, feet, or even miles. Your program should automatically create a keyframe for you since you've changed the X coordinate of the model by moving it along the X axis. If your program requires you to create a keyframe manually, do that now. We'll now refer to this spot as **Point C**.

FIGURE 13.5 *The first keyframe was created at* **Point A** *and the second keyframe was created at* **Point C***.*

STEP FOUR

Go ahead and preview your animation. The computer will automatically fill in the frames between the first and last keyframe. The most immediate advantage of using keyframes is that the computer automatically fills in or *tweens* the coordinates of the airplane at the intermediate frames between the keyframe at 0 seconds and 3 seconds.

FIGURE 13.6 *The computer* tweens *the coordinates for the airplane between* **Point A** *and* **Point C***.*

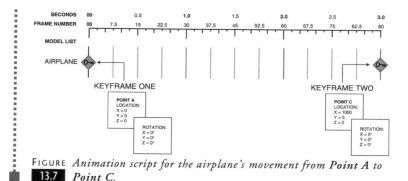

FIGURE *Animation script for the airplane's movement from **Point A** to*
13.7 *Point C.*

KEYFRAME TUTORIAL II

In Keyframe Tutorial I we created a simple animation that moved the airplane across the screen by using two separate keyframes. In this tutorial, we're going to do basically the same thing, yet add a third keyframe to illustrate further how tweening works.

If you haven't already done so, do Keyframe Tutorial I up to Step four and we'll pick up the next step with Step Five.

STEP FIVE

Move the time indicator of the animation sequencer to 1.5 seconds or frame number 45. Rotate the model of the airplane –60° on its X axis. Since the rotation along the X axis of rotation has changed, your program should then automatically create a keyframe at 1.5 seconds. If not, create a keyframe manually. Notice that your 3D application automatically calculates the X axis position for the model.

FIGURE *A keyframe is created at 1.5 seconds when the airplane is*
13.8 *rotated -60° on its X axis.*

STEP SIX

Go ahead and preview your animation. Notice that the airplane starts out level, and then gradually banks to –60° at 1.5 seconds and then gradually returns to even flight at the 3-second mark. Your 3D application automatically tweens the frames between **Point B** and **Points A** and **C**. When a keyframe is placed between two already existing keyframes, the program rubber bands the various settings. In other words the application will average the difference between the keyframes for each intermediary frame.

FIGURE **13.9** *Your 3D application automatically tweens the frames between Point B and Points A and C.*

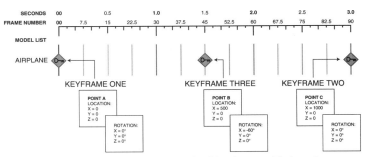

FIGURE **13.10** *Animation script showing a third keyframe added to the animation at 1.5 seconds by changing the rotation of the airplane –60° along its X axis.*

Model Hierarchy and Links

Another part of scripting an animation is setting up the models' hierarchies and links. The basic concept behind hierarchy is the parent child relationship which is defined as *wherever the parent goes, the child will follow.*

Important. During the modeling process, it's important to remember that each separate moving part of the same model needs to be on a separate layer when exported from your modeling program.

HIERARCHY

When first importing a model into an animation program, each individual part of the model that will be animated or texture mapped has to be on its own layer. Conversely, if you're using an all-inclusive modeling and animation package, try to establish this layering structure early on in the modeling process. It is up to you as the animator to create the hierarchical structure of the model from its individual layers. Many 3D animators refer to this structure as a parent–child relationship. In actuality, it can best be referred to as the parent, child, grandchild, great grandchild, and so on relationship. Once established, the hierarchy structure looks dendritic or root-like since the structure springs from the main trunk or parent and branches out to the individual children.

If we have a model of an airplane for example, which consists of a fuselage, propeller, landing gear, and wheels, each object in this model would have to be held on a separate layer. As the animator, you would want to set up the following hierarchical structure once it's imported into your animation package. The parent would be the fuselage, the children would be the propeller and landing gear. The landing gear would have its own child, which would be the wheels.

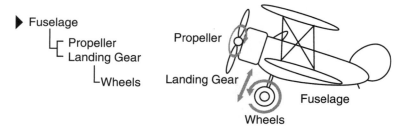

FIGURE **13.11** *The hierarchical structure of the plane has the fuselage as the parent, the propeller and landing gear as children, and the wheels as a child of the landing gear.*

The logic behind this structure is simple. The fuselage is the main parent because it is the main or largest part of the model. All of the other parts are attached to the fuselage. The propeller is a child because it has to travel wherever the fuselage goes. The propeller also has to be animated separately from the rest of the model since it should spin. The landing gear is also a child of the fuselage but has a child of its own, the wheels. The wheels need to be rotated, yet are still attached to the landing gear. When the landing gear is retracted into the airplane, the wheels will follow the landing gear.

LINKS AND COORDINATE SYSTEMS

The important question now is, once the hierarchy is established, how do we constrain the motion of the child in relation to the parent? The child in the hierarchical structure follows the parent object around when it is animated. But if we wanted to animate the child as well, what would we do. The key to animating a child object is a link. Links are used primarily when using automatic animation functions such as **Point At** and **Inverse Kinematics** to constrain movement along an axis.

Each animation package handles linking in a variety of fashions and its best to refer to your user's manual to figure out the technical aspects of the procedure. Some programs don't offer any links at all, and motion constraints placed on an object have to be defined through coordinate manipulation. On the other hand, packages such as Electric Image offer rather extensive sets of links.

T U T O R I A L

LINK AND COORDINATE SYSTEM TUTORIAL

In the earlier part of the chapter we covered the concept of individual coordinate systems for separate objects. Each model in the world of the animation has its own coordinate system. Taking this concept a step further, each child within a parent–child relationship has its own coordinate system as well. It is around the individual coordinate system for each part of the model that you need to script your animation.

STEP ONE

Start by importing the model of the guns into your animation package. Notice that the length of the model is on the X axis, with the barrels facing toward the –X direction. If the model is not pointing in the right direction, realign the model accordingly. The model is composed of seven individual layers each with its own garish color. The different colors should help you discern the separate parts of the model.

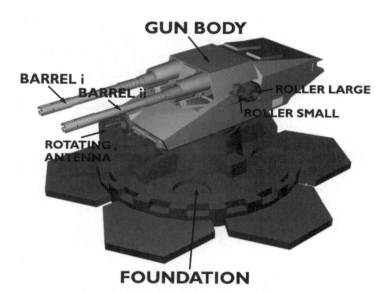

FIGURE
13.12 *The model for the gun has seven layers each with its own color.*

STEP TWO

The next step is to establish the hierarchy of the model. The Foundation layer is the parent. The only child of the Foundation layer is the Gun Body. The Gun Body has Barrel i, Barrel ii, Roller Large, Roller Small, and the Rotating Antenna layers as children.

FIGURE
13.13 *The hierarchy tree for the guns has the Foundation layer as the parent and the Gun Body layer as its only child. The rest of the objects are children of the Gun Body.*

STEP THREE

In this step, we need to realign the origins or center points for the Gun Body layer. Most animation programs set the coordinate system to default to the exact center of the object. In this case, since the Gun Body object needs to rotate on an axis slightly off center, the coordinate system needs to be realigned.

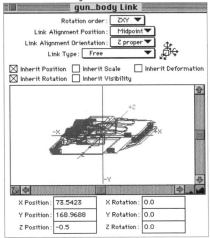

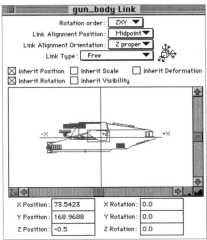

FIGURE **13.14** *Three-quarter view of the model in Electric Image 2.5 with the coordinate system at the center of the object.*

FIGURE **13.15** *Front view of the model in Electric Image 2.5 with the coordinate system at the center of the object.*

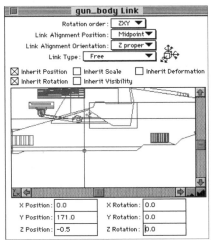

FIGURE **13.16** *Enlarged front view of the model in Electric Image 2.5 with the coordinate system realigned off center of the object.*

Programs such as StudioPro, Infini-D and Electric Image let you drag the center of an object's coordinate system to the desired location. To make life a little easier when creating the model, I placed a small cube where the center of rotation should be aligned.

STEP FOUR (OPTIONAL)

If your animation program supports complex links, then go ahead and follow the directions for this step. If not, skip to Step Five. It won't make a real difference anyway unless you are using the automatic **Point At** animation function of your application.

We need to set movement constraints for the individual parts of the model. By locking the specific axis of rotation and movement of the various parts of the model, we can make the gun perform in a more realistic manner. Figure 13.17 charts the exact links and constraints that need to be done to the model.

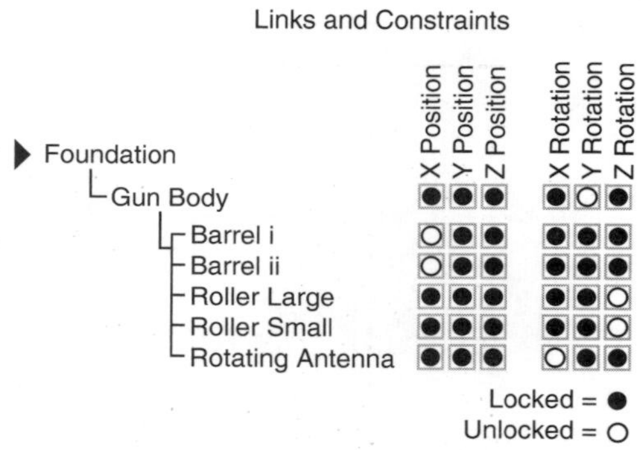

Links and Constraints

	X Position	Y Position	Z Position	X Rotation	Y Rotation	Z Rotation
▶ Foundation						
└ Gun Body	●	●	●	●	○	●
└ Barrel i	○	●	●	●	●	●
├ Barrel ii	○	●	●	●	●	●
├ Roller Large	●	●	●	●	●	○
├ Roller Small	●	●	●	●	●	○
└ Rotating Antenna	●	●	●	○	●	●

Locked = ●
Unlocked = ○

FIGURE 13.17 *Various parts of the model need to be constrained in order to use the automatic Point At animation function.*

STEP FIVE

It's now time to animate the model. Make sure that the model is in the field of view of the camera and then set up the following keyframes.

Tip. Notice that for each degree the Gun Body rotates, the children rotate 2 degrees. When the point in degrees exceeds 360° that means one rotation is equal to 360° + x°. For example 780° = 2 full rotations + 20°.

At the 3-second mark:

- Rotate the Gun Body on its Y axis –148°
- Rotate the Roller Large on its Z axis –248°
- Rotate the Roller Small on its Z axis 248°
- Rotate the Rotating Antenna on its X axis 248°

At the 4-second mark:

- Rotate the Gun Body on its Y axis 48° to the –107° point
- Rotate the Roller Large on its Z axis 82° to the –166° point
- Rotate the Roller Small on its Z axis –82° to the 166° point
- Rotate the Rotating Antenna on its X axis –82° to the 166° point

At the 5-second mark:

- Rotate the Gun Body on its Y axis –116° to the –223° point
- Rotate the Roller Large on its Z axis –232° to the –398° point
- Rotate the Roller Small on its Z axis 232° to the 398° point
- Rotate the Rotating Antenna on its X axis 232° to the 398° point

At the 8-second mark:

- Rotate the Gun Body on its Y axis 201° to the –22° point
- Rotate the Roller Large on its Z axis 800° to the 402° point
- Rotate the Roller Small on its Z axis –800° to the –402° point
- Rotate the Rotating Antenna on its X axis –800° to the –402° point

Tip. If your program supports the **Point At** animation feature, you could have created an object and pointed the Gun Body layer at the target. By doing so, you would have had to animate only the target and the Roller Large, Roller Small, and Rotating Antenna.

STEP SIX

Go ahead and do a preview of your animation. If your program supports velocity controls, try to make the velocity into
bell curves so that the action starts slow, peaks, and then
slows down near the end of the movement.

Congratulations, you've just completed a very difficult
tutorial! If you want to work on this animation further, try to
add texture maps to the model and create a scene to place it
in. If you're feeling slightly more adventurous, create flames
to flash out of the barrels when they're fired and make them
recoil slightly.

Animation Sequencers

Even though all animation packages are not created equal, after a
point they sure do look the same. The reason behind this striking sim-
ilarity is the fact that the theory behind animation on the computer is
fairly consistent. All animations are linear in nature since when they
are played back they start at the beginning and finish at the end. This
seems very elementary but you should have a grasp of this concept
before you start playing with your sequencer.

Strata StudioPro 1.5

Specular Infini-D 3.0

Electric Image Animation System 2.1

FIGURE *Examples of animation sequencers from Strata StudioPro*
13.18 *1.75, Infini-D 3.0, and Electric Image 2.5.*

Just about every animation package with the exception of a couple of programs uses a graphic linear time line sequencer. Most of them are based on the same interface design so picking up a new animation program is far easier than learning a new modeling application.

If you scripted your animation neatly enough, it can be transposed easily onto your animation sequencer. You're probably asking yourself "Why did I have to script out the animation on paper when I could have just done it on the computer?" For a simple animation, go for it, I do the same thing. But when you are working with a very complex animation, with a few dozen models with several hierarchical levels, it's easier to do it first on a big sheet of paper. It's kind of like storyboarding for the animator. Every time that you move a model and set a keyframe, you'll have to wait for the screen to update and the computer to recalculate coordinates. On slower systems with less powerful programs, this can try the patience of Ghandi.

SECTION THREE: MOTION THEORY

Objects move and that's all you need to know. Actually that's not entirely true. There are many subtitles of movement that can be difficult to notice or even replicate. Take a human being for example; the motion associated with a simple task such as walking is very complex. As each leg moves forward, a hip moves ever so slightly, the opposite arm swings forward while the other moves back, shoulders also move in rhythm with the rest of the body. To further complicate matters, the length of stride and pattern of movement are rarely the same with each step. We take natural motion for granted until we have to replicate it in 3D.

 Tip. Accurately animating the human body is one of the most difficult tasks to master in 3D. But there are several hardware-based solutions. Polhemus uses ultrasonic 3D digitizers to record actual human motion and convert it to IK data sets. A human actor has ultrasonic transmitters placed on the key joints of their body, and then the computer simply records their movements over time. These data sets can then be applied to a 3D model.

Velocity

One of the most important aspects of motion theory is the concept of velocity. Velocity is the speed at which your model or camera moves over time. The most important lesson to learn about velocity is that it is rarely constant. Sure, you will have plenty of animations when the camera simply follows an object cruising by, but for more complex work velocity control is imperative.

VELOCITY CONTROLS

To simplify velocity, we can refer to it as the speed of a model. When an object starts to move, it gradually works its way up to its cruising speed, after all not everything is shot out of a cannon. In 3D, the animator needs to have a way of handling velocity in a gradual manner. It's like slowly stepping on the gas pedal of a car rather than stamping your foot down. Imagine how unnatural it would look for a model to go from a dead standstill to speed across the screen and then suddenly stop on a dime.

Most lower end animation programs offer **Ease In/Ease Out** features for keyframes. **Ease In/Ease Out** options offer the animator a simple way of either gradually increasing or decreasing the velocity of a model. The user is able to set the percentage of time between keyframes for the object to accelerate or de-accelerate.

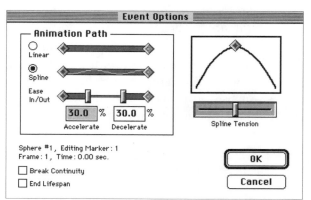

FIGURE *Ease In/Ease Out interface window from Strata's*
3.19 *StudioPro.*

More sophisticated animation packages let the user edit the velocity of a model by using a series of spline-based control points. The animator is thus able to create a user definable velocity curve for a model.

This feature is particularly useful when trying to average the velocity over a series of unevenly spaced keyframes. Spatial coordinates and also scale and rotational velocity can be tweaked.

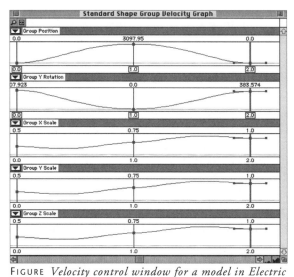

FIGURE **13.20** *Velocity control window for a model in Electric Image Animation System.*

HOW FAST IS FAST?

The speed limit in 3D space is a relative concept. Since we lack many real-world spatial cues such as depth of field, sound, and backgrounds it is often very difficult to judge how fast our model is moving or rotating. Of course, all of these effects can be added to an animation during the rendering process but at that point it's too late.

Tip. VIDI's Presenter Pro has 3D sound capabilities that enable the user to attach a sound to an object. As the object passes by the camera, which is equipped with a microphone, the sound gradually increases in pitch and volume and then fades away, mimicking the Doppler effect.

We're also looking at our model through the tiny window of a computer monitor, which even further restricts our field of view. A good example of this problem is watching a car race on television, we never really realize how fast these cars are traveling since the camera always pans to follow the car as it passes. It's not until we look at the scene in a broad panoramic viewpoint do we realize the speed of the car.

Scale

So how do we post a speed limit in 3D? The first key to this process is scale. When you're creating your object try to model in real-world units. Choose your unit of measurement, feet and inches or meters and centimeters, and then make sure that your 3D animation package can import these units. It is vitally important to have a consistent measure of distance. For example, if you have just built a model of a car that is 12 feet long, it's easier to think that you have to move the car 100 feet in 3 seconds rather than 100 units in 3 seconds, especially when you have no clue of the size of one unit. A lot of people when modeling usually just start cranking away without any thought of scale. I for one am one of those people. But before exporting my model I usually scale the object to real-world units so that I can conceptualize distance in the animation package.

Tip. Judging the speed of your animation is extremely important. One of the best methods is unfortunately trial and error. Perform periodic 320 x 240 preview animations using either bounding boxes or wireframes in order to get a rough idea of how your animation runs.

Frame Rate

Since my output is usually for television, I always think of speed in terms of 30 frames per second. So relatively speaking 15 frames is rather quick, and when played equals one-quarter of a second. Also even though one second can seem like an amazingly short period of time in reality, it can equal an eternity in 3D. Think of it this way — if I were animating a laser beam traveling from a gun barrel to a spaceship, at most I would have the beam travel the distance in 15 frames or one-half of a second.

Human Motion or Character Animation

Animating the human body in 3D is one of the most challenging tasks and it is next to impossible without IK or *inverse kinematics*. Inverse kinematics are high-level links between various parts of a user-definable skeleton. Constraints can be placed on various joints so that they stay within a specific range of motion. IK capabilities, for example, let the user drag the foot on a human figure, and then the calf, thigh, and hip follow along automatically.

When animating the human figure or any other model, there are a few tips that you should follow.

- *Anticipation.* Action just doesn't start, there are usually a few movements that lead up to the primary action. Once again the analogy of being shot out of a cannon springs to mind. It would be very boring to see a cannon sitting there and then a puff of smoke. I usually think in terms of cartoons. The cannon usually swells first and then spits out a cannon ball. On the other hand take the human figure. Before someone jumps into the air, they crouch down before springing away.

- *Exaggeration.* It's like a street mime; if they mimicked reality normally, it wouldn't be very convincing. They have to exaggerate every action so that the viewer takes notice. Take our cannon example again. If the base of the cannon swelled only slightly before spitting out the ball, it wouldn't be very interesting. Now on the other hand if the cannon swelled to almost bursting, and then elongated itself after spitting out the ball, then it would be much more exciting.

- *Follow through.* Every action has an equal and opposite reaction. If a cannon spits out a cannon ball, it's going to roll backwards a little bit. If a car comes to a screeching stop, it's going to shimmy from side to side. Inertia should always be accounted for as well. An object doesn't just come to a standstill after cruising along unless it happens to crash into a brick wall. This is where controlling velocity comes into play.

- *Overlapping action.* The world does not operate on a strict timetable. Everything starts and stops at different intervals. Try to space out your motion so that the action looks more natural. Take a walking human being for example. As the foot starts to travel forward, the calf and then the thigh start to rise. Finally the hip swings forward as well. In a scene, if you have several objects moving at the same time, it's easy to become focused on a central object.

- *Squash and Stretch.* As soft objects move, they become distorted because of inertia. Take a rubber ball for example, as it bounces on the ground, it becomes deformed. As it rebounds, it elongates itself in the direction that it is traveling. If you want to exaggerate motion, try subtly tweaking the squashing and stretching of hard objects as well.

Motion Paths

Not everything travels in a straight line. Straight lines are easy, after all it's just traveling from point A to point B. But a curved line is a little more complicated than that. Fortunately for you there is a mathematical answer to our problem. A spline is a mathematical formula that defines a curve. There are several different types of splines, ranging from hermite to Beziér to natural cubic. These splines can be used in both the modeling and animation process.

For now, all that we should be concerned about is the animation aspect of a spline. A spline consists of three major parts: the anchor points which define the beginning and end of the spline, the curve that describes the space between the anchor points, and the control handles, which allow the user to alter the shape of the curve.

 Tip. Always use the fewest number of control points or keyframes to define the arc of a curved motion path. A motion path with too many keyframes can turn out to be uneven or result in jerky motion.

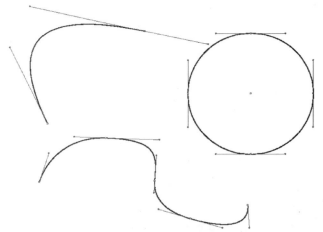

Figure *Example of Beziér splines from Adobe Illustrator 5.0.*
13.21

Animation packages handle spline-based motion paths in one of two ways. The first method lets the user adjust the shape of the curve between the two anchor points or keyframes by manipulating the tension of the spline. Most low-end animation applications use this method. On the other hand, the more sophisticated animation programs let the user manipulate the control handles of the spline to form the shape of the curve. This method offers far more control than the other technique.

SECTION FOUR: BASIC CINEMATOGRAPHY

Strap on the steady cam or climb into the cherry picker, it's time to start the camera rolling. Your motion paths for your models have all been tweaked and the individual parts of your model have been animated. Finally you'll be able to yell "Action!" and watch everything move from behind the viewfinder of your camera.

One of the first things to learn is to slow your action down. I've seen too many 3D animations that just go zipping by, and most of the action and models are totally missed just because everything has been scripted too quickly. Even though it takes time to render your animation, it's worth adding a few more hours of rendering for a few more seconds worth of action. This actually leads to the second point.

As any good director will tell you, it's better to shoot more footage than you actually need. The idea is to think ahead to your postproduction concerns. If you're stringing together several clips into one long movie, your going to have to create transitions between shots. If your clip starts right on top of the action in the scene, then your fade-in will take place during the most exciting part of the clip. A fast transtion should have 8 frames overlapping, but no less. A slow transition can last anywhere from 1 to 3 seconds. If the animation is fast paced, then a short transition will definitely do. But if the mood is slower, then a longer transition will be more appropriate.

Basic Camera Tips

If you've ever been forced to watch home movies of your friends' and relatives' vacations you can learn what to avoid in your own animations. One of the first signs of poor camera handling is the shaky hand syndrome. The picture bobbles up and down and nothing is in focus for very long. Fortunately for the 3D designer, the camera can remain as steady as a rock. Since our camera is mounted on a virtual dolly, we can even move our camera from place to place without worrying about a single wobble.

Another sign of poor camera abilities is the whiplash effect. The person shooting the movie pans around quickly from object to object in the scene, resulting in a blurry picture and a quesy feeling on the part of the viewer. Unfortunately this also happens in 3D. The trick is to make your camera pans as evenly as possible, which can be accomplished in several ways. The first way is to average the velocity of the camera's movement. For most pans try to use your velocity controls to start the pan slowly and then increase in speed and then slow down again. The shape of the velocity line should be a bell curve. A comfortable camera pan is around 45° to 50° for every second so a 360° pan around should take around 8 to 10 seconds. A more cautious or careful camera pan, where you want the viewer to notice a lot of detail in the scene, should be 15° to 20° every second. If you're tracking an object and you want the camera to pan around and follow the model, use the point at feature in your animation package and make sure that the velocity of the model is even.

A good place to learn about good camera handling techniques is in the movies. Watch how a director uses the camera in a scene. Try to notice first of all how they frame a shot, and then try to remember where they would have located the camera itself on the set. Also look for things such as how they pan to follow an object, how they link pieces of footage, and where their transitions are in a clip. Even though your virtual camera can do far more rolls and movements than a real-world one might, you might reconsider it. If the cinematography is a little too fancy, then the viewer might become distracted. The bottom line is to keep it simple. You would be surprised at how many really great animation shots involve only simple camera movement.

Basic Camera Movements

There are three basic camera movements that you should learn before moving your way up to the really fancy stuff. Once you get these down, try variations on the same theme.

ZOOM IN

The first camera shot is a simple zoom in. Position the camera a distance away from the subject and then gently zoom in on the object. Once satisifed with the speed of the zoom, another variation is to try rotating the camera slowly around the object with the camera reference point fixed while zooming in. This is perhaps the most basic camera movement to use and learn.

MODEL FLY-BY

Another technique is an object fly-by with the camera in a stationary position. The camera should be placed fairly near the motion path of the moving object. Set the camera to track or point at the object. In Figure 13.22 there are three variations on the same theme that produce different results when rendered.

In Figure 13.22A the camera is set near the center of the length of the distance that the airplane will be traveling. Depending on the speed of the airplane and the distance from the camera, the viewer will be able to see the airplane grow larger and then fly by and then grow

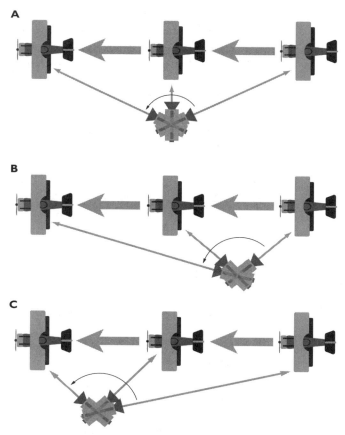

FIGURE **13.22** *The stationary camera tracks a moving object in these three scenarios. The most important factor in these three senarios is the camera placement.*

smaller. The overall feeling of the shot is that the action flows smoothly and evenly and the viewer isn't really surprised.

Figure 13.22B has the camera set toward the beginning of the motion path of the airplane. In this setup the action starts abruptly with the plane flying past fairly early in the action. This will grab the viewers' attention immediately. A good idea is to have an interesting background or model for the airplane to fly toward in the later part of the animation, shifting the viewers' attention toward the background model. A shot like this makes a good transition to a clip featuring a closeup of the background model.

Figure 13.22C has the camera placed near the end of the motion path, which gradually draws the viewers' attention in toward the subject of the animation. This is a good way to bring or introduce a model into a scene. With the model slowly growing in size and separating itself from the background, the viewer is gradually brought into the action.

You can do several vartions on this simple model fly-by. It's a good idea to try things such as banking the wings of the airplane as it approaches the camera or making the motion path incline slowly upward or downward. Remember that we should be thinking in three dimensions rather than only two. Make your motion paths take full advantage of 3D space.

CAMERA DOLLY

An alternative to the fly-by is the dolly. In movie production, a camera has to be fairly steady and level when it is tracking a moving object, especially when the camera itself is moving. Cinematographers use a dolly, which is basically a camera on wheels that is placed on top of a pair of tracks. In 3D we don't need to go to all that effort, but we do want to try to recreate the same results as a dolly.

The first type of dolly movement has the camera moving alongside the model as the model travels along. In Figure 13.23A the camera tracks the model as it goes along its motion path. The results are fairly predictable. In Figure 13.23B the camera has a higher speed than the model, and eventually passes the subject. This type of shot is great for showing the viewer more of the front end of the model. In Figure 13.23C the camera moves slower than the object eventually falling behind the subject. For obvious reasons, this type of camera footage is good for showing the back end of the model.

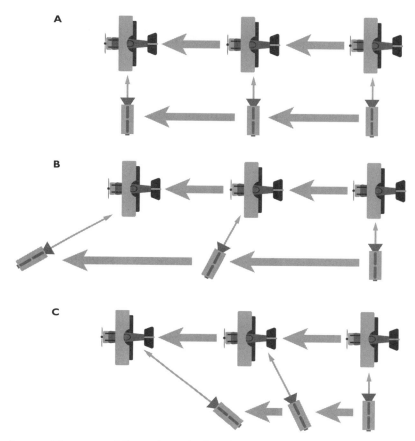

FIGURE **13.23** *The camera follows alongside the subject at different velocities to achieve varied results.*

CHAPTER REQUIREMENTS
Basic understanding of either Premiere or After Effects and Photoshop.

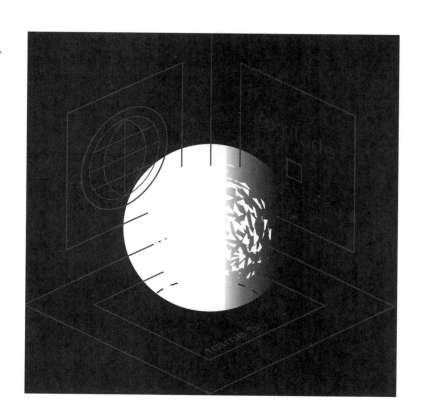

Wh_hen I think back on my misguided childhood, one of my fonder memories is that of blowing up model airplanes with firecrackers. I have always resented my parents for not giving me more munitions to play with such as dynamite and pluto-nium. For some strange reason they believed that I might blow myself up. Now that I'm a responsible adult I realize that I can't go around exploding tactical nuclear devices just for fun, but I might be able to do it for a living.... In 3D I can blow up models of entire cities or even planets and not be socially ostracized for my actions, hey, I might even win an Oscar.

This chapter covers some of the flashier parts of 3D animation: explosions, particle effects, and fire. We'll also discuss how to make your images much more interesting by using backgrounds and how to add them to your scenes in both the rendering and postproduction process.

SECTION ONE: PYROTECHNICS

Smoke, fire, explosions, sparks, and lightning — sounds like a safe neighborhood doesn't it? In this section we'll cover how to create fire, shock waves, and all sorts of mayhem for use directly in an animation. We'll learn how to play pyromaniac using particle systems, animated texture maps, and old-fashioned animation techniques.

SECTION TWO: SPECIALIZED ANIMATION FEATURES

Morphing, inverse kinematics, deformations, explosions, velocity curves, and auto-rotation — sound like a foreign language? Well it might as well be for the majority of people out there. We'll cover the basics of these features and how and when to use them.

SECTION THREE: BACKGROUNDS

Do you remember those high school musicals with the painted backdrops that looked like they were done by a crazed monkey with a box of crayons? We can do much better than that with very little effort. Learn how to create an effective background for your animation by rendering it into the scene or by compositing in postproduction.

SECTION ONE: PYROTECHNICS

Snap, crackle, and pop are some of the sounds that the average parent dreads hearing. The visual images associated with those sounds, apart from the three funny looking elves pushing cereal, can also be fairly frightening. That's what we want to do in this section — recreate the awe inspiring feel of a giant explosion or display the deadly beauty of bolts of electricity and sparks of hot metal.

We'll cover some of the basics that you'll need in your animations: fire, smoke, lightning, sparks, and explosions. There are several methods of creating these effects ranging from going out and buying a CD-ROM or specialized program to low-budget methods such as using your preexisting resources. For this section you will need a program such as Adobe's After Effects or Premiere in order to create the animated texture maps. If you're unsure about what an Alpha channel is, you might consider jumping ahead to Chapter 16, Postproduction, to get a better understanding.

Prometheus had it easy compared to what the 3D designer has to go through to get fire on the screen. Unfortunately it's not as easy as rubbing two sticks together to get a fire going. Creating fire in 3D can be accomplished using a variety of methods.

CD-ROMS

I've always believed that there's no substitute for the real thing. Whenever I texture map a model I always prefer to use scanned textures rather than artificially created ones. The results always look more realistic and it's usually a lot easier to do in the first place. When it comes to creating fire, smoke, or explosions the same premise holds true.

I honestly believe that the best method for creating these special effects is to go out and buy stock fire or explosion footage. This guarantees the fastest and most realistic results since the footage is digitized directly from film. Visual Concept Entertainment is a company that offers two CD-ROMs entitled Pyromania I and II with excellent source footage of fire, explosions, smoke, and sparks.

Tip. Visual Concept Entertainment can be contacted at VCE, 13300 Ralston Avenue, Sylmar, CA 91342; (818) 367-9187.

Pyromania comes with sets of numbered PICTs that can be compiled into QuickTime files, a task that can be done in either Adobe's Premiere or After Effects. The problem is that most files that you capture yourself or that come on a CD-ROM do not include Alpha channel support. The Alpha channel is what makes it possible to create a semitransparent texture map. For example, a typical frame of an explosion has all of the fire and sparks shot on a black background. If you were simply to use this as an animated color map, the black area would give away the rectangular shape of the map. The trick is to create an Alpha channel or transparency map from your preexisting RGB channels.

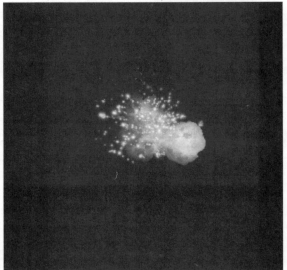

FIGURE **14.1** *This frame is from a VCE explosion movie file and was shot on a solid black background.*

EASY ALPHA CHANNELS

One method of creating an Alpha channel is chroma keying, which we will cover in Chapter 16. For now we're going to use another method. Our method works for most footage shot on a solid black background and can be accomplished in one of two ways. The first is simply to convert the RGB movie into a grayscale file and then use it as an animated transparency map for the animated color map. This process can be done in either Premiere or After Effects. The second method can be accomplished only in After Effects. By applying the **Shift Channels** Effect and then selecting **Take Alpha from Red** and **Take Red From Alpha** you can create an Alpha channel based on the predominant color in the clip.

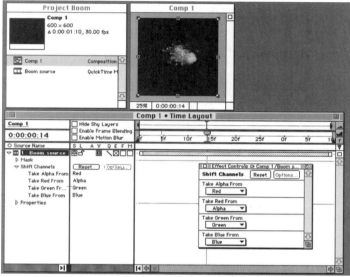

FIGURE
14.2
*An Alpha channel can be created from the RGB channels in Adobe After Effects 3.0 by using the **Shift Channels** effect.*

Tip. When you need to create the illusion of a flickering fireplace, create a rectangle and then place it directly in the hearth and then apply your animated map to the object. In addition use a projector or animated gel aimed at the back wall of the fireplace to simulate the light cast by the flames. And don't just restrict yourself to mapping explosions and fire onto 2D shapes. You can create ghostly characters out of digitized video to float around a scene using this same technique.

INSERTING THE MAP INTO THE SCENE

Once you've compiled your footage into a QuickTime movie, the next task is to integrate the explosion into your animation. The best method for using these files in your project is to create a 2D shape to map the animation of the explosion onto an area such as a square or rectangle. Keep the shape invisible until you want your object to explode and when the time comes, make it visible and play back the animation. At the same time you can either make your exploding object invisible or use an animation feature such as Mr. Nitro, which is included with the Electric Image Animation System, or Explode, which is included with Strata StudioPro. Both of these animation tools break an object up into tiny polygons and send them hurtling off into space.

The drawback to the use of mapped explosions and fire is the fact that they are simply 2D shapes. For example, it's not possible to fly through these explosions, and the illusion also tends to fall apart if the camera has time to move around the 2D shape on which the animation is mapped.

Particle Groups

What are particle groups? Particle groups are sets of computer-created objects that can be controlled via presets. The advantage to using particle groups is that the user just has to configure them only once. When using a particle system a set of global parameters defines how an entire group behaves. Since a particle group can consist of anywhere from a hundred to a hundred thousand objects, the advantages of automated features are obvious. The user does not have to animate every single particle; instead a preset such as a direction is specified with a standard of deviation assigned to it.

A particle generator can be used for anything from a simple spark to a puff of smoke, a fireworks display, or a waterfall. And depending on the software package you're using, you can also specify a user-definable model as a particle. Software that can handle particle effects on the Macintosh can be broken up into two categories: 2D and 3D. The only 3D application that offers particle groups is Electric Image. On the other hand, there are a couple of 2D video editing packages that can be used to create 2D movies of particle effects, which can be turned around and used in a 3D program.

3D PARTICLE GROUPS

Electric Image Animation System is the only program on the Macintosh that offers the animator 3D particle effects. One of the primary reasons that 3D particle groups are better than 2D maps is the fact that they can interact with the models in the scene since they are actual 3D objects. For example, it's possible to create a fountain of sparks that spurts into the air and then bounces off of a floor plane. The particle groups can be used in a variety of situations ranging from fireworks to water fountains. By adding a little bit of motion blur to the particle group it can be made to look like a flickering fire.

Electric Image also has a smoke feature that can be animated to create banks of 3D smoke or fog that you can fly through. This too is another extension of the particle effects feature of the program. Be sure to check out the animation created with particle groups in Electric Image on the CD-ROM.

```
Particle Generator by Mark Granger
     Copyright © 1994, Electric Image, Inc.
        Maximum Particles: 1000
   New Particles Per Second: 25        ± 25
         Particle Life Time: 10        ± 0
  Create Particles From Time: 0      To: 100

 H Position: 0    ± 0    Direction: 0
 Y Position: 0    ± 0    Direction: 1
 Z Position: 0    ± 0    Direction: 0

 Deviation Angle: 0    ± 2
        Velocity: 100  ± 10
     Gravity H: 0    Y: -50    Z: 0
 Y Ground Level: 0      Air Resistance: 0
  Bounce Factor: 0.5   Bounce Friction: 0.9

    Energy 1.0: [  ]   0.5: [▒▒]   0.0: [██]

         [  OK  ]   ( Cancel )
```

FIGURE **14.3** *Electric Image is the only 3D program on the Macintosh that uses 3D particle groups.*

Northern Lights Productions

To get the most out of particle groups in Electric Image, it's a good idea to use third-party developer Northern Lights Productions' plug-ins. Northern Lights has three plug-ins based on the Electric Image particle generation architecture: Zeus, Dante, and Big Dipper. Zeus lets the user create 3D bolts of lightning or electricity while Big Dipper lets the user create 3D star fields that make for stunning background visuals. Dante is a particle generation system that lets the designer use their own models as particles.

Included on the CD-ROM are two 32-bit QuickTime movies that were created in Electric Image with Zeus. These animations are of bolts of lightning striking and electricity. It's entirely possible to create your own animated maps by painting them frame by frame, but by using Northern Lights' plug-ins the process is entirely automated. Feel free to use these animations in your own work as 2D texture maps.

FIGURE
14.4
Northern Lights Productions' Zeus plug-in for Electric Image lets the user create 3D bolts of electricity or lightning.

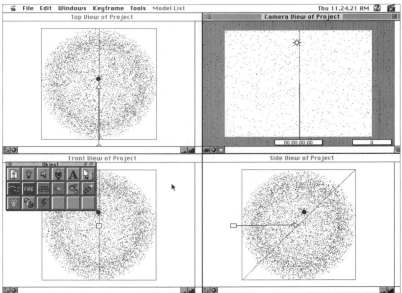

FIGURE
14.5
Northern Lights Productions' Big Dipper plug-in for Electric Image creates 3D star fields. Each star in this picture is an individual particle and can be given various spectral characteristics. Also a model can be substituted for a particle which makes creating an asteroid field a breeze.

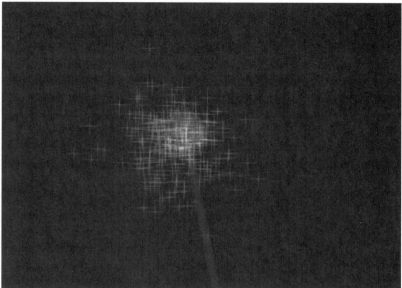

FIGURE 14.6 *Northern Lights Productions' Dante lets the user create particle effects using their own models as particles. In this image the stars or particles coming from the wand are based on a model.*

Tip. Northern Lights Productions can be contacted at 210 The Village, Suite 203, Redondo Beach CA 90277; (310) 376-4266 or Bear60@aol.com

2D PARTICLE GROUPS

So you can't afford a copy of Electric Image but you still want to use particle groups to get all of those special effects into your animations. Well, you're in luck, there are a couple of work-arounds that you can use. Instead of 3D particle effects you're going to have to settle for 2D texture mapped ones. But with a little careful manipulation and planning, a lot of people will not know the difference. One of the advantages of using 2D particle effects is lower rendering times. Since the computer only has to work in two rather than three dimensions, there are fewer numbers to crunch. To date, there are two programs that currently support 2D particle effects on the Macintosh, Strata's MediaPaint and MetaTools' FinalEffects plug-ins. The FinalEffects plug-ins only work within Adobe's After

Effects so you're going to need to budget for both the plug-ins as well as the application.

Both MediaPaint and After Effects can be though of as digital video editing tools, but in this case we can turn them around and repurpose them for our 3D applications. Since the particle groups that we're creating with these programs are only 2D images, we have to map them onto 2D shapes in our 3D scene as animated texture maps. Remember that we also have to create a transparency map so that the background of the animated texture map is not visible. Flip back a few pages to the section on Easy Alpha Channels for a more thorough description of this process.

FinalEffects

FinalEffects is a set of third-party plug-ins distributed by MetaTools for Adobe's After Effects application. The plug-ins can be used either in postproduction on top of preexisting footage, or they can be used to create animated texture maps that can be used during the rendering process. For this section we will focus on using FinalEffects to create animated texture maps.

FinalEffects offers a comprehensive array of particle groups that the designer can use to create a variety of special effects. The user can choose from different types of particles. By juggling variables such as particle life span, birth rate, and color, special effects such as smoke, dust, or fire can be created. For particle groups consisting of lines, you can create special effects such as fireworks, waterfalls, lawn sprinklers, shooting stars, or sparks. On the other hand sphere-shaped particles can be used to mimic smoke, dust, or bubbles. By combining several groups of particles such as lines and spheres, you can create your own waterfall.

If you have a copy of After Effects 3.0 or later, be sure to try the demo version of FinalEffects included on the CD-ROM. There are several tutorial files included that cover all of the effects that you've seen here, as well as some other ones not mentioned. One of the advantages of using the FinalEffects plug-ins is that After Effects automatically creates an Alpha channel for the animation, which can be used as a transparency map in some 3D programs.

Included on the CD-ROM are a few prerendered animations that you can use in your own animation. They were created with Final Effects and make excellent texture maps.

Tip. After you've created an animated texture map for smoke effects, try applying it in your 3D application using the following method. First of all make sure that you have a transparency map that corresponds to the color map. Then create three to four infinite horizontal and parallel planes. Apply a map to each plane making sure you use different coverage scales. Be sure to keep the transparency setting at high and then, voilá, instant fog.

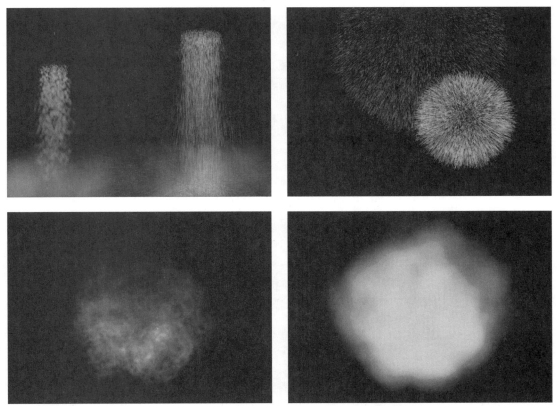

FIGURE 14.7 *The Final Effects plug-ins can be used to create a multitude of particle effects such as (clockwise starting at the top left) waterfalls, fireworks, explosions, and smoke.*

Tip. Try adding multiple particle effects to the same project. For example, try combining an explosion with smoke or sparks. For a waterfall, try combining smoke with a stream of falling particles.

Traditional Animation Methods

The most inexpensive method of creating effects such as lightning, fire, or sparks is to do it yourself. Yes, it is labor intensive, but on the other hand the results can be very high quality. Also particle groups are fairly restrictive in what they can do, for example nothing presently available for the Macintosh can create a shock wave. In this section we'll cover how to create your own specialized pyrotechnic displays using nontraditional tools and techniques. Like the other methods mentioned previously, we're going to create 2D maps and then apply them to objects in our 3D scenes.

LIGHTNING AND ELECTRICITY

Back in the days of Disney when animation was first becoming a booming art form, artists had to draw and paint each frame by hand. We're going to use some of those same techniques to create our lightning but instead of celluloid and paint, we'll use our digital canvas.

For an effect such as lightning, you can simply draw the bolt in a program such as Photoshop and then map it onto a 2D object in your 3D scene. One of the reasons that it's so easy to create lightning is that it is only on the screen for a brief moment. For example, in reality when a bolt of lightning strikes, it is visible to the naked eye for less than 1/16th of a second. Even though you think that the bolt is still visible, what you're seeing is the after effect of the bright flash on your retina.

When we create our own lightning bolt, we don't have to worry about the animation being smooth. Since the flash of lightning is on the random side, each consecutive frame does not have to precisely match the previous one. A single bolt of lightning should not last for more than two consecutive frames. At most all you really need is four bolts of lightning, which shouldn't take you more than 10 minutes to create in Photoshop.

Start by simply drawing a forky bolt of electricity using whichever color you feel is appropriate. The next step is to apply a small degree of Gaussian blur so that the bolt appears to be glowing. Repeat the process four or five more times and then import all of the individual frames into a program like Premiere. Figure out how long you want each bolt to be on the screen and then insert each frame into the time line. Render the movie and you're done. All you have to do is then map the lightning movie onto a 2D object in your 3D scene and there you have it, instant lightning.

The same method works for creating bolts of electricity. Since a bolt rarely stays in one place for any length of time, you can have them jumping all around the screen for less than a frame apiece. It is a good idea though to keep fixed start or end points for the bolts.

T
U
T
O
R
I
A
L

SMOKE AND FOG TUTORIAL

Creating convincing smoke or fog is slightly more difficult but not entirely impossible. The most convincing aspect about artificial smoke is its semitransparent nature. So it's important to remember that while we're creating the color map for smoke, we also need to create a transparency map. Also included on the CD-ROM is a copy of the Premiere project file used to create the animated smoke texture map.

STEP ONE

We will start by creating a color map in Photoshop. It's a good idea to calculate how large your puff of smoke or fog bank will be before starting. In this case, we're going to

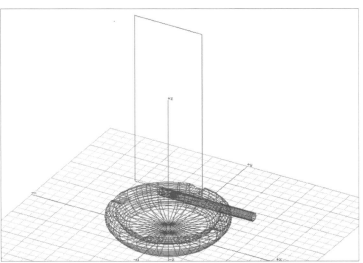

FIGURE *The 2D rectangle in the model will have an animated texture*
14.8 *map for smoke applied to it.*

create a stream of smoke coming out of a cigarette. Mind you this is no plug for the tobacco industry, so bear with me. Anyway, we have to start with a model. Figure 14.8 illustrates what our model looks like. Notice the 2D rectangular shape onto which we will map the smoke map.

STEP TWO

Do a screen capture of your model so that you can calculate the proportions of the 2D rectangle. In Photoshop, create a new document with the same dimensions as the

FIGURE *The map for the smoke can*
14.9 *be created in Photoshop in
a very short space of time
using a few tools.*

rectangle. Fill in the background black. Use the airbrush tool to paint a wavy streak of smoke. Then use a little Gaussian blur and after that the smudge tool to create the streaky stream of smoke.

STEP THREE

Create an Alpha channel for the smoke map based on the RGB color channels by copying the RGB colors into a newly created Alpha channel. You will notice that Photoshop automatically converts any colors into a grayscale image.

STEP FOUR

Save the file as a 32-bit PICT file. Import it into either Premiere or After Effects. Change the duration of the image to 5 seconds. Make sure that the output dimensions equal the dimensions of the clip. Insert the clip into the time line and then apply the **Ripple** filter. Render the clip using the same timebase as your animation. For example if your animation is at 24 fps, render the animated clip at 24 fps.

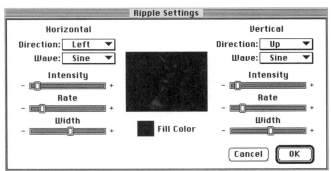

FIGURE **14.10** *By applying the **Ripple** filter to the clip in Adobe Premiere 4.0, we can create the illusion that the smoke is flowing upward.*

STEP FIVE

Import the file into your 3D application and then apply it to the 2D rectangle as a color map (Figure 14.11). Be sure to apply the transparency map as well. Render away!

FIGURE *Once the map is applied to the object and rendered it will*
14.11 *appear as if smoke if flowing upward from the cigarette.*

The illusion of fog can be created in much the same manner. Check out Chapter 8, the section on animated transparency maps, to see how to create your own animated fog.

FIRE IN AFTER EFFECTS

Unfortunately creating fire using the traditional animation methods is both a time-consuming and mind-numbing job. Each flame has to be synchronized exactly with the previous flame in order to create a convincing illusion. But there is another method that is definitely easier. To complete this tutorial you will need a copy of Adobe's After Effects with the **Displacement Map** and **Wave Warp** effects. Included on the CD-ROM is a copy of the After Effects project. A special thanks to Tim Landry (Tim_Landry@lamg.com) who thought this all up.

We will not be going through a step-by-step tutorial for this section but the After Effects project file is included on the CD-ROM. The main components of the file are a color map and two displacement maps.

By animating the postion of the two displacement maps over time, and adding the **Wave Warp** effect to the color map, a passable version of fire is possible.

FIGURE **14.12** *The color map will serve as the basis for our flames.*

FIGURE **14.13** *Displacement map one (left) and displacement map two (right).*

FIGURE 14.14 *Final shot of rendered fire.*

T
U
T
O
R
I
A
L

SHOCK WAVE TUTORIAL

For a while, you couldn't go to a movie or watch a television commercial without seeing a lens flare. Well, the latest trend in special effects is now the shock wave. Never mind the fact that an explosion in outer space would cause a spherical shock wave, a planar one is much more exciting. Included on the CD-ROM is a copy of the After Effect and Premiere project file used to create this tutorial.

STEP ONE

Before your start doing anything, take a few moments to calculate how large the shock wave will appear in your animation. You don't want to make your map too small and then notice pixelization when the image is scaled upward or made too large such that you overload your system resources.

Start by creating a 600 x 600 pixel document in Photoshop. You will be working backwards since you're creating an image of what the shock wave will look like when it has expanded to its largest dimensions. Create a ring of blue and draw in the flames on the inside of the ring. Try using either the airbrush or smudge tool for the job. Once you've completed the color map, remember to create an Alpha channel for the transparency map.

Tip. An easy way to create an Alpha channel in Photoshop 3.0 is to do all of your artwork on a layer separate from the background. Then load the transparency selection for that layer, and fill in the same selected area with white in the Alpha channel.

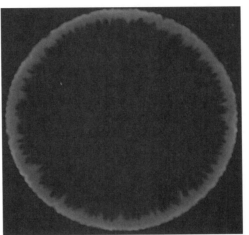

FIGURE
14.15
The color map for the shock wave is created in Photoshop. This is what the wave will look like when it has expanded to its largest dimensions.

STEP TWO
Repeat Step One two more times. You will need a total of three color maps for the project.

STEP THREE
Import all three color maps into a program such as After Effects and set the duration of the project to approximately 3 to 4 seconds. Place all three color maps into one composition. Set up a keyframe at the beginning of the time line and scale each map down to 1% of its original size. Create a keyframe for each map at the end of the time line and scale the maps back to 100% of their original size.

What you have just done is create the illusion that the wave is expanding out from a central blast area. Use the velocity controls for the scaling option and make the expansion start slowly and then gradually increase the expansion rate for the maps as they grow larger.

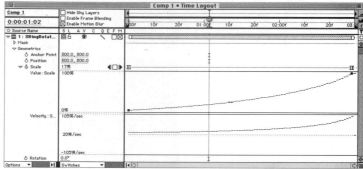

FIGURE *This is the velocity curve for the scaling of the rings in Adobe*
14.16 *After Effects 3.0.*

STEP FOUR

The next step is to give the shock wave a little more movement. Create a keyframe for each one of the rings at the start of the time line. Now skip to the end of the time line and create another set of keyframes.

At the end of the time line, set the rotation of the bottom-most ring to –90°. For the middle ring, set the rotation to 90°. For the top ring set the rotation to 180°. Set the time line back to the start of the animation. Set the opacity of the middle ring to 49% and the top ring to 24%.

What you have just done is rotate the rings at various speeds and also make the upper two rings semitransparent so that the lower rings will be partially visible when rendered.

You might also want to animate the opacity of all three rings to fade away to 0% at the end of the animation so that it appears as if the shock wave is gradually dissipating.

STEP FIVE

Render your shock wave animation and then apply it to a square-shaped 2D object in your 3D application.

FIGURE
14.17
The shock wave texture map can be added to a scene along with an animated lens flare for added effect.

Tying It All Together

Now that you've figured out how to use pyrotechnics in your animations by using animated maps, particle effects, or stock footage, all you need to do now is make it convincing. Try adding other tricks such as synchronizing a lens flare with your explosion. Another tip is to use a semitransparent sphere that expands outward and disappears within a couple of frames to simulate a different type of blast effect. Also try using the animation features such as Electric Image's Mr. Nitro, Strata's Explosion plug-in, or Infini-D's Explode animation assistant in combination with these recently acquired effects to create the illusion of shrapnel or debris.

SECTION TWO: SPECIALIZED ANIMATION FEATURES

While each animation program is unique in the features that it offers, there are some common tools that automate many of the more mundane tasks faced by the 3D animator. These automated functions take a lot of the unpleasantness out of animation. For example, imagine if you had to animate every single particle in a group of 10,000 objects.

Your mind would freeze up and your brains would come dripping out your nose. Well, maybe not, but you get the general idea. In this section we will explain some of the more popular automated animation tools available today.

- Align to path
- Velocity curves
- Explode
- Inverse kinematics
- Deformation
- Morph
- Metaballs

Align to Path

Automated animation tools are definitely work-savers. The most common automated feature available in just about every animation package is **Align to Path** or **Auto Rotate**. If you wanted to script an animation of an airplane flying through the friendly skies, weaving amongst the clouds and gently banking while it turns, you would need to use the **Align to Path** feature.

The first step would be to create a motion path for the airplane, which is as simple as moving the time line forward and then moving the airplane in space. The problem is that the airplane wil be continually facing forward no matter where it is on the motion path.

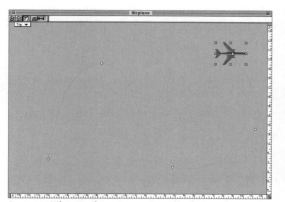 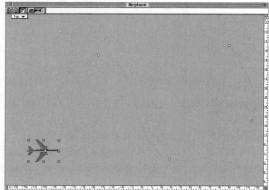

FIGURE *The airplane is continually facing forward regardless of its location on the motion path.*
14.18

The hardest part of creating this animation would be manually aligning the body of the airplane in the direction in which it's traveling. Fortunately we can use the automated animation tool, **Align to Path**. The computer automatically aligns the body of the model in the direction it is traveling. Strata StudioPro does one better and also automatically banks the model on the curves.

FIGURE **14.19**   *Strata StudioPro offers **Align to Path** and **Bank on Turn** animation features.*

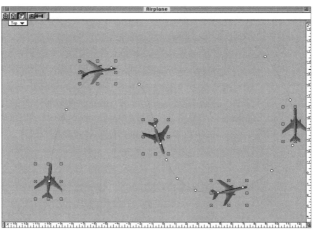

FIGURE **14.20**   *With **Auto Rotation** animation features, the process is almost completely automated when a model is aligned to a motion path.*

Velocity

As mentioned in the previous chapter, velocity curves are one of the most vital animation tools needed by the 3D designer. Velocity is the speed at which a model travels and as we know from past experience, velocity is rarely constant. For example a race car speeding around a track tends to slow down right before a curve and then accelerates through the straight-a-ways. When it comes to animating an object such as a race car, you could manually set the velocity of a model with a set of keyframes, but chances are the motion would not be smooth.

The best method for controlling the speed of a model is a velocity curve. Some programs use this high-end feature while others still rely on the older **Ease In/Ease Out** tool. A velocity curve plots the speed of a model between keyframes, and lets the user drag an anchor point on the curve to change the velocity of a model. There are several velocity curves for different parts of the model, for example, positon, rotation, and scale all have separate curves.

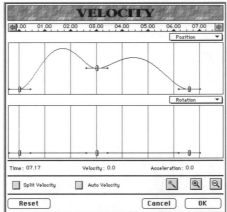

FIGURE **14.21** *The velocity controls from Specular Infini-D 3.0 let the user set the velocity of a model's postion as well as rotation.*

Explode

Making things go boom is one of the greater joys in my life. But imagine how difficult it would be if I had to animate every single piece of shrapnel in an explosion. Thankfully all of the major animation packages available today offer some form of automatic explosion. How does this automated explosion process work? It's actually fairly simple.

Your program facets your model into tiny little polygons, and then scatters them in space. Depending on the application the user can configure the strength of the blast, amount of gravity and wind resistance, and the lifetime of the polygons.

Perhaps the most well-appointed animated explosion tool can be found in Electric Image's Mr. Nitro. The user can not only set features mentioned above, but can also create two-directional blast waves to destroy the object.

FIGURE *Electric Image's Mr. Nitro explosion plug-in offers*
14.22 *the most options for destroying your model.*

The major drawback to any animated explosion effect is the fact that the debris from the explosion looks computer generated since all of the objects are composed of three- or four-sided polygons. Many first-time animators tend to just destroy a model completely with an automated explosion, which looks very unreal. There is a better alternative.

It involves more modeling but the hard work is worth it. For example if we wanted to destroy a model of a building, we would first start by modeling the outside shell of the building. The next step would be to model a skeleton of the inside of the building that consists of the girders and plumbing. Also for an added dimension of destruction we could model parts of the building that might come flying off in a blast such as a radio tower or bath tub.

When it finally comes time to animate the scene, keep the skeleton model invisible. Use your animated polygon explosion to destroy the shell of the building. At that point make the inside skeleton visible and send your radio tower hurtling toward the camera. Key in a bright flash of light and there you go, instant destruction.

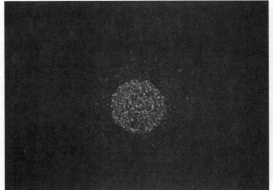 

FIGURE
14.23 *The first shock wave hits and starts to blow outward (top). The second wave starts on the object (left). The entire model is blown to smithereens (right).*

Inverse Kinematics

If you want to do character animation on a computer, you need a program that supports inverse kinematics. What are inverse kinematics or IKs? IKs are an advanced form of links that join groups of objects together. In the case of character animation IK links join a foot to a shin, a shin to a thigh, a thigh to a hip, and so on. Links are the glue that binds your model into a single group. Flip back to Chapter 13 to the section titled Model Hierarchy and Links if you're feeling a little fuzzy about this topic.

By creating a series of IK links or chains between objects, the user can build a skeleton. This skeleton in turn can be animated. You're asking yourself "What's the difference between IK and normal links?" Well with IK links, the user can place certain constraints on the movement of the joints between the objects as well as create a certain type of elasticity between the links. For example if you wanted to move a character's leg forward, you would drag the foot. The calf, thigh, and hip would follow along automatically.

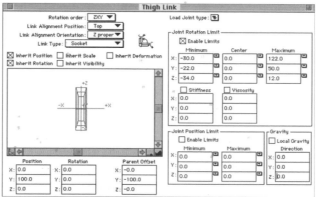

FIGURE **14.24** *Electric Image 2.5's joint linkage interface allows the user to set up and control hierarchical motion and inverse kinematics.*

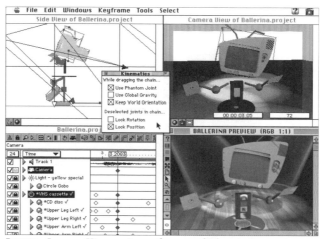

FIGURE **14.25** *Inverse Kinematics, a feature of Electric Image Animation System 2.5, lets animators create lifelike movement in the joints of animated characters.*

Deformations

Nothing in the world of 3D is constant, and that includes geometry. It might look a little strange but we can take a model of Big Ben, for example, and then squash, stretch, or even bend it into all sorts of various shapes. These special effects are more commonly known as deformations.

The way that your application handles deformations depends entirely on the type of animation package you are using. Strata's StudioPro and Specular's Infini-D, which are combination modeling and animation packages, let the user create deformations with the modeling tools. For example, the most common pair of deformations, squash and stretch, can be applied using the scale tool.

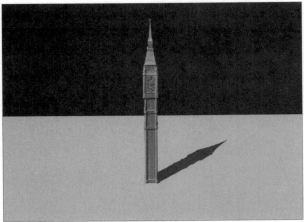

FIGURE 14.26 *Squash and stretch deformations can be applied with the scale modeling tool in both StudioPro and Infini-D. Squash (top) and stretch (bottom) renderings from StudioPro 1.75.*

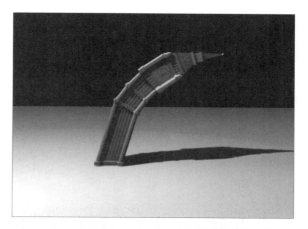

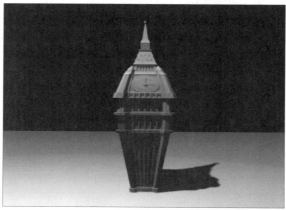

FIGURE 14.27 *Electric Image 2.5 offers the user a wide variety of deformations from which to choose: Bend (top), bulge (middle), and twist (bottom) are just a few samples of what is available with this program.*

Electric Image, which is a dedicated animation program, has tools specifically created for deformations. The user has a variety of different types of deformations to choose from ranging from Bézier spline-based deformations to taper and twist. One advantage that Electric Image has over the other programs is the amount of control as well as the area affected by the deformations.

Deformations are particularly useful when trying to anthropomorphosize (instill human characteristics in inanimate objects) objects in animations. We've all seen animations of dancing cereal boxes and bottles of mouthwash, they were all done with animated deformations.

Morph

For a while, one of the most popular animation special effects was the *morph*. A morph is when one object transforms into another. Vertices from one model are matched to corresponding vertices on another model, and the program gradually interpolates an amorphous blob between the two. Like the page turning transition is to the video editor, or cheese whiz is to the gourmet, the Morph falls into the same sort of category for the 3D designer. There are a couple of programs on the Macintosh that can handle morphing, but it is generally restricted to models based on the same spline object.

Metaballs

Metaballs are the most questionable animation feature on the Mac. While other platforms such as the SGI have applications that take full advantage of metaballs for modeling, no Mac application has truly proved them useful. Metaballs are spherical models that have their own specific animation characteristics. They behave like a liquid with a high surface tension. Whenever one or more metaballs approach they bond to form a larger volume. Some programs even offer control parameters such as speed and gravity. The question is, what do you do with them?

SECTION THREE: BACKGROUNDS

A good background can make or break a rendering. The key of course is knowing how to create a good one. Nowadays there are literally thousands of third-party developers dedicated to producing CD-ROMs full of high-resolution imagery. A lot of this imagery can be used royalty free in your productions. The primary advantage to the use of stock footage in your 3D production is that it is easy to use. You don't have to go out and photograph a landscape, develop the film, and then scan it into your computer. Another benefit is that a photographed background definitely makes an image seem more real.

Applying a Background in a Scene

The most simple method of inserting a background into a scene is to use the **Add Background** feature found in your 3D rendering programs. Most programs let the user load a 2D image into their application, which will be used as the background when the scene is rendered.

Tip. Make sure that the dimensions of your background match the dimensions of the final rendering. If your background is too small, it will appear pixelated; too large and your system has to deal with more information than it needs to.

Tip. Use your background image as an environment map for an added degree of realism.

The question is, do you really want to add the background now? Adding a background to a 3D scene can add a fair amount of rendering time to your project especially when dealing with an animation. Its is usually a better idea to render your animation first with the background as an Alpha channel and then composite the image later in postproduction. We'll cover this topic in Chapter 16.

Using Models as Backgrounds

The problem with using a 2D image as a background is that the camera action might not match a still background image. You could add a moving video clip as the background in postproduction if you render the scene with an Alpha channel. Unfortunately you will then have to match the action in the composited background to the rendered action in the foreground such as a camera pan or zoom.

Perhaps a better alternative, which provides the most realistic results, but at the cost of increased rendering times, is to use 3D objects as canvases on which to paint a background. By using this method the camera can interact with the background and the designer does not have to worry about the foreground and background being synchronized.

T
U
T
O
R
I
A
L

ENVIRONMENT SPHERES

Imagine you want to create an animation of a spaceship gliding through the universe. In the background you want a nebula and maybe even a dusting of stars. You could draw a rectangular image but it would be a big pain to animate and synchronize it properly to the action in postproduction. Fortunately there is another method available.

STEP ONE

Start by creating your color maps in Photoshop. Paint one color map for the nebula, and two separate maps for the star field. Make the aspect ratio of the nebula 1:2 and 1:1 for the star field. Be sure to create an Alpha channel or transparency map for each image.

Tip. An easy way to create a star field is in Photoshop. Create a new document and then use the **Noise** filter. Set the level to around 32. Then invert the image and adjust the levels to get the desired number of stars.

STEP TWO

In your 3D application, create three concentric spheres. Make each sphere slightly larger than the one inside. The size or scale of all three spheres needs to be very large relative to the size of the models in the animation. All of your models need to fit easily within the three spheres with plenty of room to spare. Also be sure that your light source is located within the spheres as well.

Apply the color map for the nebula on the inside sphere using spherical mapping. Apply a color map for the stars onto each of the two outer spheres using cubic mapping. The use of cubic mapping reduces the chances of spherical distortion at the poles and the equator. Be sure to apply a transparency map to each sphere so that the one behind it is visible.

FIGURE
14.28
Color map for the nebula (top) and color maps for the star field (left and right).

STEP THREE

Depending on the rendering algorithm and 3D application, you might have to create a specular, ambient, and diffuse map for each sphere. Do a test rendering to see which are necessary. Also, if available in your 3D package, turn off shadow casting and receiving for each sphere.

By creating three concentric spheres with color maps, you have a passable 3D environment for your animation. All of the action for the animation can be set within the three spheres. Since each sphere is slightly larger than the next, it provides an element of depth. As a camera pans around the scene, the nebula and both star fields appear to be layered with a paralax effect.

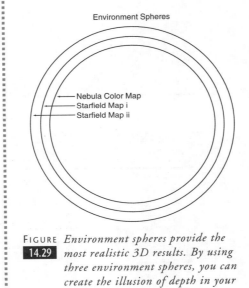

Environment Spheres

Nebula Color Map
Starfield Map i
Starfield Map ii

FIGURE **14.29** *Environment spheres provide the most realistic 3D results. By using three environment spheres, you can create the illusion of depth in your background.*

ENVIRONMENT SAUCERS

Another method used to create a convincing background image is to scale an environmental sphere along its Y axis so that it becomes more saucer shaped instead of spherical. By also adding a 2D square or rectangle in the center of the saucer you can create a ground plane. Apply sky textures such as clouds or stars to the sphere and maybe even a terrain model to the ground plane. All of the action in the animation should take place between the top of the saucer and the middle ground plane.

Tip. Be sure to add the illusion of depth of field and haze by using fog in your renderings. Set the outer perimeter of the fog to be slightly less than the radius of the saucer.

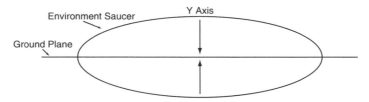

FIGURE *All of the action should take place between the top of the saucer*
14.30 *and the middle ground plane.*

INFINITE PLANES

There is yet still another method for creating a background for your scene. Create two infinite planes that are oriented on the X, Y axes. Script all of the action in the scene to occur between the two planes. If you want to make the animation a little bit more dramatic, apply an animated texture map to the planes. The drawback to using this technique is that the image does appear slightly flat.

Environment Mapping

You're probably wondering why the section on environment mapping is in this chapter rather than in the chapter on texture maps. The reason is that while an environment map is indeed a specific type of map, it isn't handled in the same way as a regular texture map. An environment map is an image that is mapped onto an invisible sphere that surrounds your entire scene, and is used by your 3D rendering application as a reflection.

If we created a highly reflective object in a 3D scene, the object would reflect all of the other models around it. The problem arises when dealing with objects that you don't see. For example, imagine a shiny teakettle sitting on your kitchen table. The kettle reflects everything in the room such as the stove, the counter top and the lights. But the kettle also reflects the things that we can't see when we look at the kettle. Our limited field of view only takes in the kettle and the table that it's resting on. But the kettle reflects other objects such as the picture on the wall behind us, or the chandelier hanging from the ceiling. Of course, we don't want to model all of this stuff just for the sake of a reflection, that's why we turn to environment maps.

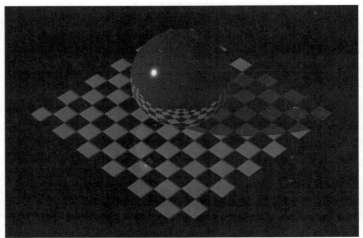

FIGURE 14.31 *Rendering of a scene in StudioPro with no environment map applied.*

FIGURE 14.32 *Rendering of a scene in StudioPro with an environment map of a room applied. Notice that the reflections on the floor are more realistic as well.*

Environment maps can be anything from a scanned image to a rendering of a scene. Most programs let the user either choose from a set of predefined maps or allow the user to load their own. To get the most accurate results in a scene, it's a good idea to create your own environment map. Creating your own map is as simple as doing a quick rendering of the scene on which you're working. If you're concerned that the reflective object might show up flaws in your rendered environment map, take the map into Photoshop and apply a little Gaussian blur or distortion to the image. By using this method, the reflections in the final rendered scene will be based on the exact same color palette as the scene itself.

Perspective Matching

One of the more useful features of 3D design is creative visualization. It's tremendously easier and faster to design a product such as a toaster or a skyscraper in 3D than it is to go out to a model shop and have one built. The client can also be taken on a fly-through of a building, for example, complete with marble floors, glass windows, working lights, and fountains. The scale modeler would be hard pressed to do the same.

One of the more specific visualization tasks for the 3D designer is digital compositing. Digital composting places 3D objects into 2D photographed scenes. For example, an architchtural firm might want to see what a group of kiosks looks like in a lobby. Of course it is cheaper to model the kiosks in 3D than to construct life-size mock-ups.

MODELING

The first step in this process is to make sure that your modeling is accurate. Use real-world dimensions and if you can use a CAD file as your template. The idea is to be able to place your models accurately within the scene. Not only do you need to model your kiosks, but it is a good idea to also model some of the larger feature objects in the scene. For example, you should model the escalator and some of the walls, but don't waste your time with objects such as ashtrays or potted plants. The larger objects will help you align the model's perspective later on with the photograph.

FIGURE *The kiosks will be inserted into a photograph of the actual scene. The*
14.33 *lines on the floor are from a 2D DXF file from the building's architect*
and were used to match the perspective of the model to the photograph.
In the final rendering they were made invisible.

THE PHOTO SHOOT

The next step is to go out and photograph the scene itself. Make sure that you take a floor plan with you so that you can mark where your camera is located. Measure and record the height of the camera off the floor. It is also vital to remember the lens size, focal length, and film type so that you can later match it in your 3D application. It's a good idea to walk around the space so that you can figure out where the light is coming from, and the type of lighting being used. For example, figure out if the space is lit by incandescents or natural lighting. Also record the time of day so that you can match your solar angle and shadows.

Another good idea is to take three ping-pong balls with you to the photoshoot. Place them somewhere in the scene where they can be easily removed in postproduction. Place the balls a fair distance apart in the location, they will be used later to triangulate the scene. Make sure that you record where you placed them. For example: "10' in from the right on the north wall, 5' up from floor." When you get back to your studio create a model for each ball in the 3D scene. These anchor points are vital if you don't have any other references such as a CAD file!

MATCHING THE PERSPECTIVE

Now comes the hardest part and, unfortunately, it's all trial and error. Set your 3D camera to the exact same settings as your real-world camera. But don't rely completely on the numbers, use your eyes to judge the scene. Your 3D camera uses an algorithm to determine focal length and perspective and it might not exactly match the settings of your real camera.

Scan the photograph of the scene into your computer. Make sure that the dimensions of the 3D camera window correspond to that of the scanned photograph. Import the photo into your 3D application and then use it as a background. Try to line up the 3D ping-pong balls and the real ones in the photograph. Do your test renderings in wireframe so that you don't have to wait too long for the image. Finally, keep on doing it until you get it right. Try to match the parallel lines in your model with the lines in the photograph, those are the best indicators of a good match.

When you feel that you've gotten everything aligned, render the scene with the background as an Alpha channel and then composite the background.

Tip. Electric Image and Infini-D have a feature that lets the user see the background image in the camera window. This feature is invaluable when trying to match perspectives since you do not have to wait for a rendering to see if your lines match.

FIGURE **14.34** *The kiosks were rendered with the background as an Alpha channel and then composited in Photoshop.*

15 Rendering

The rendering process occurs when the computer finally takes over and you can just sit back and watch. It's kind of like sending out film to be developed at the local photo shop. The rendering process can take anywhere from minutes to even days when the scene is complex. The more lights, texture maps, and model geometry that you add to a scene, the longer the amount of time that you will have to wait for the image to be rendered.

Unlike photography where you only get one chance at taking a picture of a scene, it is commonplace for the 3D designer to take quick multiple renderings of a scene before committing to a final shot. In 3D we don't have the luxury of a camera's viewfinder or WYSIWYG (what you see is what you get) — and it's very rare to be able to get a scene completely right on the first try.

Tip. The rendering process should be thought of as an interactive process. When you're either modeling or applying your texture maps it's important to stop and do a quick rendering of your model from time to time.

SECTION ONE: RENDERING ALGORITHMS

You'll learn how to choose the right rendering algorithm for your animation. The difference between Raytracing and Phong and the advantages and disadvantages of each are discussed, along with the fabled "Raydiosity."

SECTION TWO: CONFIGURING THE COMPUTER

Take a few minutes now to save yourself a couple of hours later. Learn how to configure your computer for rendering.

SECTION THREE: SPECIAL RENDERING CONSIDERATIONS

Render farms, multiple processors, and SGI rendering engines are covered.

SECTION FOUR: OUTPUT RESOLUTIONS

We discuss how to set the frame rate, screen size, and bit depth of your animation relative to mulitmedia, television, and print applications.

Section One: Rendering Algorithms

Many types of rendering algorithms are available and each one serves a unique purpose to the 3D designer and should be used in specific situations. But before we get into the different types of rendering algorithms available, we should cover how your computer actually renders a scene. This information isn't absolutely essential to comprehend or even know, but it will give you a good understanding of how rendering works.

Surface Normals

Every model that you will ever render will be composed of polygons. Even your spline-based models are first converted to polygons before rendering. Most programs use either three- or four-sided polygons to define the surface of a model. A polygon can be broken down into two separate parts: vertices and lines. The vertices are the points that define the start and end of a line. The length and number of lines determine the shape and size of a polygon. Groups of polygons are then used to create shapes such as a spheres or cubes.

When it comes time to render a scene, either one or several *normals* are assigned to every single polygon in the model depending on the rendering algorithm. A normal is a perpendicular vector that is used by the rendering algorithm to determine the orientation or direction of the polygon. Depending on the type of rendering algorithm used, a normal is assigned either to the center of a polygon or to each one of the individual vertices that compose a polygon. Normals are then used to determine the intensity or shade of the polygon or the pixel that it is assigned to by the rendering engine.

Normals, polygons, and verticies are all used by your rendering engine to create an image.

The following is a list of the more popular types of rendering engines available on the Mac:

- Wireframe
- Hidden line
- Flat shading
- Gouraud shading
- Phong shading
- Ray tracing
- Radiosity

Wireframe

The wireframe rendering option is available in just about every single 3D package today. When either modeling or scripting an animation, you're usually looking at a wireframe preview of the model. When a scene is rendered in wireframe mode, you can only see the edges or lines that compose the polygon. It's kind of like a skeleton view of the scene. You are able to see both the front and back faces of a model since none of the polygons are rendered as solid.

Wireframe rendering is useful for viewing the motion and placements of models in an animation. One of the drawbacks to previewing an animation in this mode is that it is often difficult to see if one model passes through another. The advantage is that wireframe is often the fastest rendering option available.

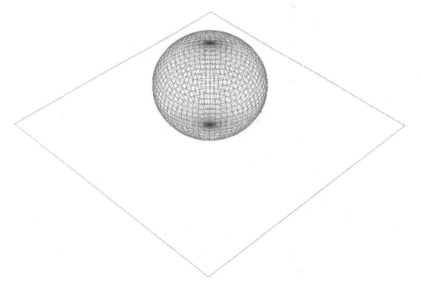

FIGURE **15.1** *Wireframe rendering lets you see all of the geometry that composes the surface of a model. Notice that the rear faces of the sphere are visible.*

Hidden Line

Hidden line is like the wireframe mode except that the polygons that are obscured by other geometry are not visible. Hidden line is useful for determining the spatial orientation of an object. In wireframe mode, it's often difficult to discern whether you're looking at the top or bottom of a model. By using hidden line you will be able to tell how and where your model is located in a scene.

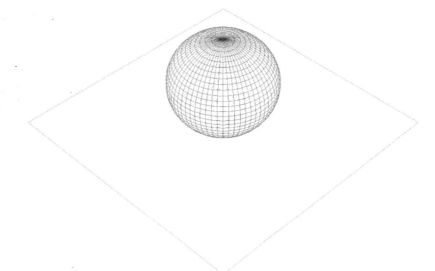

FIGURE *Hidden line rendering hides the geometry that is obscured by other*
15.2 *geometry.*

Flat Shading

Flat shading assigns a normal to the center of each polygon and then shades the polygon with one uniform color. The object tends to look very faceted since it is not smoothed. The advantage of using flat shading is that you can determine the intensity and placement of light sources without having to commit to a higher level rendering algorithm, which would be more time consuming. Flat shading is perhaps the best choice of rendering algorithm to use for a preview animation (see Figure 15.3 on the following page).

Gouraud Shading

Gouraud shading works by interpolating the intensity of the normals that are located at the vertices of each polygon, and then averaging the intensity for the entire surface of each polygon. Even though the object appears to be smoothly shaded when rendered, the primary disadvantage of Gouraud shading is that texture maps often appear to be muddy and the edges of an object are often faceted. Specular highlights are also prone to artifacting.

FIGURE *Lighting intensity is assigned in a uniform manner for each polygon.*
15.3

FIGURE *Texture mapping with Gouraud shading tends to be muddy and the*
15.4 *object often appears faceted around the edges.*

Gouraud shading is useful for getting a rough idea of the color and texture mapping of an object. Even though Gouraud is one of the faster rendering engine, I usually prefer to render an object in Phong shading because of the higher image quality (Figure 15.4).

Phong Shading

Phong shading assigns a normal to each vertex in a polygon and then creates a set of new normals for the entire face of the polygon. Each normal is used to calculate an intensity value for each pixel in the face of a polygon.

Phong shading is truly the workhorse of the animation world. While the image quality is not as high as Raytracing, Phong shading is by far much faster. Rendering time is perhaps the number one concern to the 3D producer working under deadline, and in many cases it is not cost effective to use Raytracing to complete a project. Phong shading is relatively fast and the image can even rival Raytracing when the designer is skilled enough. The drawback to Phong shading is that both reflections and shadows are not as precise as they would be with a Raytracing algorithm.

FIGURE *Phong shading is the best choice of a rendering algorithm when*
15.5 *rendering a long animation.*

QuickDraw 3D will begin to use a hybrid Gouraud/Phong rendering algorithm as its rendering engine. The quality of the QD3D-rendered image is good enough to judge the placement of texture maps, colored light sources, reflections, and transparencies. However, it is not refined enough to be used in the final product.

Raytracing

Ray tracing is unlike all of the other rendering algorithms available. A ray is cast backwards from the camera lens, to the object, and then, depending on the level of reflection, transparency, or amount of refraction, to another object or light source. The number of bounces is know as recursion and the higher the number of recursions, the more accurate the image but the longer the rendering time. Each ray cast from the camera corresponds to a pixel in the final image.

Raytracing is the most accurate of all of the rendering algorithms available for production work. Reflections, shadows, and refraction are calculated according to real-world physical parameters and are very exact. The drawback to Raytracing is that it is generally slow in comparison to the rest of the rendering engines. For longer animation

FIGURE *Ray tracing is the most exact yet the slowest of all of the rendering*
15.6 *algorithms.*

projects it would be a better decision to use Phong. But when it comes to doing still images, a Raytracing algorithm is a better choice since the image is not moving and has to stand up to closer scrutiny by the viewer.

Radiosity

Developed at Cornell University, Radiosity takes Raytracing one step further. Radiosity calculates *interobject illumination* or color bleed. For example, if you placed a red ball on top of a piece of white paper, you would be able to see a red tint on the paper where the ball is resting. On the Macintosh platform, the only version of Radiosity available is in Strata StudioPro and is their own version, which is named Raydiosity. Either Radiosity or Raydiosity cannot be seriously considered for full-scale production work because of the amazingly long rendering times associated with both algorithms.

Tip. You can fake Radiosity by placing a low-intensity radial light near the object that is receiving a color bleed from another object. Make sure that the color of the light matches the color of the object casting the glow. Another work-around is to change the specular color of the object that is receiving the color bleed to match that of the color of the casting object.

SECTION TWO: CONFIGURING THE COMPUTER

Once you've finished setting up the scene and you're ready to hit the render button, take a few minutes to set up your computer. These few minutes you take now can save you hours in the long run. Here's a checklist of things that you should do before starting a long rendering project:

- Turn your computer into an island unto itself and take it off of any established network. You don't want any interruptions from automatic file archiving software or other pesky users trying to access your files. The worst case scenario would be for your computer to crash and lose all of the work already rendered. There is less chance of this happening if your computer is on its own.

- Disable any extensions not in use. You'll save yourself a couple of megabytes worth of RAM, which you should dedicate to your rendering application anyway.
- Disable any automatic software such as screen savers, fax software, and automatic shutdown options. Screen savers don't do anything anyway and they interfere with the processor. Fax software can interrupt the rendering process and crash your computer, which can ruin hours if not days worth of work. Don't forget to turn off power-saving options such as automatic shutdown features. Think about what would happen if you have your computer shut itself down every night at twelve and you have a rendering set to go all weekend. You won't be too happy on Monday morning. The only thing that your processor should be doing is rendering!
- Try to batch or queue renderings rather than rendering them from the application. Every window that is open or application that is running slows down rendering time. Many applications such as Electric Image, StudioPro, and form•Z let the user batch render files. This is a more efficient rendering method since you don't have the overhead of the animation or modeling application.

SECTION THREE: SPECIAL RENDERING CONSIDERATIONS

At the higher end of the 3D spectrum there are unique solutions to the problems of long rendering times. And every software developer has taken a different approach to this dilemma.

Rendering Farms and Multiprocessors

The old expression goes "Two heads are better than one." And in 3D the axiom stands true. A rendering farm is simply a group of networked computers dedicated to rendering animations. Depending on how the software is configured, the farm can handle the rendering process in one of two ways.

The first method is called *distributed rendering,* in which the chunks of the project are automatically distributed among the members of the farm. Each computer renders a certain number of frames and then sends the information back to the server. The second method uses the concept of parallel processing. All of the separate computers work as one, breaking down a single frame of animation and working on it at the same time. In this case the processing power of the farm increases geometrically rather than arithmetically.

With the advent of the DayStar digital multiprocessor machines, up to four 604 PowerPC processors can be installed in one computer. Unfortunately the increase in processing power is arithmetic and true parallel processing won't surface until late 1997 when Apple releases its next version of its operating system.

SGI Rendering Engines

The limitations of processing power of the PowerPC are always evident especially when compared to the SGI platform. And the old expression goes "If you can't beat them, then join them." Some software applications such as Electric Image and Hash Inc's Animation Master offer separate rendering engines that can take advantage of the computational power of the SGI platform. The advantage of this setup is that the user can work under the easy-to-use Mac OS and then turn around and take advantage of the SGI's processing power without having to learn too much UNIX.

Hardware Acceleration

In the past, companies such as YARC Systems offered specialized hardware rendering acceleration boards for certain software applications. Rendering times were dramatically faster than on the older 68K machines. When the PowerPC came about, the difference in rendering speed between the two was marginal and the boards soon lost favor. But now new hardware called the HYDRA has been introduced by YARC that once again accelerates rendering faster than many PowerPC processors. The major drawback is software support for these new boards.

Section Four: Output Resolution

The old saying goes "Garbage in, garbage out." Choosing the correct resolution for your image or animation is vitally important. Whether you're using the final output for multimedia, print, or television you need to work at the highest possible resolution possible. When it comes time to render an animation you're often faced with a myriad of different screen sizes and ratios, frame rates, dots per inch, and bit depth. For the uninitiated this can be a very confusing moment. Even worse, as each of these fields increases, so do your rendering times. You don't want to spend too much time rendering a file, but on the other hand you don't want to sacrifice image quality either.

Multimedia

Several factors affect the playback of animations targeted for multimedia applications. Your first consideration is the medium used to deliver the project. Developing an animation for a CD-ROM is vastly different from an animation used for a kiosk. The key to producing an animation for a CD-ROM title is judging the lowest common denominator. Not everyone will have a superfast and well-equipped computer like yours, and the playback of the animation depends entirely on hardware considerations.

The biggest bottleneck in multimedia is the CD-ROM drive itself. Optimizing animation for delivery on CD-ROM is discussed in depth in Chapter 16, Postproduction. For now, what you need to decide on is the frame rate and screen size of your animation. A good rule of thumb is to render at 320 X 240 at a frame rate of 24 to 26 fps. It's best to have too much footage at a higher quality than not enough. You will probably want to reduce the bit depth, frame rate, and screen size later, but for now you should keep the quality as high as possible. Also do not use a lossy codec on your animation.

Tip. A lossy codec is one that reduces the size of the file at the cost of resolution. The only QuickTime compressor that you should be using for now is Animation set to its highest quality settings. If you're tight for space, settle for JPEG. It does lose some resolution, but not a tremendous amount.

For multimedia kiosk projects your options are a little bit better since you already know the capabilities of your delivery platform. If the kiosk uses a hardware compressor/decompressor such as Radius's VideoVision Studio card or Targa's TrueVision board, your animation's quality should be kept high. The resolution should be 640 X 480, at 30 fps, with 24-bit color. If you're not planning to use a hardware codec your maximum screen size should be 320 X 240 and the frame rate up to 24 fps with a 16-bit color depth.

On the other hand, I prefer to keep all of my animations at 640 × 480, 30 fps, 24 bit, regardless of the type of project. It's fairly easy to alter any of these parameters in postproduction in a minimal amount of time. The advantage is that if I ever decide to port my animation to any platform the source material will be already prepared.

Television

Rendering an animation for broadcast television delivery can be fairly tricky at times and here are several issues that need to be dealt with in order to guarantee a successful project.

Color

The first issue is color. Your multiscan computer monitor gives you a greater range of colors to choose from, which can be a problem when converting an animation to NTSC. Also colors such as some shades of red tend to bleed when displayed on an NTSC monitor. When rendering an animation, go ahead and use the full 24-bit color palette. The palette can then be converted into a NTSC safe palette in postproduction. The screen size should be 640 × 480 and the frame rate 29.97 fps or 30 fps depending on your output device. Unfortunately the term "frames per second" can be slightly misleading. The next section will explain the concept of interlaced fields.

Interlacing

The major problem with converting an animation to NTSC is dealing with interlacing. What is interlacing? Well, it all goes back to how your multiscan computer monitor and interlaced television monitor display images.

A computer monitor is composed of thousands of horizontal lines which draw the image displayed on the screen. The lines are refreshed or redrawn on the screen from top to bottom every fraction of a second, fast enough that you probably don't notice. Once the electron gun reaches the bottom of the screen, it starts again at the top working downward. This is why when you see video tape shot of a computer monitor, you probably notice that the image on the monitor appears to be scrolling downward. The reason is that the video camera only records an image at 29.7 frames per second while the computer's refresh rate is much higher.

Multiscan Computer Monitor
Scan Lines

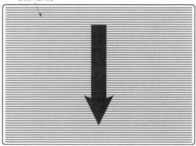

FIGURE
15.7
A multiscan computer monitor starts by drawing scan lines at the top of the screen and then works its way downward.

A television screen on the other hand is interlaced and is composed of 525 scan lines. One frame of video is made up of two separate fields or sets of scan lines. The two fields are composed of two sets of alternating scan lines. An NTSC monitor starts by displaying the Upper Field or Field #1 first. Once this field is displayed on the screen then the Lower Field or Field #2 is displayed. The fields are alternated at 60 cycles per second. So even though one frame is displayed at 30 frames per second, each frame consists of two fields and each field is on screen for 1/60th of a second.

Interlaced Television Monitor
Scan Lines

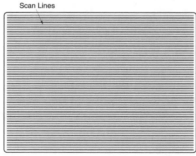

— Scan lines for Field #1 or Upper Field
— Scan lines for Field #2 or Lower Field

FIGURE
15.8
An interlaced television screen displays 60 fields or 30 frames per second. The two fields are composed of two separate sets of alternating scan lines.

Rendering for an Interlaced Monitor

So you're probably wondering how to create an animation for an interlaced or television monitor. There are a couple of methods. The first is to not worry about it at all. Several postproduction applications can interpolate the second field from the first. The drawback to this method is that the animation will not be as sharp or smooth as an interlaced animation. The second method depends on your 3D application. Some programs such as Electric Image let you render an interlaced animation file. If you don't have this interlacing feature and you want to interlace your animation, there is a work-around. You will need to render the file at 60 frames per second and then interlace the animation in a postproduction application such as Adobe After Effects. After Effects will take alternating frames and use them in the lower field. Unfortunately rendering times will be doubled using this method.

 Tip. When or if HDTV ever arrives on these shores, the dimensions of the screen are 2130 x 1152 pixels.

PIXEL RATIO

At the high end of the video spectrum you also have to consider pixel ratio. The horizontal to vertical ratio of a computer pixel is square or 1 to 1 but for various high-end video formats the pixel ratio can be rectangular. For example, Sony's D-1 component digital format has a pixel ratio of 2 to 1. The only program that supports a variable pixel ratio is Electric Image. Generally speaking this should not concern any but the extremely high-end user.

Film

Rendering an animation for delivery on film is technically easier to grasp than rendering for television. The frame rate of film is 24 frames per second; the problem is calculating the aspect ratio and the resolution at which to render.

The method used to get computer graphics to film is the digital printer, which can be found only at the high-end postproduction houses. Depending on the grain of the film and the type of digital printer used, the resolution and aspect ratio of the animation will vary. Listed below is a rough reference to the aspect ratios you should be working at to output to the various film types. Be sure to check with your postproduction house to see if the dimensions are suitable and to find out their recommended resolutions.

Film Type	Aspect Ratio
Super 8mm	4:3
16mm	18:13
Super 16mm	5:3
35mm slide film	3:2
35mm full	4:3
VistaVision	3:2
65mm	16:7
IMAX	6:5
70mm	2.19:1
Techniscope	2.35:1

Print

The trick to printing an image is knowing the maximum output resolution of your printing device. If your color copier or Fiery printer can support up to 300 dpi, then you should render your image at a slightly higher resolution just so you have a margin of error. The problem is that most 3D programs aren't configured to render to a specific dpi number; instead they are designed to render to a specific screen size. The trick is being able to calculate a certain screen size so that you end up with the right dpi.

The screen resolution of the average Macintosh monitor displays 72 dpi, which is dots or pixels per inch. If you want to render a 640 x 480 pixel image at 300 dpi the first step would be to divide the output resolution by 72.

300/72 = 4.17.

The next step would be to multiply both the horizontal and vertical dimensions of the image by 4.17 and then that would be the new screen size. Once the image is rendered you can then adjust the dpi and image size in a program such as Photoshop. Most people simply multiply the horizontal and vertical dimensions by 100 so that they have a little leeway when it comes to manipulating the image in postproduction.

CHAPTER

16 Postproduction

CHAPTER REQUIREMENTS
Basic understanding of either Premiere or After Effects and Photoshop.

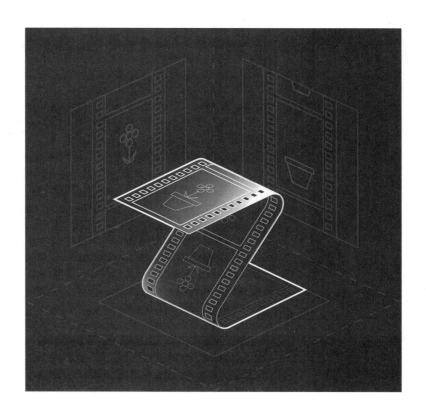

Congratulations on making it this far. The modeling, texture mapping, lighting, and then rendering stages were long and complex, but finally it's almost done. All of your clips have been rendered and they're waiting to be strung together. In this section we'll finish what we've started and put the final touches on our work.

SECTION ONE: POSTPRODUCTION SOFTWARE

Learn all about your software tools After Effects and Premiere. What is QuickTime and all of the associated codecs? Going for the high road, we'll learn about hardware video editing suites.

SECTION TWO: DIGITAL COMPOSITING

Your best friend is the Alpha channel. Learn how to use the Alpha channel to composite footage or create your own. If there is no Alpha channel in your video, try using chroma keying instead.

SECTION THREE: PREPARING FOR OUTPUT

Learn how to optimize your animation for CD-ROM, televison, and how to deal with the big ugly interlacing issue.

SECTION FOUR: OUTPUT METHODS

Now that you've finished your animation, how do you get it off of your computer onto video tape? All about frame-accurate solutions, CD-ROMs, and interlacing.

SECTION ONE: POSTPRODUCTION SOFTWARE

The entire world of digital postproduction can find its roots in the old analog tape rooms that used to service the broadcast industry. It wasn't so long ago that tape editors had to use several racks of frame-accurate tape recorders to create a project. The minimum requirement was at least three tape decks, the A/B decks to play the source material, and the C deck to record it all. Lengthy EDLs (edit decision lists) were necessary to tell the decks which footage to play and record. To get any special effects, more expensive hardware was necessary to perform even the simplest transition or wipe. To say the least it was not fun, easy, or cheap.

Welcome to the world of nonlinear digital editing. All of your clips are at your fingertips. Your source footage is held on a hard drive so that means you don't have to sit and swap tapes out of a series of expensive frame-accurate tape decks. Also since all of the information is digital, there is no generation loss. Finally, we have a wealth of special effects to choose from that can make the most seasoned tape editor green with envy.

| **Editing Software** | Our primary tools in this world of nonlinear editing and postproduction are Adobe's Premiere and After Effects. Both of these programs have a wealth of features that can accomplish all of our requirements. In the previous chapters we had mentioned both of these programs in reference to creating texture maps, but in this section we're going to use these programs as our postproduction workhorses. Any serious 3D designer needs a copy of either one or both of these programs. For this chapter we're assuming that you have a basic understanding of Premiere. There are some tutorials for After Effects as well, but they are not as detailed. Both After Effects and Premiere project files are included on the CD-ROM that correspond to each tutorial. There is also a demo version of Premiere that you can use if you don't have a copy of either program. |

Each program has specific uses in the world of nonlinear editing and postproduction, and it wouldn't be excessive to have both programs in your studio. Some feature sets do overlap, but each application has its own strengths and weaknesses, yet as a whole both programs complement each other.

AFTER EFFECTS 3.0

After Effects has been traditionally thought of as a 2D video animation program, yet the interface is remarkably like a 3D animation program with a keyframe-based linear time line. Special effects such as warping, rippling, opacity, scale, and numerous filters can be applied to video or animation clips with keyframes and then altered over time. Multiple mattes or layers can also be animated. The best feature of this program is the level of control afforded to the user. Numeric fields and velocity curves control just about every feature of this application. The drawback to After Effects is the rather spartan and sometimes counter-intuitive interface.

PREMIERE 4.0

Adobe's other signature product is Premiere. This application is reminiscent of the traditional tape editing environment with two A/B tracks. The user has a variety of different special effects and transitions to choose from which makes stringing together a series of clips a breeze. While Premiere does have many of the same features as After Effects, it does lack the same level of control and precision. The primary strength of Premiere is that it is an excellent editing tool for both video and sound, and the interface is very intuitive and easy to use.

QuickTime and Codecs

All that we can do on our computer in terms of animation probably would not be possible without the magic of QuickTime. QuickTime is a system-level extension that is available on both PC and Mac platforms that makes handling video or animation files easy. QuickTime writes to a common file format that is accessible in just about every video and 3D application available to date. Even though our completed animation might seem like one single file, it is really composed of many individual frames as well as a sound track. The QuickTime format manages to squeeze the entire animation into one tiny little package or file.

Another benefit to QuickTime is the file size. By using codecs, the user can set the resolution, data rate, and the size of an animation. A codec, otherwise known as a compressor/decompressor, is what allows you to play back your animations on the desktop. If you try to play back an animation that has not been compressed, you'll notice that frames will be dropped or the motion will appear ragged because the amount of information is simply too much for your computer to handle.

CODECS

Most users are familiar with software-based codecs. There are specialized hardware-based codecs available but they do require separate boards or cards. In the case of software codecs, anyone with a computer can use them. A software codec comes in a variety of different forms, each one suited for specific applications.

Cinepak

Cinepak is the best choice for playback from a CD-ROM drive and you can usually get a good playback rate upwards of 320 x 240. The drawback to this codec is the fact that compression times can often be long and the image quality is somewhat low.

Apple Video

Generally a better quality than Cinepak, but it tends to take more storage space and has a slower display rate.

Animation

This is the best codec for saving or storing an animation. This format is lossless and can handle bit depths to 32 bits. However, it is not fast enough to handle most playback situations and should be used as an archiving or intermediate codec.

JPEG

Developed by the Joint Photographic Experts Group, JPEG is the next best codec for storing an animation. This format is lossy so you will lose some resolution but the image quality remains good. If you don't have the storage space but you want to keep a high image quality, use JPEG. Some specialized video boards use JPEG as a codec.

MPEG

MPEG offers a fairly high image quality comparable to VHS video. MPEG can handle full-screen video at 24 bits. The drawback is that you will need both a hardware compressor and decompressor.

Graphics

Graphics is used when the target platform can only handle 8-bit graphics. It's a lossless format and is fairly slow.

None

Kind of self-explanatory. None uses no compression at all and is completely lossless.

Resolution

Garbage in, garbage out. Remember that phrase. No matter what codec you eventually decide to deliver your animation with, you have to maintain the highest possible resolution throughout the entire production process. That's why I always recommend rendering all of your animations at 640 × 480 with 24-bit color and a 30 fps frame rate even if they will be played back from a CD-ROM.

Tip. It's often faster to render at 320 × 240 for CD-ROM production but I like to work with higher quality images just in case I have to repurpose the animation.

Any image correction, special effects, or editing needs to be done at the highest possible quality. You shouldn't be editing together 8-bit clips of video, or compositing a 16-bit file on top of a 24-bit image. Yes, it does require a tremendous amount of storage space to keep all of these files but the end product will suffer otherwise. Also if the specifications change in midproject you won't have to go back and rerender all of your source material if you stay at 24-bits. And even though you might want to use Cinepak as your codec you should only work with a lossless codec during the postproduction process. An animation that has been compressed and then recomposed again will look terrible.

Hardware Editing Suites

One of the primary disadvantages of editing animation or video on the desktop using strictly software methods is speed. As you probably have already noticed, your computer tends to become bogged down when playing back an animation that is larger than 320 × 240. The computer cannot handle that amount of data being shuttled along from your hard drive to the CPU. The primary culprits for this trickle of data are:

- Hard drive speed
- SCSI port speed
- Codec

The question is, how do I get full-screen video on my desktop? First of all let's break down an animation into its key components. One second of animation is composed of 30 frames and each frame is equal to approximately 1 megabyte of information uncompressed. If your hard drive can only transfer information at 2 megabytes per second then there's the first problem. The next problem is the SCSI port speed. A

SCSI-1 port is the standard interface used to connect a hard drive to a computer's motherboard. A SCSI-1 bus can only pass around 2 MB/sec. Sounds like we're trying to pass a watermelon through a garden hose.

HARDWARE-BASED CODECS

The first solution in reducing the data flow is to use a codec or compressor/decompressor. A codec can reduce the size of your frame, but at the cost of either resolution or decompression speed. QuickTime offers a variety of different software-based codecs but none of them is fast enough to handle full-screen video at 30 frames per second. That's why we have to turn to hardware-based codecs.

Companies such as TrueVision, Data Translation, Radius, and Avid all offer a variety of cards that have hardware-based codecs that can handle the rigors of playing back an animation as well as digitizing or capturing video. The quality of the image varies according to the compression ratio of the board. You can buy a low-end board that can play back a full-screen animation for approximately $2000. The drawback is that the image quality is not too clear because the compression ratio is fairly high. Generally speaking the low end boards do not have a good enough quality for professional broadcast results, yet they do offer a means for previewing an animation. To get the best possible image quality, you have to use less compression. Using less compression means that more information has to be transferred at any given time. Hardware-based codecs or video editing boards can reduce the data steam down into the 2 MB to 5 MB per second range. Unfortunately that's not small enough for the average system to handle. The solution involves throwing even more hardware at the problem.

While the average computer user is content with the trickle of information moving from the hard drive to the computer, the video or animation professional needs to move data at a rate that would seem like a fire hose in comparison. The average hard drive that comes with a computer has a data transfer rate in the 1- to 2-MB per second range which for the video professional is not even close to being suitable. The solution is twofold: Replace the SCSI-1 bus and find a faster hard drive.

SCSI-1 vs. SCSI-2

In 1985, even before the finishing touches were made on the old SCSI-1 format, engineers were working on the much faster SCSI-2 specifications. The differences between the two formats are numerous and the technical specifications are bewildering even for the most computer savvy. If you do manage to muddle through all of the technical jargon and cryptic phrasing, the primary difference, relevant to digital video, between the two formats can be summed up in a few sentences.

SCSI-2 can pass information along in 16-bit blocks as opposed to the 8-bit blocks that SCSI-1 can handle. The obvious advantage is that the SCSI-2 format can handle twice as much information in the same space of time as the SCSI-1 format. But it doesn't just stop there since SCSI-2 also has two distinct options that can increase the data stream. SCSI-2 has the option of being configured as both fast and wide. By using two SCSI-2 buses, a Wide configuration can transfer 32 bits of data instead of 16 bits. The fast option means that information can be transferred in a synchronous rather than an asynchronous manner. In more simple terms this means that the SCSI-2 bus does not have to wait for the first block of 16 bits of information to be transferred before starting to send the next block of 16 bits. Fast SCSI-2 can support up to 10 MB/sec and when combined with the wide format can go upwards of 40 MB/sec. When purchasing either a hard drive array or SCSI-2 card, be sure that they support both the fast and wide formats in order to get your money's worth. Another advantage of SCSI-2 is that it supports up to 15 SCSI addresses per bus. When it comes to setting up arrays of multiple drives those extra address will enable you to add more than you could under the seven addresses allocated under SCSI-1.

While most stock computer systems come equipped with SCSI-1 buses, the video professional usually has to add these. Several companies offer PCI-based cards such as Atto's Silicon Express IV and FWB's JackHammer. Of course these cards are useless unless there are high-speed drives to back them up.

THE ARRAY

While the hard drives that comes with most computer systems are more than capable of handling spread sheets and word processors, in the realm of digital video they would never last a moment. The hard drive industry has recently been producing low-cost, high-speed AV drives that are ready for the challenge of digital video. An AV drive does not experience T-Cal or thermal recalibration and has a sustained data transfer rate often in the 3 to 4 MB/sec range, which for a 5- or 10-second clip might be sufficient. But for any lengthy project exceeding 2 to

3 minutes, an AV drive would not be able to handle the load. That's where the array comes in handy.

An array is simply a pair or more of hard drives working in tandem that the computer recognizes as a single device. By *striping* several devices, which is also referred to as RAID level 0, the burden of both reading and writing information can be passed on to several devices instead of just one. An array can consist of just about any number of devices on the same SCSI bus. Taking this a step further, several arrays on multiple SCSI buses can be striped together to form an array of arrays, increasing the data transfer rate of the entire unit.

Tip. One of the major caveats of a dual-channel structure is both the termination and cabling issue which has plagued the SCSI format since its introduction. As more devices are added to an array, more cabling is then necessary and termination becomes even more difficult to configure. Keep your cables short in order to stave off future problems.

Section Two: Digital Compositing

Your best friend in the world of digital compositing is the Alpha channel. The Alpha channel has a variety of different uses depending on your application and the file format that you choose to use. For example, many 3D applications allow the designer to use a texture map with an Alpha channel. The Alpha channel can then be used as a grayscale texture map. On the other hand, in postproduction, the Alpha channel is used primarily as a transparency selection. But before we get too involved with all of the various uses of the Alpha channel, we should cover what it is and how to create one.

What Is the Alpha Channel?

There are literally hundreds of different types of graphics file formats available today ranging from TIFF to Targa to JPEG. For Macintosh users we should be mostly concerned with the PICT file, which is the platform standard. Photoshop or DeBabelizer can read and write to most of the formats available, but chances are your 3D application can only load PICT files for texture maps or backgrounds.

A PICT file can be written as a 32-bit image with 8 bits of information reserved for the red, 8 bits for the green, and 8 bits for the blue channels. Each channels can support up to 256 shades of the respective color, and when each channel is combined with the others you have a palette of 16.7 million colors with which to work. But you're probably saying to yourself, 8 + 8 + 8 only equals 24, where are the other 8 bits? The last 8 bits of information are reserved for the Alpha channel.

Tip. Now of course you don't need to use all of the channels available to you with the PICT format. For example, you can have a 24-bit image that has 16.7 million colors and no Alpha channel, or a 16-bit image with only thousands of colors, or even an 8-bit image with 256 colors.

But if the red, green, and blue channels control the color of an image, what does the Alpha channel do? The Alpha channel is an invisible 8-bit grayscale channel that can be used for selection or transparency information as well as for 3D texture mapping data. Sounds a little complex? It really isn't, believe me.

T
U
T
O
R
I
A
L

ALPHA CHANNEL TUTORIAL
The best way to learn all about the Alpha channel is with Adobe's Photoshop 3.0. There's a tryout version on the CD-ROM if you don't have a copy. Photoshop is one of the best tools for both texture map creation, postproduction, and general graphics work.

STEP ONE
Start by launching Adobe's Photoshop 3.0. Make sure that the **Channels** floating palette is on the screen. If it isn't go to the **Window** menu, select **Palettes**, and then **Show Channels**.

STEP TWO
Open the image of the spaceship. The image was rendered with the background as an Alpha channel, which is a common feature found in most 3D applications.

STEP THREE

Go to the **Select** menu and choose **Load Selection**. When the dialog box pops up make sure that **Channel #4** is selected in the pull-down **Channel** menu. You have just loaded the Alpha channel. The spaceship should have become selected in the image window. Now you can copy this information into another document, or choose to change the background image without disturbing the image of the spaceship.

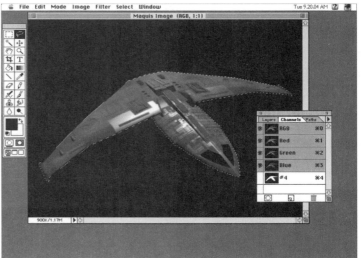

FIGURE *The Alpha channel can be used to separate the foreground image*
16.1 *from the background. Most 3D applications let the user render the background as an Alpha channel.*

Tip. The Photoshop format supports up to 24 separate Alpha channels for one file while the PICT format only supports 1.

STEP FOUR

Now that you've seen how the Alpha channel works, we can now find out what it looks like. Go to the **Channels** floating palette and click once on the channel that is labeled **#4**. This loads the Alpha channel into the image window. Notice that the Alpha channel consists only of shades of gray. Areas that are white are loaded into the selection while areas that are black are not. The in-between shades of gray are semitransparent. Notice that the white area in the image corresponds to where the spaceship is located in the foreground, while the black area matches the background.

FIGURE
16.2
The Alpha channel only uses shades of gray. Areas that are white are loaded into the selection while areas that are black are not.

STEP FIVE

Try painting or scribbling a few lines in the Alpha channel. Click once on the **RGB** channel in the **Channels** floating palette. Repeat Step Three. Notice that the changes that you made in the Alpha channel are now loaded into the selection.

Tip. When rendering your animation, be sure to use a codec that supports 32-bit images or an Alpha channel if you intend to composite a background in postproduction. The Animation codec is the best choice to use.

The advantages of using Alpha channels are numerous. For example, you can render your entire animation with the background as an Alpha channel and then substitute anything that you want in postproduction. By using this technique you're given more leeway from the design perspective since you don't have to commit to a background image and you reduce rendering time as well.

OTHER USES FOR THE ALPHA CHANNEL

In 3D design, the Alpha channel can also be used to store information. For example, in the RGB channel you can store the color map for the texture while in the Alpha channel you could keep the transparency or bump map. The advantage of this system is that it's easier to deal with one map instead of two. Several 3D applications ranging from Infini-D to Electric Image can use 32-bit texture maps.

Creating Your Own Alpha Channel

There are several ways to create your own alpha channel and the first method is automatic. For example, when you're rendering an animation, your program should let you render the background as an Alpha channel. The Alpha channel should then be automatically saved into the file. If your 3D program doesn't support an Alpha channel as a background, then don't despair, there is a work-around.

T
U
T
O
R
I
A
L

RENDERING AN ALPHA CHANNEL

OK so your 3D application doesn't support an Alpha channel and you want to create one so that you can apply some special effects in postproduction. The first step is to render your animation normally as a 24-bit file. The next step is to make a copy of your original animation project. Open the copy of the project and do the following:

STEP ONE
Delete all of the light sources in your scene.

STEP TWO
Select all of the models in your scene and remove all of the texture maps and then make your objects completely white and the background color black.

STEP THREE

Turn off all of the rendering special effects such as shadows, transparency, and bump mapping.

STEP FOUR

Set the ambient light value to 100% or completely white.

STEP FIVE

Choose a relatively fast rendering algorithm such as Phong. Render the animation. Voilá, the animation will look exactly like an Alpha channel. We'll cover how to add this clip to your animation in the next section.

SWITCHING CHANNELS

Another situation that might occur is if you want to create an Alpha channel for a video clip. Take, for example, some of the footage that comes with VCE's Pyromania CD-ROM. Some footage has an explosion shot on top of a black background. The footage doesn't have an Alpha channel but you definitely need one in order to create a transparency map. We could chroma key out the background, which we'll cover in the next section, but this method is slightly better. One caveat: These two methods will only work on footage shot on top of a black background and that has only bright colors in the foreground.

Method One

This is the easiest method and works well for 3D applications that do not support Alpha channel transparency maps. Take the clip into either DeBabelizer, After Effects, or Premiere and convert it to grayscale. Since the background is black, it will be completely transparent when applied as a map. You might have to adjust the levels of brightness and contrast in order to set the correct amount of transparency. =

Method Two

This method will require Adobe's After Effects. Import your clip into the program and then apply the effect **Shift Channels**. Select **Take Alpha**

from Red and **Take Red from Alpha.** By using this technique you can create an Alpha channel based on the predominant color in the clip.

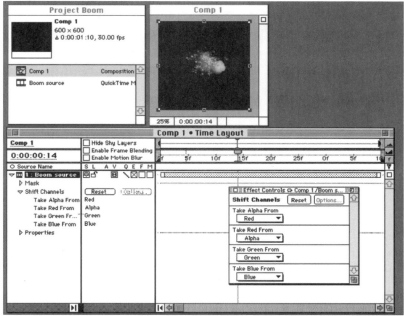

FIGURE *An Alpha channel can be created from the RGB channels in Adobe After*
16.3 *Effects 3.0 by using the **Shift Channels** effect.*

T
U
T
O
R
I
A
L

ADDING AN ALPHA CHANNEL INTO A CLIP

How do I add an Alpha channel to a 24-bit clip? Well you're going to need a special program for that task, and it's Equilibrium's DeBabelizer. A Lite version and a demo version of DeBabelizer are included on the CD-ROM. You will need a fully fledged copy of DeBabelizer to get the this task done but it's another one of those essential programs that will make your life easier.

Let's say that you have created an Alpha channel for a clip by converting the animation into a grayscale file. Rename your RGB or color animation Color Animation and the grayscale file Alpha Animation.

STEP ONE

Launch your copy of the DeBabelizer application. Go to the **Scripts** menu and select **New**. When the **Edit Script** window pops up, go to the **Palette** menu and select **Channels** and then select **To Original Alpha**.

Next go to the **Edit** menu and select **Clear**. The **Edit Script** window should look like the image in Figure 16.4. Name your script **Alpha Add Script** and save the script.

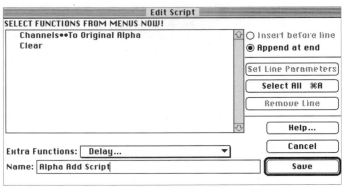

FIGURE *Use Equilibrium DeBabelizer's automatic scripting*
16.4 *functions to create an Alpha channel for your 24-bit file.*

STEP TWO

Go to the **File** menu and select **Batch** and then **Place and Save**. You will now need to create two new **Batch Lists**. Create the first batch list and add the Color Animation file to the list. Name the list RGB Batch List and then save the list. Create another new batch list and add the Alpha Animation file to the list. Name the list Alpha Batch List and then save the list.

STEP THREE

Select the **RGB Batch List** in the left side of the **Batch Place & Save** dialog box. On the right side of the box, select the following parameters:

Do Script: Nothing
Place: image in same position
List: Alpha Batch List
Script: Alpha Add Script

Select the file type that you wish to save the file to such as QuickTime or PICTs. Make sure that you choose a lossless codec or 32-bit file format or all of your work will be for naught. Click the **Do It** button and then you're finished.

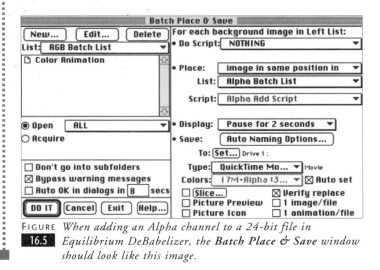

FIGURE *When adding an Alpha channel to a 24-bit file in*
16.5 *Equilibrium DeBabelizer, the **Batch Place & Save** window should look like this image.*

T
U
T
O
R
I
A
L

COMPOSITING WITH AN ALPHA CHANNEL

In the previous section we discussed what an Alpha channel was and how to create your own. We also covered how to load an Alpha channel in a still image. In this section we're going to take an animation that we have previously rendered and composite the action over another image. Once again, the key to our success is the Alpha channel.

To get the most out of this section you will need a program such as Premiere or After Effects. If you don't have either one, you're in luck. A tryout version of Premiere is included on the CD-ROM.

When the animation that we will be using was rendered, the background was rendered as an Alpha channel. In order for our animation file to retain the Alpha channel information, the Animation QuickTime codec was used since it is both lossless and supports a 32-bit file format. Remember that a 32-bit image is the same thing as saying that the image was saved with an Alpha channel.

Step One

Launch your copy of Adobe's Premiere. You can either start a new project file or load the project file that is included on the CD-ROM. Choose the output resolution you want from the presets.

Step Two

Import the files titled Background PICT and Rendered Movie into the project. Set the duration of the Background PICT clip to 4 seconds.

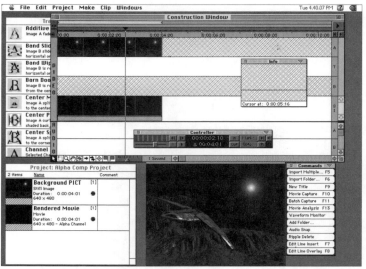

Figure 16.6 *With Adobe Premiere 4.0 we can composite an animation created with an Alpha channel over another image.*

STEP THREE

Place the Background PICT clip into track **A**. Place the Rendered Movie clip into track **S1**. Select the Rendered Movie clip by clicking on it once in the project window. You will know that the clip is selected by the floating marquee that flashes around the perimeter of the clip (see Figure 16.6).

STEP FOUR

Go the **Clip** menu and then select **Transparency**. In the **Transparency Settings** dialog box select **Alpha Channel** from underneath the **Key Type** pop up menu. If you want a preview of what the composited image will look like, click on the third button from the left underneath the **Sample** window. Go ahead and click the **OK** button.

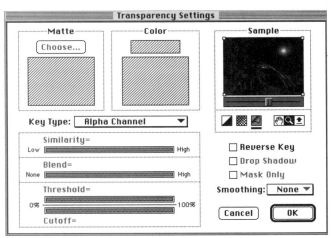

FIGURE **16.7** *In the **Transparency Settings** window in Adobe Premiere 4.0 you can set the type of keying for a clip. In this case we are keying out the background Alpha channel.*

STEP FIVE

Go ahead and render your movie. This time it should only take a few seconds. The advantage of using this postproduction compositing method is that you save in initial rendering time and also have flexibility in terms of a background image.

FIGURE *The background image was created in MetaTools Bryce and was*
16.8 *then composited underneath an animation in Premiere 4.0.*

Shadow Masks

There are a few problems associated with compositing an animation in postproduction. First of all the reflections in the 3D animation sometimes do not match the image in the background. The best solution in this case is to use the background image as the environment map during the rendering process. The second problem unfortunately is not as easily solved. Shadows can be a major cause of headache if not handled properly. The problem is one of how we transfer a shadow from an animation, yet at the same time leave the background of the animation behind.

The idea of this exercise is to use a shadow created in a 3D program as a shadow on top of the image that you're using for background in postproduction. The solution lies in a shadow mask.

PLANNING

Before you even launch your 3D application you need to take a good long look at your background image. Try to figure out a couple of things such as where is the light source coming from and the angle of the ground plane. You will need to match the perspective of the 3D environment to the 2D background image.

FIGURE
16.9
When looking at the background image, try to calculate the angle of the ground plane, and the direction and color of the light source.

MODELING

Yes this method of creating a shadow mask involves some modeling, but don't worry, it's nothing too extensive. The idea is to create a model of the ground plane that matches the image in the background. For most cases a simple 2D rectangle will do.

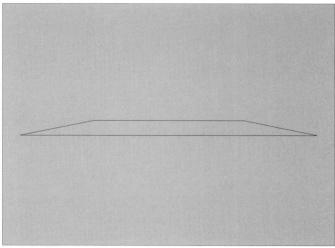

FIGURE
16.10
When creating a model of the ground plane, make sure to match the angle of the ground plane in the photograph.

LIGHTING AND RENDERING

Once the model of the ground plane is complete, bring your 3D model into the scene. Try to match both the lighting angle as well as the color of the light source to the background image. The next step is to render the scene twice. The first time make the ground plane invisible and render the background as an Alpha channel. This animation supplies the color image for the final product.

FIGURE *The first rendering should have only the model in the*
16.11 *scene and the background rendered as an Alpha channel.*

The next step is slightly more complicated. Save a copy of your animation project and then work from the copy. Make the ground plane visible again and remove all texture maps from the entire scene. Apply a completely white material to all of the objects in the scene including both your model and ground plane. Make this white material able to reflect 100% of diffuse and ambient light. Turn off all of your rendering effects such as bump mapping and specularity but keep shadows turned on. Set the background color to be completely white as well. Increase the ambient light level to approximately 75%. This number will take a little bit of trial and error to get right.

Render the animation for the shadow mask. You will probably have to adjust the levels of the animation so that the balance between the black and white areas is more defined.

FIGURE
16.12
Once the shadow mask animation is rendered the levels of the animation will have to be adjusted so that there is a higher contrast.

T
U
T
O
R
I
A
L

COMPOSITING THE SHADOW MASK

The final stage in the process is to bring all of the pieces together. All of the images used in this tutorial are on the CD-ROM. The project files are saved for both Premiere and After Effects so you can either load the projects or start from scratch. For the sake of this lesson we will use Premiere to composite the shadow mask.

STEP ONE

Load all three files into Premiere: Background, Foreground, and Shadowmask. Place the Background clip into track **A**. Place the Shadowmask clip into track **S1**. Select the Shadowmask clip by clicking on it once in the project window. You will know that the clip is selected by the floating marquee that flashes around the perimeter of the clip.

STEP TWO

Go the **Clip** menu and select **Transparency**. In the **Transparency Settings** dialog box select **Multiply** from underneath the **Key Type** pop-up menu. The **Cutoff** slider bar controls how dark or light the shadow will be. If you want a preview of what the composited image will look like, click on the third button from the left underneath the **Sample** window. Go ahead and click the **OK** button.

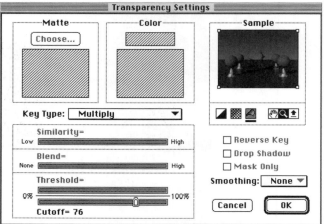

FIGURE **16.13** *The first step is to composite the shadow mask in Adobe Premiere 4.0 over the background image. By using the **Multiply** command in the **Transparency** setting dialog box we can composite our shadow.*

STEP THREE

Create a virtual clip of the Background and Shadowmask area. Drag the virtual clip to the right and place it into track **A**. Add the Foreground clip into track **S1**. Select the Foreground clip by clicking on it once in the project window. You will know that the clip is selected by the floating marquee that flashes around the perimeter of the clip (Figure 16.14).

STEP FOUR

Go to the **Clip** menu and select **Transparency**. In the **Transparency Settings** dialog box select **Alpha Channel**

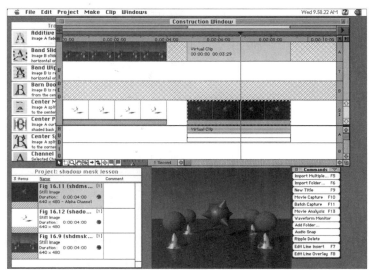

FIGURE
16.14
By creating a virtual clip in Adobe Premiere 4.0, we can then composite the foreground image over both the background and the shadow mask.

from underneath the **Key Type** pop-up menu. If you want a preview of what the composited image will look like, click on the third button from the left underneath the **Sample** window. Go ahead and click the **OK** button.

STEP FIVE

Hey, you're done. Go ahead and render the image if you want. The process might seem a little complex but it does get easier with time. For those After Effects users out there, here are the settings that you can use for compositing a shadow mask:

- Apply the **Set Matte/Levels** effect to the background clip.
- Set **Take Matte from Layer:** to the shadowmask clip.
- Set **Use for matte:** to **Luminance**.
- Adjust **Matte Output Black Level** to control the darkness or lightness of the shadow.

FIGURE *A shadow mask can be composited over a background image in*
16.15 *either Premiere or After Effects using a variety of methods.*

Chroma Keying

Now what do you do if you don't have an Alpha channel to work with? We've all seen our local weather person on television standing in front of a moving map of the country complete with thunderstorms and tornadoes. What most people don't realize is that the weather person is being composited directly over the footage in real time. OK so we can't easily do something like that in real time with our computers just yet, but we can use the same technique. That technique is referred to as *chroma keying*.

Behind the weather person is usually a blue or orange screen that does not match any shade of their hair color, skin tone, or clothing. The entire idea is to find a shade of blue or orange that completely contrasts with the coloring of the subject. What the television director then does is replace the background color with the weather map. We can do the same thing in 3D.

For example, let's say that we have a really groovy animation and we want to place a person in front of it in postproduction. The first step of course would be to render the animation. The next step would be to shoot the footage of the actor.

LIGHTING CONSIDERATIONS

When shooting footage of an actor in front of a blue screen there are a few things that you should know about color and lighting. First of all you don't have to use a blue screen at all; you can use any shade you want. But once again the idea is to come up with a color that is completely contrasts the coloration of the actor. The next important thing is that you have to make sure that the blue screen is evenly lit. If there are several shades of blue in the background, then it will be difficult to chroma key out the screen. You also have to backlight the figure by placing a light source between the screen and the actor. If you don't then the actor might have a blue halo from the reflected light from the screen, which would cause artifacting around the edge of the actor. Finally make sure that your actor does not have any clothing that matches the color of the screen. If there are any color matches the actor might end up with a hole in his or her body when the scene is composited.

PROCESSING THE FOOTAGE

Once the footage is shot and digitized into your computer, use either Premiere or After Effects to composite the two images. You use the exact same method as compositing with an Alpha channel except that you choose the chroma key option instead. Then the background color is simply replaced with your animation.

Rotoscoping

Not all of the animation that you do will be in 3D and that's where rotoscoping comes in. *Rotoscoping* is traditionally thought of as painting on top of either animated frames, video, or even film. Why rotoscope? Well for complicated animations of humans or animals, it's often a good idea to use a guide. By painting a simple stick figure skeleton over actual footage, the animator can create a guide to use as a reference later in the production process. Another use for rotoscoping is adding special effects to video or an animation in the postproduction process. For example, lightning bolts, fire, or even particle groups can be added to a rendered animation. Unfortunately a lot of these effects need to be drawn by hand, which can be a time-consuming process.

DEBABELIZER

A number of methods are available for rotoscoping images. Most applications automatically save an animation using the QuickTime format. To be able to work with an animation in a program such as Photoshop, it needs to be converted into a series of PICTs. Equilibrium's DeBabelizer is perhaps the best application suited for this job. DeBabelizer can read a QuickTime file and then convert it into a series of sequentially named PICT files. After that all you need to do is open each PICT in a program such as Photoshop and you're ready to paint. Once you're finished with your files you can then use DeBabelizer to recompile all of the files into on QuickTime movie.

STRATA MEDIAPAINT AND FRACTAL DESIGN PAINTER

The drawback to using the previous method to rotoscope a movie is that you have to decompile the QuickTime file and then recompile it when you're finished. Another issue is that you have to be able to manage a large quantity of individual PICTs all at the same time. Wouldn't it be nice to be able to paint directly on top of a QuickTime movie?

Well that's where both MediaPaint and Painter come into the picture. Both programs let the user import a QuickTime movie into the application. In Painter users have the entire array of natural painting drawing tools at their disposal. On the other hand MediaPaint has a few cool particle effects tools that can save some serious time in the long run. If you're interested in rotoscoping, check out these two programs.

Adding Special Effects

Sometimes you just don't have the tools or special effects available in your 3D animation program. If you don't have lens flares or particle effects, don't worry you will. Through the wonders of postproduction you can add a lens flare or raging waterfall to your animations. The process is as simple as adding a filter or an effect to a clip.

T
U
T
O
R
I
A
L

LENS FLARES

You can use a lens flare for a variety of purposes, ranging from simulating a strong light source to mimicking the flash of an explosion, to a distant sun in the night sky. You can add a lens flare to a still image in Photoshop with a click of a button. But for an animation we need a little more than that, we want an animated lens flare. By using Premiere we can animate the position and intensity of a lens flare over time. For this tutorial we'll use an animation of the shock wave that we produced in Chapter 14.

STEP ONE

Import the clip of the shock wave into Premiere. Drag it into either track **A** or **B** on the time line.

STEP TWO

In this step we're going to do a little splicing. We want to apply a filter to only the front end of the clip. If we don't cut the clip into two separate segments any filter that is applied will be applied to the entire clip. Zoom in on the project window and view the clip in two-frame increments. Select the **Razor** tool from the palette in the lower left corner of the project window. Go to the clip in the project window and then click once underneath frame number 16 or time index 0:00:00:16.

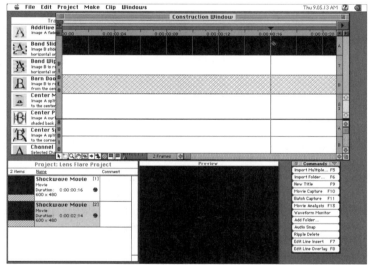

FIGURE
16.16 *Using the **Razor** tool in Adobe Premiere 4.0, you can cut your clip into several pieces. A filter can be applied to each piece over time.*

STEP THREE

Select the first clip on the time line by clicking on it once. You will know that the clip is selected when a floating marquee surrounds the clip. Go to the **Clip** menu and select **Filters**. Scroll down the list of filters available till you reach **Lens Flares**. Select **Apply** and when the **Lens Flare** window pops up select the **105mm prime** radio button and set the **Brightness** level to 10%. Click and drag the x in the preview window to center the flare in the scene. Click the **OK** button and click **OK** once more in the **Filters** window.

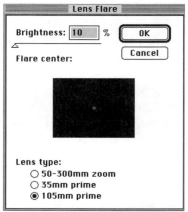

FIGURE **16.17** *The **Lens Flare** filter in Premiere 4.0 can be used for a variety of special effects ranging from a distant sun to an explosion.*

STEP FOUR

Select the **Razor** tool again and cut the first clip at frame number 5 or time index 0:00:00:05.

STEP FIVE

Select the first clip and then select **Filters** from the **Clip** menu. You will notice that even though you cut the former clip into two pieces, it still retains the filter that you had applied to it. Select the **Lens Flare** filter from the right side of the menu and then click on the **End** button in the **Settings Section**. When the **Lens Flare** window pops up, set the **Brightness** level to 171%. Click the **OK** button and then click once again in the **Filter** window. You have just animated the lens flare brightness over time.

STEP SIX

Select the middle clip in the project window then select **Filters** from the **Clip** menu. Select the **Lens Flare** filter from the right side of the menu and then click on the **Start** button in the **Settings Section**. When the **Lens Flare** window pops up set the **Brightness** level to 171%. Click the **OK** button. Click on the **End** button in the **Settings Section**. When the **Lens Flare**

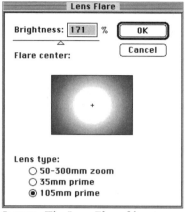

FIGURE **16.18** *The **Lens Flare** filter in Premiere 4.0 can be animated over time by changing the start and end settings for the filter.*

window pops up set the **Brightness** level to 10%. Click the **OK** button and then once again in the **Filter** window.

STEP SEVEN
Go ahead and render your movie. By creating three separate clips and applying filters, you've animated a lens flare filter over time. Position and intensity can also be animated.

PARTICLE GROUPS

Included on the CD-ROM is a demo version of MetaTools' Final Effects. Take it out for a test drive and see if you like it. For a more in-depth look at Final Effects read Chapter 14, Animation Special Effects, in the section named Pyrotechnics.

SECTION THREE: PREPARING FOR OUTPUT

Once all of the editing, splicing, and compositing have been finished, you have to get your footage ready for the playback device. Even though your computer might be able to play back the animation, someone else's might not.

Multimedia

Multimedia comes in many shapes and sizes. This all-purpose buzzword is used for everything from CD-ROMs to video on demand via cable hookups. Our major concern in this section is optimizing our animations so that they can be played back under the various formats of multimedia.

CD-ROM

There are several methods of delivering an animation in a multimedia format and the type that is most familiar to everyone is via CD-ROM. The playback of animations is most affected by the low data transfer rate of the CD-ROM. The playback of video requires an almost constant data stream. If it's interrupted the movie will drop either frames or sound. One of the most commonly used solutions is simply to reduce the amount of information that has to travel from the CD-ROM to the computer. Software-based codecs shrink the data stream by reducing the size of the files that have to travel through the CD-ROM bottleneck. Apple's QuickTime offers a variety of lossy codecs that sacrifice image quality for speed. The goal of the developer is to get the most colors, largest screen, sharpest image, and highest constant frame rate possible for video.

 Tip. You've probably noticed that many of the animations included on the CD-ROM are in an Electric Image Fastloader format. Fastloader does not depend on QuickTime and is Electric Image's custom codec. It can handle a higher frame rate and screen size but at the cost of RAM. All animations are preloaded into RAM to guarantee optimum playback. If you're having problems playing back a Fastloader file, you probably don't have enough RAM. All animations have also been compressed with the Animation codec so you can recompile them at your leisure.

On the other hand, the developer also has to optimize the animation for the lowest common denominator. It's for this reason that it is imperative to understand who your target audience is. Generally speaking the average computer owner only has a 2X speed CD-ROM drive and a monitor depth of 8 bits. The image quality will be poor, the screen size small, and the frame rate low for an animation being played back under those conditions. Playback quality also depends entirely on the type of processor playing back the animation. A PowerPC CPU can handle more information that an older 040 machine.

Data Transfer Rate

How do you decide on a codec, screen size, and frame rate? Measure the data transfer rate of your target device and then go from there. Once you've calculated the average data transfer rate of your target device, you can start optimizing your animation. Just about any hard drive formatting application comes with a benchmarking utility that will be able to tell you the average read times for either a hard drive or CD-ROM device. But make sure that you take around 10% to 15% off of the top because of the overhead of the operating system.

Optimizing Your QuickTime Movie

To start optimizing your movie you're going to have to make a few hard decisions. Something has to go: either frame rate, bit depth, or screen size. As each one of these items is reduced, so is the data rate. Two

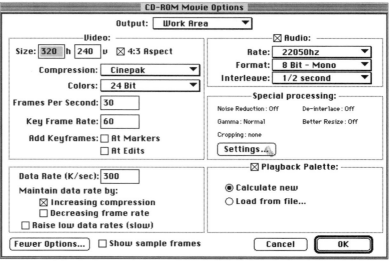

FIGURE *Adobe Premiere 4.2 has a new tool that optimizes QuickTime movies*
16.19 *for playback from CD-ROM.*

programs spring to mind when it comes to handling this reduction issue: Equilibrium's DeBabelizer and Adobe Premiere. Of the two, Premiere offers slightly better control over targeting data rate. In version 4.2 of Premiere, Adobe introduced a new tool that optimizes QuickTime for CD-ROMs. Features such as screen size, codecs, and gamma controls have been integrated into the tool. Once the data rate has been set, all you have to do is wait for the program to compress your files.

Kiosks

One of the primary advantages for the multimedia developer when creating an animation for a kiosk is that the specifications for the target device are set. Also animations can be stored on a fast hard drive which offers higher frame rates as well as screen sizes. Another feature is that an animation can also take advantage of hardware-based codecs.

Television

So you've rendered your animation at 640 x 480 at 30 fps and you want to output it to television. The problem is that your computer and TV handle video in completely different ways. There are two major issues when preparing an animation for television: NTSC legal colors and interlacing. If you haven't already done so, flip back to Chapter 15, Rendering, and read the section on interlaced images.

NTSC Legal Colors

Believe it or not, your computer can display more colors than your TV can. Also certain colors such as some shades of red tend to bleed when viewed on a television monitor. The trick is to convert your animation's color palette into something more digestible for NTSC broadcast. Just about any program ranging from Premiere to DeBabelizer can handle this task. The point of this section is simply to remind you to convert your animations before outputting them.

Interlacing

It's not completely true when someone states that NTSC broadcasts at 30 frames per second. In reality, one frame of video consists of two separate fields. This springs from the fact that in the old days when technology was not as advanced as it is now, the electron gun that shot an image onto the screen was not capable of doing it in a single pass. So instead half of the image was drawn and then 1/60th of a second later, the second half was drawn. The two halves then formed one whole frame. And so things stayed.

Anyway we have to have some means of interlacing our animation for this archaic format. The first method is to do nothing at all. Several programs such as Premiere and After Effect can output an interlaced file by interpolating the second field. What occurs is that the program copies the information from the first field into the second field. The drawback to this method is that the motion in the animation might appear choppy when played back.

Tip. If your 3D application cannot render at 60 fps, set the frame rate to 30 fps and then double the duration of the animation.

The next alternative is more visually appealing but also more time consuming. It means going back to your rendering application and rerendering your animation at 60 frames per second. Once the rendering is complete, bring the animation into either Premiere or After Effects. Both programs can then take an alternating frame and convert it into the lower field. The file can then be output as an interlaced animation.

If you can't afford a copy of either AfterEffects or Premiere, there is a low-cost alternative to creating an interlaced animation. McQ Productions/Software Systems offers an application named OutFielder that coverts a 60 fps animation into a 30 fps interlaced file. A unlockable demo version is included on the CD-ROM.

Tip. McQ Productions can be contacted at PO Box 1676, San Mateo CA 94401; (800) 659-4755.

Film

My only advice about either rendering or outputting to film is to contact your local postproduction service bureau. Your resolution depends entirely on their digital printer and the method of delivery varies from company to company. Some prefer DAT, others ABEKAS, and some are even content with SyQuest cartridges. But be prepared to pay anywhere from $45 to $120 dollars per frame.

SECTION FOUR: OUTPUT METHODS

The hardware used to output to film is too expensive for the average animation studio to keep on hand and using a CD-R (Recordable CD-ROM) for multimedia is as simple as copying from one drive to another. The last piece of the project that can still be done in house is moving all of that information from the computer to video tape.

Frame-Accurate Tape Decks

There are a couple of methods that you can use to output your animation to videotape. The first method is to use a frame-accurate tape recorder in conjunction with a video card. McQ productions offers a software solution called MacAnimator Pro. MacAnimator Pro is a software-based video animation controller that can manage a frame-accurate editing recorder with SMPTE time code and RS-422 control via a serial cable. Each frame of the animation is output via the video board to the tape deck, and the software controls the entire process. This method guarantees the highest possible output available for midrange users. MacAnimator Pro also can record and capture uncompressed video. There's a demo version of MacAnimator Pro included on the CD-ROM that can be used with any RS-422 deck.

The drawback to this method is that outputting to video in this manner requires a fairly expensive tape deck. Also there is a tremendous amount of wear on both the tape as well as the heads in the deck. Another issue is that the process can be fairly time consuming. And if one frame is somehow missed or corrupted, you will have to start the process over.

Digital Video Editing Suites

As mentioned previously in the section on Hardware Editing Suites, digital video is fairly accessible on the desktop. Companies such as Avid, DataTranslation, and Radius offer a variety of solutions. These editing suites offer the user a great means of previewing an animation as well as a solid editing environment. In terms of outputting an animation, all of these suites can output a NTSC video signal in real time.

The drawback is that the image quality is not as sharp as that offered by the frame-accurate solution, and the price of both the boards and the high-speed arrays can easily reach into the 20K price range.

APPENDIX
A

Index of 3D Companies

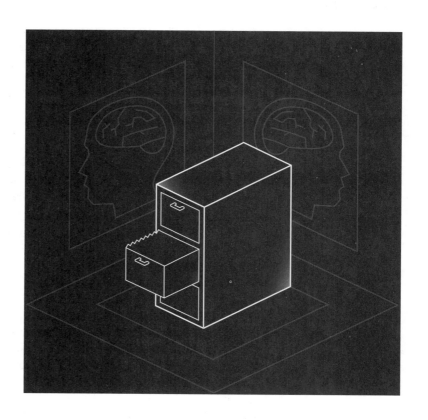

Alias Research Inc.
SKETCH!
3D modeling and rendering application.
110 Richmond Street East
Toronto Ontario M5C1P1
V: 416.362.9181
F: 416.362.0630

Artbeats
Tilable textures and backgrounds on CD-ROM.
PO Box 709
M.C. Oregon 97457
V: 800.444.9392
V: 503.863.4429
F: 503.863.4547

Adobe Systems Inc.
PHOTOSHOP
2D image manipulation and creation application.
PREMIERE
Non-linear video editing application.
ILLUSTRATOR
2D PostScript creation application.
AFTER EFFECTS
2D video animation and special effects application.
TEXTUREMAKER
Texture creation application.
1585 Charleston Road
Mountain View CA 94039
V: 415.961.4400
F: 415.961.3769

Artifice Inc.
DESIGN WORKSHOP
3D visualization tool for architectural applications.
PO Box 1588
Eugene OR 97440
V: 503.345.7421
F: 503.346.3626

Ashlar Inc.
VELLUM 3D
CAD
1290 Oakmead Parkway, Suite 218
Sunnyvale CA 94086
V: 800.877.2745
F: 408.746.0749

Asym Technology
ZOOM
CAD
924 Carl Road
Lafayette CA 94549
V: 510.943.6157
F: 510.943.3213

auto•des•sys
FORM•Z
3D modeling and rendering application.
2011 Riverside Drive
Columbus OH 43221
V: 614.488.9777
F: 614.488.0848

Byte by Byte Corp.
SCULPT 3D
Modeling and rendering application.
39225 West Baker Lane, Suite 3229
Austin, Texas 78759-5321
V: 512.305.0360
F: 512.305.0371

Data Translation
MEDIA100
Non-linear hardware editing suite.
V: 508.460.1600
F: 508.481.8627

DayStar Inc.

Genisis MP

Multi-processor Macintosh computers.

5556 Atlanta Highway

Flowery Branch GA 30542

V: 800.962.22077

F: 404.967.3018

Dynaware USA Inc.

DynaPerspective

CAD

950 Tower Lane Suite 1150

Foster City CA 94404

V: 800.445.3962

F: 415.349.5879

Electric Image Inc.

Electric Image Animation System

3D Animation and Rendering Application.

117 East Colorado Blvd Suite 300

Pasadena CA 91105

V: 818.577.1627

F: 818.577.2426

Equilibrium Technology

DeBabelizer

Batch processing and conversion for image files.

3 Harbor Drive Suite 111

Sausalito, CA 94965

V: 415.332.4343

F: 415.332.4433

Fractal Design

Painter

2D image creation program using natural tools such as brushes and textures

Poser

3D parametric human body modeler.

335 Spreckels Drive, Suite F

Aptos CA 95003

V: 408.688.5300

F: 408.685.8528

Form & Function

Wraptures Volume One and Two

Tilable texture maps and backgrounds on CD-ROM.

1595 17th Avenue

San Francisco CA 94122

V: 415.664.4010

F: 415.664.4030

Hash Inc.

Animation Master

3D character modeling, rendering, and animation application.

2800 East Evergreen Blvd.

Vancouver, WA 98611

vox: 206.750.0042

fax: 206.750.0451

Intergraph Corp.

MicroStation Mac

CAD

289 Dunlop Blvd.

Huntsville AL 35894

V: 205.730.2700 or 800.345.4856

F: 205.730.9491

Kandu Software

CADMover

3D file conversion application.

2305 North Kentucky Street

Arlington VA 22205

V: 703.532.0213

F: 703.533.0291

Knoll Software

CyberMesh

Photoshop plug-in for 3D terrain and mesh creation.

PO Box 6887

San Rafael CA 94903

V: 415.453.2471

F: 415.499.9322

Macromedia Inc.
EXTREME 3D
3D modeling, rendering and animation application.
600 Townsend St.
San Francisco CA 94103
V: 800.945.4601
F: 415.442.0190

MetaTools
KPT BRYCE
3D terrain modeling, rendering, and animation application.
KPT FILTERS
Photoshop plug-in filters useful for creating texture maps.
6303 Carpinteria Ave.
Carpinteria, Ca 93013
V: 805.566.6296
F: 805.566.6385

Mira Imaging, Inc.
HYPERSPACE
3D digitizing software.
2257 South 1100 East, Suite 1A
Salt Lake City Utah 84106
V: 800.950.6472
F: 801.466.4699

Mike Clifton
SCULPTOR
Shareware 3D modeling application.
1013 Thistle Ct.
Sunnyvale CA 94086

Northern Lights Productions
ZEUS, DANTE, BIG DIPPER
Animation plug-ins for Electric Image Animation System.
210 The Village, Suite 203
Redondo Beach CA 90277
V: 310.376.4266
F: 310.372.5236

Onyx Computing
TREE PRO
3D parametric modeling application for trees and shrubs.
10 Avon Street
Cambridge MA 02138
V: 617.876.3876
F: 617.868.8033

Pixar
MACRENDERMAN
High end rendering engine for RIB models.
SHOWPLACE
Scene building application with a GUI interface for MacRenderMan
TYPESTRY
3D type modeling and rendering application.
1001 West Cutting
Richmond CA 94804
V: 510.236.4000
F: 510.236.0388

RayDream Inc.
1804 North Shoreline Blvd
Mountain View CA 94043
V: 415.960.0766
F: 415.960.1198
RayDream Designer
3D modeling, animation, and rendering application.

Specular International
INFINI-D
3D modeling, animation, and rendering application.
LOGOMOTION
2D type modeling, animation and rendering application.
479 West Street
Amherst MA 01002
V: 800.433.7732
F: 413.253.0540

Strata Inc

STUDIOPRO
3D modeling, animation, and rendering application.
STRATA MEDIAPAINT
Video special-effects and rotoscoping application.
2 West St. George Blvd.
Ancestor Square, Suite 2100
St. George UT 84770
V: 801.628.5218
F: 801.628.9756

The Valis Group

PIXEL PUTTY
3D modeling, rendering and animation application.
2270 Paradise Drive
Tiburon CA 94920
V: 415.435.5404
F: 415.435.9862

Viewpoint DataLabs

3D models.
870 West Center
Orem UT 84057
v: 801.224.2222
f: 801.224.2272

Virtus Corporation

VIRTUS WALKTHROUGH/PRO
3D architectural visualization and animation.
VIRTUS ALIEN SKIN
Texture creation application.
118 Mackenan Dr
Suite 250
Cary NC 27511
V: 800.847.8871
F: 919.460.4530

Visual Information Development Inc.

PRESENTER PRO
3D modeling, animation, and rendering application.
136 West Olive Avenue
Monrovia CA 91016
V: 818.358.3936
F: 818.358.4766

Visual Concepts Engineering Inc.

PYROMANIA
CD-ROM of explosions and fire.
13300 Ralston Ave
Sylmar CA 91342
V: 818.367.9187
F: 818.362.3490

Virtual Reality Laboratories, Inc.

VISTAPRO
3D terrain modeling, animation, and rendering application.
2341 Ganador Court
San Luis Obispo CA 93401
V: 805.545.8515

YARC Systems Corp.

QuickDraw3D accelerator board.
975 Business Center Circle
Newbury Park CA 91320
V: 805.499.9444
F: 805.499.4048

Glossary

3D DIGITIZERS

Hardware device used to digitize real world models or objects into the computer. The user inputs X, Y, Z coordinates and creates a mesh surface which represents the surface of the actual object. There are four major types of 3D digitizers available: mechanical arm, ultrasonic, magnetic resonance, and laser.

PARTICLE GROUPS

Groups of points or models created in a 3D or 2D application that can be used to create special effects such as fire, fog, smoke, sparks, or water. Particle groups are usually animated by one global set of parameters or behaviors.

3DMF FORMAT

The 3D MetaFile format was created by Apple Computer as a part of their QuickDraw 3D package. The 3DMF format handles high end geometry such as NURBS, texture mapping information, animation characteristics, lighting, and hierarchy.

ACCENT LIGHT

A light used to highlight or draw attention to a specific part of a scene. Usually a spotlight or point light source is used.

ALPHA CHANNEL

The Alpha Channel is the last 8 bits of information stored in a 32 bit image. The first 24 bits are used to store the RGB color information while the last 8 bits define a 256 shade grayscale image. This grayscale image or Alpha Channel can be used to carry transparency information for post production compositing or for advanced texture mapping in some 3D applications.

AMBIENT LIGHT

Ambient light is the light reflected from the part of the object in shadow. The ambient light feature in your 3D program controls the color as well as the intensity of the ambient light reflected from your model. Ambient light is often referred to as the color of shadow.

ANGLE OF INCIDENCE

The angle at which the rays of light cast from a light source intersects the surface of an object. As the angle of incidence approaches 90° the surface of an object becomes more evenly illuminated.

ARRAY

Two or more hard drives that have been striped using RAID level 0. An array acts shows up as one volume, with information written in an alternating fashion across both devices. Arrays are generally used for digital video applications that require a high data transfer rate.

ATTENUATION OF LIGHT

The rate at which a light falls off. The attenuation of light is the square of the distance traveled. As an object travels twice as far away from a light, it receives a quarter of the illumination.

AV HARD DRIVE

A high speed high capacity hard drive capable of sustaining an increased data transfer rate. AV drive usually do not experience thermal recalibration which causes an interruption in the data stream.

AXONOMETRIC VIEW

A method of looking at a scene in 3D modeling that is completely without perspective. Otherwise known as an orthographic view.

BIT DEPTH

The number of colors in an image is measured in terms of bit depth. An 8 bit image has 256 colors, a 16 bit image thousands of colors, and a 24 bit image millions of colors. A 32 bit image is a 24 bit image with an 8 bit Alpha channel.

BOOLEAN FUNCTIONS

In 3D modeling, Boolean functions let the user add or subtract two intersecting volumes. The four major types of Boolean functions are Union, Difference, and Split and Intersection.

BUMP MAP

An 8 bit grayscale image that is used to simulate surface texture in the rendering process by manipulating surface normals. A bump map creates the illusion of texture, but does not alter the surface geometry of an object.

CD-R

A recordable CD ROM. A laser is used to burn of an layer of organic dye on the surface of a CD-R encoding the information on the disc. CD-Rs have a shelf life of around 100 years.

CEL

A single frame of animation. A cel or celluloid is a transparent piece of film that is used by a traditional 2D animator as a canvas.

CHROMA KEYING

The process in post production of replacing a specific color in a clip with another image or piece of footage.

CINEPAK

A codec commonly used for compressing a clip for playback from CD ROM.

CODEC

A codec or compressor/decompressor is used to reduce the file size of a clip by using a variety of algorithms. Codecs can be either software or hardware based.

COLOR DEPTH

See Bit Depth

COLOR MAP

A color image that is used to color or cover the surface of a 3D object.

COLOR TEMPERATURE

The color of a light can be described in terms of temperature. Blue or purple fall into the category of cool, while reds and yellows warm.

COMPOSITING

The process of overlaying one image over another in the post production process.

Cubic Mapping

A method of applying either a color or texture map to an object. Cubic mapping applies a map in a cubic fashion. Another way of visualizing this is that a map is applied to the six faces of an imaginary cube around an object.

Cylindrical Mapping

A method of applying either a color or texture map to an object. Cylindrical mapping applies a map in a cylindrical fashion, much like wrapping a Tootsie Roll in a wrapper.

Deformations

An animation or modeling feature that lets the user distort a model using a variety of methods. A model can be deformed by twisting, squashing, stretching or even bending on a spline.

Depth of Field

A term used to describe the phenomenon that as an object recedes into the distance it becomes out of focus.

Diffuse Color

The diffuse color of an object is the color seen when an object is completely illuminated. Diffuse color is often referred to as the actual color of an object.

Displacement Maps

A displacement map is a grayscale image that is used to alter the surface of an object. Unlike a bump map which only disturbs an object's surface normals, a displacement map actually distorts surface geometry.

Distributed Rendering

A feature of rendering applications that distributes the burden of rendering an animation over several computers.

DXF

An aging 3D file format that is supported by the majority of 3D applications. The Drawing eXchange Format, originally developed by Autodesk, lets the user save a models geometry, color, and layer information in one file.

Edge Density

A rendering feature that controls the density or opacity of an object's outer or inner regions

ENVIRONMENT MAP

A color map that is applied to an invisible sphere in a 3D scene. An environment map is the image that is reflected in a reflective object.

EXTRUDE

A modeling feature that lets the user create a 3D object out of a 2D shape. The extrude modeling feature is most like a real world pasta machine pushing a 2D shape along a straight line.

EXTRUDE ON PATH

A modeling feature that lets the user create a 3D object out of a 2D shape by pushing a 2D shape along a line, path or curve.

FALLOFF

See Attenuation

FIELD OF VIEW

The number of degrees used to describe the amount of the surroundings visible from the front of a camera lens.

FIGURE GROUND

A technique used to judge the composition of an image. By rendering a scene in silhouette the viewers eye is not distracted by color or content.

FILL LIGHT

A light source used to fill in shadowed or dark areas in a scene.

FLAT SHADING

A rendering method that shades a polygon as a solid color.

FOCAL LENGTH

The distance from the front of a lens to the focal point of a camera. As the focal length of a camera increases, the field of view decreases.

GEL

A transparent piece of colored film that is used to cover a spotlight. In a 3D scene with a gel, a texture or pattern can be used to obscure a light source to create a pattern in the shadow.

GOBO

A 3D object or model placed in front of a light source that is used to create a pattern in the shadows.

INDEX OF REFRACTION

The amount of distortion applied to an image when seen through a transparent object.

INTERLACED FRAME

NTSC television delivers an interlaced frame. An interlaced frame or image is composed of two fields alternating at 60 fields per second.

INVERSE KINEMATICS

Complex joint structures that connect groups of objects. Inverse kinematics are used for tasks such as character animation. As a child that is grouped using IK is moved, the parent objects are also moved according to a variety of preset links and constraints.

JPEG

A lossy codec that stands for Joint Photographic Experts Group that is used mostly for still images. The quality of the image is fairly high, but decompression times can be high unless assisted by specialized hardware.

KEY LIGHT

The main light in a 3D scene. Usually the shadow casting light source.

LATHE

A modeling tool that is used to create a 3D object out of a 2D shape. The lathe tool is much like a carpenter's lathe with a 2D template being used to form the profile of an object.

LENS FLARE

The starburst pattern that appears when a camera lens is pointed directly at a strong light source.

LOFT

A 3D modeling tool that is used to create a 3D shape out of a series of 2D ribs.

LOSSY CODEC

A codec that reduces image quality when it compresses an image.

METABALLS

A 3D modeling feature that lets the user create a model out of a group of spheres. The spheres have variable degrees of gravity or attraction that distorts the surface of the spheres.

MORPH

A 3D animation feature that lets the user transform the geometry of one model into the geometry of another model.

MOTION BLUR

The blurring of a fast moving object when captured on video or film.

MOTION PATH

The path taken by an animated model.

MPEG

A fairly new codec used for digital video transmission. MPEG or Motion Pictures Expert Group codec is a lossy codec.

NURBS

Non Uniform Rational B-Splines. A type of weighted spline used for modeling purposes.

PARALLEL LIGHT SOURCES

A light source that mimics the parallel beams of light cast by a distance light source such as the sun.

PERSISTENCE OF VISION

The illusion of movement created by rapidly changing still images.

PERSPECTIVE MATCHING

Matching a virtual camera's fov, aspect ratio, height and placement to that of a photograph.

PLANAR MAPPING

A method of mapping that projects a 2D image in a flat or planar manner onto the surface of a 3D object.

POINT LIGHT SOURCE

Point or radial light sources emit light in a spherical or radial manner from a fixed point in space.

PRIMITIVES

The basic building blocks of 3D. Primitives are used to form the most rudimentary shapes of a model. Cubes, spheres, cones, and tori all fall into the category of primitives.

RAYTRACING

One of the most realistic methods of rendering a scene. Raytracing follows or traces a ray of light from the camera lens out to the objects in a scene providing the most accurate shadows and reflections.

ROTOSCOPING

The process of drawing images on top of animation.

SEAMLESS MAPS

See Tilable Maps

SPOTLIGHT

A light source that casts a conical shaped beam of light.

STORYBOARDING

The process of putting ideas to paper. Storyboards are usually quick sketches that describe the action in a scene.

SURFACE NORMAL

An imaginary ray that is set perpendicular to the surface of a polygon. Surface normals are used by a rendering engine to determine the color and angle of a polygon.

TILABLE MAPS

A color or bump map that has matching edges that can be repeated along the X and Y axis with showing a seam.

TWEEING

The automatic process that a 3D animation program uses to calculate the intermediary frames between two keyframes.

Index

2D Boolean function 100
2D particle groups 381
3D text
    transforming to 2D shapes 105
3D Boolean functions 54
3D digitizers 31, 98, 127
3D face 95
3D MetaFormat 96
3D particle groups 378
68K 24

A

Accent light 260
Adobe 98, 161, 219
After Effects 3.0 219, 220, 431
Alien Skin Textureshop 161
Align to Path 394
Aligning a bitmap 141, 166
Alpha channel 94, 437
    creating 441
    rendering 441
    tutorial 438
Ambient color 142, 144
Ambient light 245, 282
Ambient value 143, 144

Angle of incidence 248
    tutorial 248
Animated bump maps 225
    tutorial 226
Animated color maps 220
Animated flash of light tutorial 222
Animated maps 177, 218
Animated reflectivity maps 214, 222
Animated transparency maps 228
Animation 7, 16, 433
    computer-based 346
    sequencers 360
    tools 58
Anticipation 365
Apple 26
Apple video 433
Archival storage 35
Array 436
Artbeats 161
Artificial lighting 285
Atmosphere 266
Atmospheric conditions 280
AV drives 436
Avid 435
Axonometric 78

B

B-splines 96
Back light 258
Backgrounds 402
Balance 94
Bevel 52
Big dipper 379
Bit depth 163
Black lights 247
Boolean functions 39, 42, 54, 100, 102
 2D 100
 3D 54
Booleans and text tutorial 109
Bottle label tutorial 189
Brick wall tutorial 197
Bryce 112
Bump maps 177, 194
 examples 204
 using 193, 196

C

CAD lighting 268
Canyon tutorial 118
Casting call 70
Cave tutorial 118
CD-R 36
CD-ROM 6, 424, 460
Cel 345
Cel-based animation 346
Center of interest 93
Central processing unit (CPU) 24
Chairs tutorial 273
Character animation 364
Chroma keying 454
Cinematography 367
Cinepak 433
CISC 24
Clock accelerators 26

Clones 26
Codecs 432
Color depth 29
Color maps 155
Color temperature 239
Complex colored gels 298
Complimentary colors 238
Composition 93, 445
Configuring your computer 73
Coordinate systems 348, 355
Creating 3D text from 2D shapes tutorial
 105
Creating a terrain tutorial 114
Creating custom gels tutorial 295
Creating ribs with EPS templates 111
Cubic mapping 158, 164
Custom gels
 creating 295
Custom maps 141
 creating 162
CyberMesh 114, 126
Cylindrical mapping 158, 164

D

Dante 379
DAT 36
Data transfer rate 461
Data translation 435
Daystar digital 25, 30, 423
DeBabelizer 219, 220, 225, 455
Dedicated terrain modelers 112
Deformations 400
depth of field 275, 280, 338
 tutorial 339
Desk lamp tutorial 312
Diffuse color 142
Diffuse maps 177, 193
Diffuse spaceship tutorial 193

Diffuse value 144, 145
Digital compositing 437
Digital video editing suites 464
DIMMs 28
Displacement mapping 204
Distributed rendering 422
Dolly 370
Dummy objects 91
DXF 95

E

Ease in/ease out 362
Easy alpha channels 376
Edge density 314
Editing software 431
Electric Image Fastloader 7
Electricity 384
Encapsulated PostScript 98
Environment mapping 407
Environment saucers 406
Environment spheres 404
EPS 54, 98, 99
    templates 98, 99
Equilibrium 219
Exaggeration 365
Explode 396
Exporting 94
Extensions 74
Extensions Manager 74
Extrude 47
Extrude on Path 48

F

Fading cube tutorial 228
Falloff 252
Field of view 333
Figure ground 94
Fill light 258

Film 427, 463
FinalEffects 381, 382
Fire 388
Flash of light tutorial 214
Flat shading 417
Flatbed scanner 30
Fluorescent 286
Fly-by 369
Focal length 332
Fog 274
Follow through 365
Form & function 161
Formats 7
FOV 333
Fractal Design 130
Frame-accurate tape decks 464
FreeHand 98, 99

G

Gears tutorial 104
Gels 291
Global location 273
Glow 144, 150
Glow maps 177, 206
Glowing radial and spotlights 309
Glowing sign tutorial 206
Gobo of stars tutorial 307
Gobos 291, 306
Gouraud 29
    shading 417
Graphics 433
Grayscale bitmap terrain 114
Grazed light 260

H

Halogen 286
Hard drives 33
Hardware acceleration 423

Hardware editing suites 434
Hardware-based codecs 435
Hidden line 416
Hierarchy 353, 354
Hotspot 252
HSL color model 237
Human body 99, 130
Human motion 364

I

Illustrator 98, 99
Index of refraction 144, 149
Infinite planes 407
Interlacing 425, 462
Inverse kinematics 355, 398
Iomega 32

J

JPEG 433

K

Kai's Power Tools 161
Key light 258
Keyframes 346, 349
    tutorials 350, 352
Keyman 346
Kiosks 462
Knoll Software 126

L

Laser digitizers 129
Lathe 44
Layers 78
Lens flares 319, 456
    types 320
Light attenuation 249

Light sources 240
    types 241
    visible 308
Light studio setup
    3 lights 257
    4 lights 260
Lightbulbs 286
Lighting 15, 57
Lightning 384
Link and coordinate system tutorial 355
Links 353, 355
Loft 53
Lossy codec 424

M

Macromedia 98
Magento optical 34
Magnetic digitizers 129
Mail order 23
Mapping
    background 178
    basics 141, 155
    types 156
Material color theory 142
Materials 140, 141
McQ Productions 463
Mechanical arm digitizers 127
MediaPaint 381, 456
Memory Control Panel 74
Metaballs 402
MetaTools 112, 161
Mirror 52
Model resolution 80
Modeling 14
    process 82
    software 38

tools 42
Modeling complex 2D shapes tutorial 102
Models 7
Modern Memory Manager 75
Monitors 28
    depth 76
Moonlight 274
Morph 402
Motion blur 342
Motion paths 366
Motion theory 361
MPEG 433
Multimedia 17, 424, 460
    kiosk 424
Multiple processor cards 30
Multiprocessors 422
Muybridge, Eadweard 63

N

N x M Mesh 95
Names 80
Neon 287
Nontraditional storyboard 69
Northern Lights Productions 379
NTSC
    legal colors 462
    safe palette 425
NuBus 25
NURBS 96

O

Object coordinates 348
Onyx 132
Optimizing 461
Origin 83
Orthographic 78, 329

Outer space 281
Output resolution 423
Overlapping action 365
Overmodeling 81

P

Painter 456
Parallel lights 241
Parametric modeler 130
Particle effects 221
Particle groups 378, 459
PCI 25, 26, 28
Persistence of vision 13, 345
Perspective 78, 328
Perspective matching 409
Phong 29
    shading 419
Physical properties 144
Pinnacle 35
Pixar 204
Pixel ratio 427
Planar mapping 157, 166
Point or radial lights 244
    attenuation of 251
Pollution 280
Polygonal based modelers 39
Polyline 95
Poser 130
Postproduction 16
    software 430
PowerPC 24
Premiere 219, 220, 432
Primitives 42
Print 428
Product design 18
Projector box tutorial 302

Projectors 291, 301
Proportions of maps 164
Pyromania 221, 375
Pyrotechnics 375

Q
QuickDraw 3D 25, 59, 96
    accelerator cards 29
    API 29
QuickTime 432

R
Radiosity 5 7, 421
Radius 435
RAID 435
Rain 281
RAM 27, 73
Raytracing 420
Reflectivity 144, 147
    maps 177, 213
Removable storage 32
Rendering 16, 57
    algorithms 415
    alpha channel 441
    farms 422
RenderMan 96, 204
Resolution 434
RGB color model 235
RIB 96
Rippling reflection tutorial 217, 304
RISC 25
Rotoscoping 345, 455
Rough draft 90
Rounding tool 52

S
Scene building 15
Screen savers 77

Script 63
Scripting your animation 346
SCSI-1 435
SCSI-2 435
Seamless maps 160, 161
Seasons 272
SGI rendering engines 423
Shadow masks 448
    compositing 451
Shadows 253
Shift channels 376
Shock wave tutorial 390
Simple boolean tutorial 100
Simple gels 291, 293
    tutorial 291
Skin 53
Smoke and fog tutorial 385
SMPTE time code 64
Snow 281
Sodium vapor 287
Software sources 220
    all-inclusive packages 38
Solar angle 269
Sony 32
Space station tutorial 209
Spaceship color mapping tutorial 167
Spaceship tutorial 152
Specular 161, 219
Specular color 142, 143
Specular maps 176, 180
Specular spaceship tutorial 182
Specular value 144, 146
Specular window tutorial 181
Spherical mapping 159, 165
Spline 366
Spline-based modelers 40
Spotlights 243
    attenuation of 252

Squash and stretch 365
Stained glass tutorial 298
Storyboarding 14, 64
Striping 437
Submarine tutorial 304
Sunlight 268
Surface maps 155
Surface normals 415
Sweep 48
SyQuest 32
System 7.5 3, 27
System Folder 73

T

T-Cal 436
Taper 51
Television 425, 462
Terrain modeling 98, 112
    other uses 124
    creating 114
Terrainman 114
Terrazzo 161
Text-shaped bump map tutorial 202
Texture creation applications 161
Texture mapping 7, 15, 58, 140, 155, 176
TextureMaker 161, 217, 219, 220, 225, 305
TextureScape 161, 219, 220
Thermal recalibration 436
Tiles tutorial 200
Tiling maps 160
Toy soldier tutorial 84
Transparency 144, 149
    maps 176, 185
    tutorial 186
Tree generators 99
Tree modelers 130
Tree tricks tutorial 134, 136
Tree professional 132

Tree tricks 134
TruevVision 435
Tube lights 246
Tutorials 6
    adding an alpha channel into a clip 443
    alpha channel 438
    angle of incidence 248
    animated bump maps 226
    animated flash of light 222
    booleans and text 109
    bottle label 189
    brick wall 197
    canyon 118
    cave 120
    chairs 273
    compositing with an alpha channel 445
    creating 3D text from 2D shapes 105
    creating a terrain 114
    creating custom gels 295
    desk lamp 312
    diffuse spaceship 193
    depth of field 339
    environment spheres 404
    fading cube 228
    flash of light 214
    gears tutorial 104
    glowing sign 206
    gobo of stars 307
    keyframe 350, 352
    lens flares 456
    link and coordinate system 355
    modeling complex 2D shapes 102
    projector box 302
    rendering an alpha channel 441
    rippling reflection 217
    shock wave 390
    simple boolean 100
    simple gel 291

smoke and fog 385
space station 209
spaceship 152
spaceship color mapping 167
specular spaceship 182
specular window 181
stained glass 298
submarine 304
text-shaped bump map 202
tiles 200
toy soldier 84
transparency 186
tree tricks 134, 136
Tweening 346
Twist 51

U
Ultrasonic digitizers 128
Underwater 283

V
Vacuum 282
Velocity 362, 396
    controls 362
Video sources 219

Views 79
Virtual camera 332, 335
Virtual memory 74
Virtual reality lab 112
Virtus 161
Vistapro 112
Visual concept entertainment 375
Visual concepts engineering 219
VRAM 29

W
Wireframe 416
Working storage 31
World coordinates 348

X
Xaos Tools 161

Y
YARC Hydra 25
YARC Systems 423

Z
Zeus 379
Zoom in 368

With Fractal Design Poser, Art Really Does Imitate Life

Poser—The Remarkable Figure Design Tool

Fractal Design Poser™ is the extraordinary art creation tool that lets you design with the human form. Developed for graphic artists, illustrators, designers and multimedia mavens, Poser is the perfect tool for integrating the human figure into your creations.

Fast and Versatile

Use Poser to easily create, pose and view an infinite variety of human models from any direction. Poser's figures are remarkably adjustable— each body part can be independently scaled and tapered to suit your exact needs. Poser is an ideal time-saving tool for developing concepts, laying out storyboards or creating a virtual photo shoot.

It's the Perfect Companion

Poser is designed to work with the paint, image-editing and 3D programs you use now—Fractal Design Painter,® Adobe Photoshop,™ RayDream Designer™ and Specular InfiniD.™ Poser saves PICT files with a mask defining the figure outline for paint programs, DXF files for use in 3D modeling programs, and RIB files for sophisticated rendering software.

Fractal Design

Poser

To order or find out more about Poser, call:

800.297.COOL

FRACTAL DESIGN CORPORATION

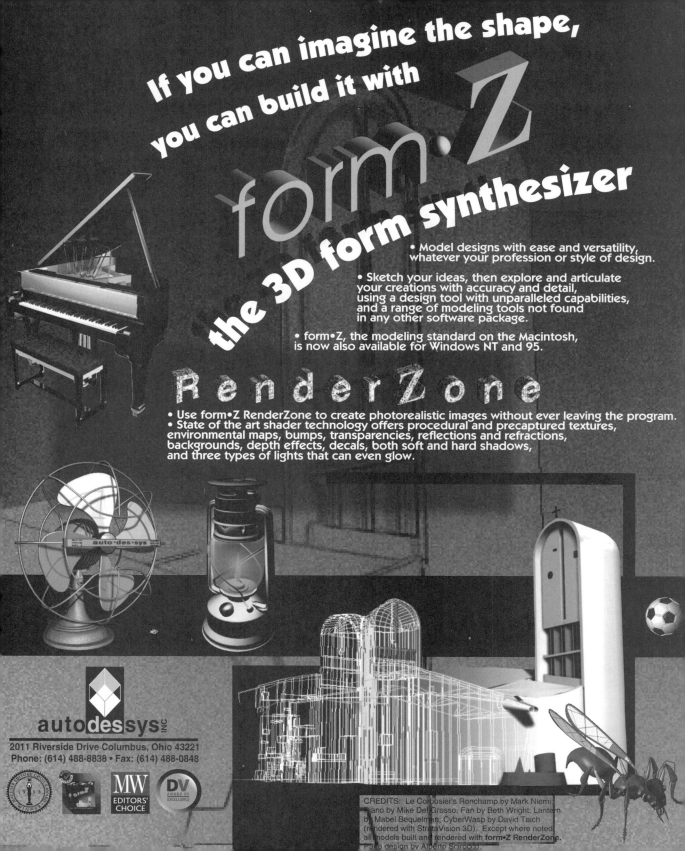

KPT Final Effects Stars as After Effects Plug-in

Put yourself in the director's chair with KPT Final Effects.™ A sophisticated collection of 28 video plug-ins for Adobe After Effects, KPT Final Effects transforms basic video compositions into spectacular presentations for output to film, videotape or CD-ROM with unprecedented realism and finesse.

Hollywood loves it! Major television networks, motion picture studios, and game developers rely on After Effects and KPT Final Effects every day. Any digital video professional can create visual effects on the Macintosh that were formerly available only on workstation-level video editing systems often costing hundreds of thousands of dollars. At just $695 suggested retail, KPT Final Effects pays for itself after only a few frames!

Here's how. Near real-time previews eliminate costly mistakes such as unnecessary renderings. Get productive and save money by making creative decisions using on-screen previews at your desk. Optimize creative control and pay production houses only for required work.

Instead of tired canned effects, KPT Final Effects' plug-ins offer an unlimited number of dynamic combinations, with interactive control over even subtle compositing details. As the effects master, you have full control over every KPT Final Effects element. Its particle system unleashes incredible animation possibilities, ranging from simple explosions to sophisticated smoke screens. Use familiar controls to create particle generation from a logo or any source. Controls can even be dynamically animated to create dramatic special effects.

At last, you don't have to be a physicist to create outrageous video effects! "Once you've used KPT Final Effects," says Keith Zentner, Adobe After Effects product manager, "you'll wonder how you ever got by without them."

To find out more, call us at
1-800-472-9025
Mention Dept. FB1N

MetaTools™
formerly HSC Software

805.566.6220 fax: 805.566.6367
Contact us in cyberspace:
metasales@aol.com
http://www.metatools.com

Introducing Macromedia Extreme 3D

Extreme 3D is the only program that does it all. Spline-based modeling. Dynamic animation. Distributed, cross-platform rendering. Even post-production.

Everything's integrated and included. 500 fonts, a CD with cool Wraptures® textures, 150 material pre-sets, and pre-built models. And at only $699 SRP, it's an extreme value.

As easy as icon-based Extreme 3D is to learn and use, the power to create amazing 3D artwork is infinite. With a scaleable interface, Extreme 3D works in layers—the more accomplished you become, the deeper you go into the world of 3D.

So to easily take your Power Mac, Windows 95, Windows NT, and Windows 3.1 designs to a higher level, get Extreme 3D. We'll even send you a free Showcase CD*, where you can see Extreme 3D and other Macromedia products in all their splendor.

FREE SHOWCASE CD-ROM*
1-800-326-2128

Or Catch Us On The Net:
http://www.macromedia.com/

EXTREME 3D

FREEHAND

DIRECTOR

AUTHORWARE

SOUNDEDIT 16

FONTOGRAPHER

MACROMEDIA®

Tools to Power Your Ideas

The Best in 3D Just Got *Faster!*

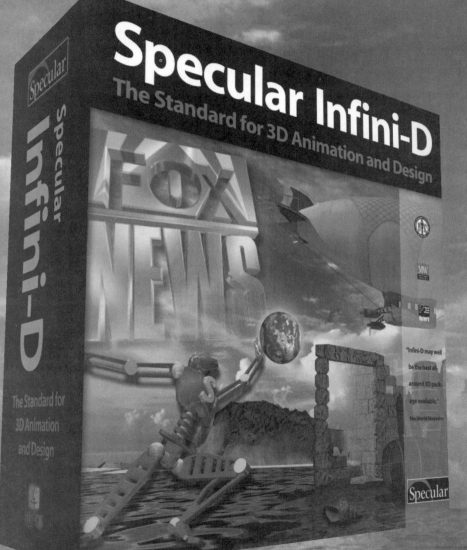

Specular Infini-D
The Standard for 3D Animation and Design

Specular Infini-D
The Standard for 3D Animation and Design

"Infini-D may well be the best all-around 3D package available."
MacWorld Magazine

Freeform Graphics &
Animation Software

THE VALIS GROUP

P.O. Box 831, Tiburon, CA 94920-0831   415.435-5404   FAX: 415.435-9862   AOL: VALISGROUP   AppleLink: VALIS